Changing Worlds, Changing Nations

Changing Worlds, Changing Nations

The Concept of Nation in the Transnational Era

EDITED BY

JOEL KUORTTI
OM PRAKASH DWIVEDI

RAWAT PUBLICATIONS
Jaipur • New Delhi • Bangalore • Hyderabad • Guwahati

ISBN 978-81-316-0519-6

Published by
Prem Rawat for **Rawat Publications**
Satyam Apts, Sector 3, Jawahar Nagar, Jaipur 302 004 (India)
Phone: 0141 265 1748 / 7006 Fax: 0141 265 1748
E-mail: info@rawatbooks.com
Website: www.rawatbooks.com

New Delhi Office
4858/24, Ansari Road, Daryaganj, New Delhi 110 002
Phone: 011 2326 3290

Also at *Bangalore, Hyderabad* and *Guwahati*

Typeset by Rawat Computers, Jaipur
Printed at Chaman Enterprises, New Delhi

Contents

Contributors

Letizia Alterno is the Editor-in-Chief of the Raja Rao Publication Project, which is currently preparing the publication of a centenary collection of Rao's works in collaboration with OUP India. She is associated with the Department of English and American Studies, University of Manchester, UK, and is the author of *Raja Rao: An Introduction* in the *Contemporary Indian Writers Series* (2011). Her publications include several articles and volume contributions on the work of Raja Rao. She is the author of Raja Rao's obituary published in *The Guardian* after the writer's death on 8 July 2006 and an article on the legacy of Rao's work published in May 2011 by *The Times of India*. She is currently editing a critical anthology that explores the significance of Rao's production today, the title of which is *Raja Rao's Work in the Transnational Era*.

Yanoula Athanassakis received her Ph.D. from UC Santa Barbara's Department of English. Currently, the College of Creative Studies Literature Fellow at UC Santa Barbara, she is working on her manuscript, entitled "Global Corporealities: Immigration and the Body in Contemporary US Narratives". In her work she explores the connections between somaticism, immigration, US citizenship and globalization. She is also the Associate Managing Editor for Special Forums for the *Journal of Transnational American Studies*

(*JTAS*) – an online publication, co-sponsored by Stanford and UC Santa Barbara.

Laksmisree Banerjee is Pro-Vice Chancellor at the Kolhan University. She completed her studies and obtained her Doctoral degree at the University of Calcutta. She has published several books and research articles. Besides being an academic, administrator and teacher, she is an acclaimed Indian writer in English, and a vocalist. Her primary research areas include Commonwealth and American Literature, World Women's Poetry, Gender and Postcolonial Studies, Creative Writing, Indian English Literature as well as Indian Classical Music and Culture Studies. She has lectured, recited and sung extensively in several universities and cities all over the world. She has devoted her entire life to enlighten students in the classroom and beyond.

Om Prakash Dwivedi is Assistant Professor in English at MITS (a deemed university in Rajasthan). His research papers have appeared in such reputed international journals as *Transnational Literature* (Australia), *Journal of Asia Pacific Studies* (USA), DOST (University of Turin, Italy) and *The Journal of Contemporary Literature* (Allahabad, India). Apart from several papers and articles published in critical anthologies, he has edited two books, *The Fiction of Amitav Ghosh: An Assessment* (2010) and *A Spectrum of Indian English Literature* (2010). He is presently working on a project, *The Other India: Narratives of Terror, Communalism and Violence.*

Devarakshanam Betty Govinden is Senior Research Associate in the Faculty of Education at the University of Kwazulu-Natal, South Africa. An academic, researcher and creative writer, she has written and published in the fields of education, literature, theology, and interdisciplinary research. Her recent critical publications include *A Time of Memory: Reflections on Recent South African Writing* (2008), *Sister Outsiders: Representations of Identity and Difference in Selected Writings by South African Indian Women* (2008), and *Words on Water – Reflections on Recent Writing* (2010).

Tuomas Huttunen is a researcher in the Department of English at the University of Turku, Finland. His recent work concentrates on the ethics of representation in contemporary literatures in English. His publications include essays and articles on V.S. Naipaul, Amitav Ghosh and M.G. Vassanji and the volumes titled, *Seeking the Self: Encountering the Other: Diasporic Narrative and the Ethics of*

Representation (2008, co-edited with Kaisa Ilmonen, Janne Korkka and Elina Valovirta) and *The Ethics of Representation in the Fiction of Amitav Ghosh* (2011).

Joel Kuortti is Professor of English at the University of Turku, Finland. He is also Adjunct Professor of Contemporary Culture at the University of Jyväskylä, Finland. His research areas include post-colonial theory, Indian literature in English, transnational identity, and cultural studies. His most important publications are *The Salman Rushdie Bibliography* (1997), *Place of the Sacred: The Rhetoric of the Satanic Verses Affair* (1997), *Fictions to Live In: Narration as an Argument for Fiction in Salman Rushdie's Novels* (1998), *Indian Women's Writing in English: A Bibliography* (2002), *Tense Past, Tense Present: Women Writing in English* (2003), *Writing Imagined Diasporas: South Asian Women Reshaping North American Identity* (2007), and *Reconstructing Hybridity: Post-colonial Studies in Transition*, co-edited with J. Nyman (2007).

Jopi Nyman is Professor and Head of English at the University of Eastern Finland in Joensuu, Finland. His research interests cover Anglophone literatures and popular culture. He is the author of several monographs and edited collections. His recent publications include the monograph *Home, Identity, and Mobility in Contemporary Diasporic Fiction* (2009) and the edited essay collection *Post-National Enquiries: Essays on Ethnic and Racial Border Crossings* (2009). His current research projects explore literature and globalization, human-animal studies and food narratives.

Nishi Pulugurtha is Head and Assistant Professor in the Department of English, Brahmananda Keshab Chandra College, Kolkata. She has worked at the University of Calcutta where she earned her Ph.D. degree on Coleridge's poetry. Her post-doctoral work dealt with the effect of English on the intellectual life of Bengal and on poetry written in English by Bengalis in the 19th century. She is currently working on Indian diasporic literature in the US at the Indian Institute of Advanced Study, Shimla and has completed a project on the poetry of the diaspora. Her monograph on Henry Louis Vivian Derozio was published last year. Her areas of interest are British Romantic, postcolonial, diasporic, and Indian English literatures, on which she has published extensively. She writes on travel and literary articles for *The Statesman*, Kolkata.

Madina Tlostanova is Professor of History of Philosophy and Director of the Center for Transcultural Studies at Peoples'

Friendship University of Russia. Besides numerous articles, she has authored four books in Russian: *Multicultural Discourse and US Fiction of the Late 20th Century* (2000), *Living Never: Writing from Nowhere: Post-soviet Literature and the Aesthetics of Transculturation* (2004), *From the Philosophy of Multiculturalism to the Philosophy of Trans-culturation* (2008), *Decolonial Gender Epistemologies* (2009); and three in English: *A Janus-Faced Empire. Notes on the Russian Empire in Modernity Written from the Border* (2003), *The Sublime of Globalization? Sketches on Trans-cultural Subjectivity and Aesthetics* (2005), and *Gender Epistemologies and Eurasian Borderlands* (2010).

Anna-Leena Toivanen completed her doctoral thesis in literature studies in 2010. In her dissertation, she discussed the production and authorship of the Zimbabwean writers Yvonne Vera and Dambudzo Marechera in the context of the Zimbabwe crisis. Her post-doctoral research project is focused on the intertwinement of transnational mobility, globalization and the failures of postcolonial nationhood in Anglo- and Francophone Sub-Saharan African women's writing. Her articles have recently appeared in *Research in African Literatures* and *Postcolonial Text.*

Christine Vogt-William studied English, German and Psychology at the University of Essen, Germany. From October 2002 till June 2008, she was a junior lecturer and research assistant at the Department of New English Literatures and Cultures at the Goethe University of Frankfurt, Germany. She spent a year (September 2006 to August 2007) at the University of York, England as a Marie Curie Gender Graduate Fellow and completed her doctoral thesis on 'Women and Transculturality in Contemporary Fictions by South Asian Diasporic Women Writers'. She has published on South Asian diasporic women's literature from the US, Canada, England and the Caribbean. She is the co-editor of and contributor to *Disturbing Bodies* (Berlin, Trafo Verlag, 2008), an essay collection on artistic and literary representations of deviant bodies, as read by scholars of literary and cultural studies, using contemporary feminist and queer theories. Her other fields of academic interest include Indo-Caribbean women's poetry, Bollywood films, Asian diasporic fusion music and J.R.R. Tolkien's fantasy works. Vogt-William was also a Visiting Scholar at the Department of Women's Studies at Emory University, Atlanta, Georgia, from 2008 to 2010. After having taught in the Postcolonial and Media Studies Department at the University of Muenster, Germany, from November 2009 till September 2011, she is currently working on her post-doctoral project (University of Frankfurt, Germany) entitled, *Twins in American and Anglophone Literatures: Negotiating Selves, Space and Gender.*

Laurenz Volkmann studied at Erlangen University, Germany, where he received his Ph.D. in English literature. He also studied at Miami University of Ohio as an exchange student, and worked at Manchester University for two years. Between 1992 and 2004, he taught at the Universities of Würzburg, Bielefeld, Hanover and Paderborn. Currently, he is Professor of EFL Teaching at Friedrich-Schiller-Universität Jena. His major publication (Habilitation) is a profound study of *homo oeconomicus* in English literature from the Middle Ages to the 18th century. He has published articles on a wide range of topics, from Shakespeare to Leonard Cohen's poetry, and from Madonna as an icon of postmodernism to German techno music.

Introduction

JOEL KUORTTI AND OM PRAKASH DWIVEDI

Beginning Transnationalism

The contemporary world is strongly demarcated by barbed wires and boundaries. The marked function of these concrete and conceptual, physical and ideological barbed wires and boundaries is to safeguard oneself from the onslaught of enemies outside, to define one's territorial-cum-cultural identity, and to inseminate the concept of a nation itself.[1] Obviously, they create a contested space within which the 'natives' practise their own tradition and culture. One pauses a while at this juncture and speculates about what makes nations and their boundaries so seductively euphoric and historically persistent. Even though any given nation-state is a singular entity, its singularity always becomes problematic because of the diversity already existing within itself, as we can perceive when we consider for example countries like India, South Africa, the United Kingdom or the United States, with subversion of one community by the other(s). The very concept of nation, thus, becomes contentious, and the nation at times turns into a space of contestation between communities, ethnicities, and religions. The core problem of the nationalistic discourse, however, remains the same: how to keep one's (implied) identity intact. Ostensibly, we can notice that the problem of identity is all the time either at stake, both within and outside the nation, or it can be said to be 'liquid' or 'fluid', to put it in sociologist Zygmunt Bauman's terms.[2]

The situation, as noted above, is none too happy and clearly exposes the dualism of the nation-state.[3] The ongoing process of identity (de)construction is centripetal in a consideration of the literature(s) being produced in the contemporary era of transnationalism. The term 'transnationalism' sounds simplistic, yet it is not so explicit in nature and is apparently enveloped in myriad confounding applications.[4] Transnationalism, as it is largely understood, is a concept that disrupts and scatters the idea of centrality and periphery. It may properly be conceived as a kind of relationship between nation-states, a crossing of national borders, a cultural/political interplay between different national cultures, or a mode of mobility of transnational subjects. To be more precise, transnationalism means a form of multi-nationalism – something that shares cultural connections with more than one nation. In a way, transnationalism does not subscribe to the view expressed by the speaker in the American poet Robert Frost's well-known poem, "Mending Wall" (1914) wherein, he says, "Good fences make good neighbors."[5] Fences are needed for the individual nation-states, not for those individuals, including writers, thinkers and political leaders, who are motivated by transnational – and more widely transcultural – ideological ideas, as neighbours who have no use for fences.

At the moment, the concept of nation is undergoing drastic changes. In this postcolonial era, globalization has brought in its train many new concepts for taking stock of this process. One of these concepts is that of transnationalism which is instrumental in conceptually breaking asunder national boundaries. It operates across the globe and, within the cultural field, it also helps to facilitate the birth and development of new literatures in the world. All over the world, transnationalism has compelled authors – especially immigrant, diasporic, or indeed transnational authors – not only to work on their identities but also change their languages. In this process, the use of English language has come handy to the immigrants in the rapidly transforming world. The postcolonial authors have been churning out new forms of 'english'[6] in their works, thereby enhancing its role as a global resource. There is something profoundly ironic in the way English, which was a borrowed language for the erstwhile colonized countries and peoples, is now constructing a new identity for them. However, in the fast-changing global scenario, this language is also changing rapidly in order to adjust itself to the new needs and demands of the literary world and this change is encouraged and accelerated by the new literatures that have taken up English as their chosen media of literary communication. Within the framework of the present anthology, among writers who have taken up the challenge are Raja Rao and Salman Rushdie who have both provoked writers and readers to work English for their own purposes. While Rao comments that "[w]e cannot write like the English. We should not,"[7] Rushdie urges further that the English "language, like much else in the newly independent societies, needs to be decolonized, to be remade in other images,"[8] and that "[t]o conquer English may be to complete the process of making ourselves free."[9]

It is within this transcultural moment and juncture that this work aims at discussing literary works that challenge existing notions of nation, nationalism, and national identity. In the following pages, we provide a brief introduction to the articles included in this anthology. After that, there are some concluding remarks as to the possible applicability of the notions discussed here and some contemplation of future trajectories. It is our hope that the book as a whole, and the individual articles on their own, would spark some new discussion and analysis of literary works in view of transnationalism.

The Structure of the Anthology

The present anthology consists of thirteen articles that from their particular perspectives consider the feasibility of nation-states in our transnational era and examine the role of language and culture in seeking a new identity for them. The book focuses on the Indian context as a case study of the thematics but it extends necessarily this nationalistic framework to reflect on other, wider contexts. As for the work's structure, we want to follow this opening up of the contextual framework, beginning from the historical Indian issues, moving into the problematization of the context, and finally considering other contexts and the ways in which these might influence our perception of the theme of transnationalism.

The first article, "Postcolonial Somaticism in Kiran Desai's *The Inheritance of Loss*" by Yanoula Athanassakis focuses on the material and immaterial forms of knowledge as found in Kiran Desai's novel of 2006. The novel becomes a patchwork of three main narrative strands – globalization, immigration and postcolonial politics. The article applies theories of feminist somaticism, calls in question the methodological framework of transnationalism, and avers that Desai's novel should also be read as a work on global immigration and the US politics of citizenship. The second article, "Partition, Private Lives and Co-Wives: Women, Modernity and Nation in Shauna Singh Baldwin's *What the Body Remembers* and Manju Kapur's *Difficult Daughters*" by Christine Vogt-William explores the question of polygamy in the days of the struggle for India's independence as discovered in the two novels under discussion. The writer thinks that both the texts address modernity and tradition with regard to women's positions and gender expectations at the time of national freedom. The ensuing third article, entitled "The Cane Is Singing: South African Indian Literature on Indenture," by Betty Govinden, presents a detailed account of recent South African Indian writings, in the context of the contemporary socio-cultural politics. It broadly examines the performances of Indianness against the backdrop of colonial, apartheid and post-apartheid forces and influences, and mainly focuses on the historical experience of indenture as depicted by South African Indian writers in their fictional works. The paper winds up the discussion by emphasizing the value of a comprehensively comparative approach to current literary studies. The fourth article by Letizia Alterno, entitled "Problems of Representation in Raja Rao's *The Great Indian Way: A Life of Mahatma Gandhi*" constructs the figure of Gandhi in a multitude of representations such as 'the British Gentleman', 'the Coolie Barrister' and 'the Satyagrahi'. It is common knowledge that Gandhi played a very vital role in India's struggle for independence and in the making of Indian nation, and the analyses of these various representations of Gandhi enhance the understanding of the complexity of his character.

The fifth article, "Memory and the Transformation of Identity: Meena Alexander's *Fault Lines*", by Nishi Pulugurtha begins with a consideration of the idea of home, which refashions one's identity in a diasporic condition. Home may be geographical space, a historical space, or an emotional sensory space. In considering the question of home or homelessness – which is more appropriate in the context of Meena Alexander's *Fault Lines* (1993), a memoir indeed – Nishi Pulugurtha forwards the view that the parameters of time, community and nation are of great importance. Meena Alexander, who is a diasporic writer now living in America, bases her *Fault Lines* on the idea of displacement overpowering the immigrants. The article under review takes into account some important questions of identity formations in view of changing nations. The sixth article, "Nation as the Persistent Centre of Meaning: Dambudzo Merechera and the Zimbabwe Crisis" is by Anna-Leena Toivanen. As the article shows, in his writings, the Zimbabwean author, Dambudzo Marechera has criticized nationalist thinking in the transnational era and envisaged alternative ways of conceiving identity. His personal experiences of exile underline his transnational poetics. In the article, the transnational impulse is studied especially in the light of the national impulse. The seventh article by Tuomas Huttunen, "The Ethics of Representation in *The Glass Palace* by Amitav Ghosh", studies the ways in which Otherness is represented in *The Glass Palace* (2000) from the viewpoint of ethics. It attempts to highlight the relationship between the self and the Other. Ghosh's novel under consideration tries to transcend the borders between nations, ideologies, ethnicities and religions. Moreover, there is an effect on this sort of transcendence in areas that have not been previously explored in mainstream fiction or historical writing. An intermediate viewpoint is created in the novel by yoking together Western ideologies and technologies and the heterogeneous histories of the areas of India, Burma and Malaysia.

The eighth article, "Transnational/Transcultural Subjectivities and Chronotopes in Diasporic Literature," by Madina Tlostanova, takes a more comprehensive and generalizing view of the topic. It problematizes the concept of diaspora and diasporic literature as travelling terms and pleads for the use of 'transculturation' as a befitting term to describe the post-diasporic subjectivity and aesthetics. It examines the aesthetics of transculturation with an emphasis on time and space and offers examples from the works of Indian, South African, Russian, Turkish and other writers. The ninth article, "Globalizing European Peripheries: The Transnational and the Translocal in Monica Ali's *Alentenjo Blue*" by Jopi Nyman, considers the extent to which current trends of globalization affect the building of European identities, and for this purpose Monica Ali's second novel, *Alentejo Blue* (2006), is closely analysed. In the light of the works of anthropologist James Clifford, and the contemporary sociologists Ulrich Beck and Saskia Sassen, the novel tries to examine the problematics of migration and the altered meanings of centre and periphery. Obviously, the identities of European nation-states are changing fast today because of global and intra-European flows of migration producing new cultural expressions. When the novel is read in a transnational framework, it unfolds silenced histories of mobility and links village life with the ways of the wider world in order to counter dominant views of cultural contact and unilateral globalization. The tenth article on "Teaching a Transcultural/Transgeneric 'Classic': Hanif Kureishi's *My Beautiful Laundrette*" by Laurenz Volkmann, takes up the question of teaching Kureishi's *My Beautiful Launderette* (1985) in a classroom having non-native speakers and of fostering students' inter/transcultural competence. Before examining the production of the film and providing a brief plot summary, the contributor makes efforts to assess Kureishi's place of importance in British cultural set-up and surveys some of his major themes. The article also shows how Kureishi subverts his audience's expectation about race, class, ethnicity and sexuality. Furthermore, it provides some practical suggestions for using various methods in evoking students' interest in the text and the film.

The eleventh article entitled "Nations of the Soul and Female Poetic Activism" by Laksmisree Banerjee, highlights the female poetic texts as powerful indicators of a new artistic and ideological brand of Nationhood, which is called here 'Nations of the Soul'. These texts bring to the fore the suppressed feminist histories, experiences and problems. They cut across the barriers of time and apace and evince a certain novel way of defining nation, nationhood and narration. The article deals, among other things, with such vital questions as canon *versus* counter-canons, homogeneity *versus* heterogeneity, centre *versus* periphery, and soul *versus* body. The feminist studies of women poets picked up from diverse territories display an irrepressible female consciousness born of a resonant poetic activism in them. The twelfth article, "Changing Worlds/Changing Words: The Language of Experiment in Salman Rushdie's *Midnight's Children*", by Om Prakash Dwivedi focuses on the global use of English in the transnational era. In the Indian context, English was introduced in the colonial period (precisely, 1835) in educational institutions by Lord Macaulay to produce office-clerks and interpreters, but later on a rich crop of talented creative writers grew up to add a new dimension to the development of English literature. After quoting Kamala Das's famous poem "An Introduction" to underscore the importance and effectiveness of English in personal/official communication and literary expression, the article proceeds to examine Salman Rushdie's innovative use of English as a language and the fantastic representation of history in *Midnight's Children* (1981): the individual history of Saleem Sinai being mixed with the national history of India. The thrust area of the contribution is to demonstrate how far Rushdie uses English as an experimentalist and how far he has been able to adapt his language, his words, to the changing demands of transnationalism. The anthology concludes with Joel Kuortti's article, "Salman Rushdie's Transnational Layers," which shows how British literature needs a new definition in the light of substantial contributors of numerous postcolonial writers of the former Empire. The article highlights Rushdie's fresh and novel way of writing fiction, which won for hi, among other things, the coveted Booker Prize in 1981 for *Midnight's Children*, and which opened up fresh vistas of narrativization. Rushdie, an Indian by birth, deals with England, English language, and Englishness. Hence, transnational layers of language and literature can be discovered in his fictional writings.

Beyond the Nation?

The present anthology of critical articles aims at conceptualizing the identity of the nation-state and pinpointing the conception that the borders of the nation-state are ever shifting, extending and transforming in order to create a new world order, a wider territorial zone, in the contemporary transnational era. The title of the book, *Changing Worlds, Changing Nations: The Concept of Nation in the Transnational Era,* underlines the transforming status of the discourse of nationalism and transnationalism. The realities and identities of people – the changing worlds – are taking place and are influenced by the changes taking place in the varying dimensions of the state culture – the changing nations.

This view is powerfully articulated by two important critics, Judith Butler and Gayatri Chakravorty Spivak, in their book *Who Sings the Nation-State?* (2007). These critics express their view as follows:

> If the state is what "binds", it is also clearly what can and does unbind. And if the state binds in the name of the nation, conjuring a certain version of the nation forcibly, if not powerfully, then it also unbinds, releases, expels, banishes.[10]

Here Butler and Spivak clearly hint at the dualism of the nation-state, the barriers of which are breaking asunder day by day in the face of the emerging forces of globalization, commercialization and multiculturalism. Their understanding is that national(istic) emblems are obsolete, and that in a world of rapid migratory movements and shifting allegiances, caused by economic, political, military, cultural, climatic and other changes, the nation-state has become a provisional place, especially for the immigrants and the entrepreneurs, the academics and the politicians, who frequently and with varying degrees of ease, cross the national borders and settle down, temporarily or permanently, in another country. Some of the immigrants gifted with the power of imagination turn out to be good writers who nostalgically or otherwise recall "imaginary homelands"[11] – to borrow a phrase from the celebrated novelist Salman Rushdie – and richly recreate them in their writings. These diasporic writers try their best to adjust their language in accordance with the changing concept of the nation-state, to keep in rhythm with the shifting paradigms of temporal and spatial realities.

In the existing discourse of postcoloniality, certain transnational formations and strands of migration tend to get represented more often and with more emphasis while other forms are marginally present, or are silenced. It is our hope that the contributions here would enable us to find some new avenues of thinking on the matter, and to connect matters that do not automatically get connected. There is an ethical call that needs to be addressed if we are to maintain the relevance of discussions of postcolonial and transnational issues.

Notes

1. There is an innumerable wealth of definitions of 'nation' and 'nationalism'. Benedict Anderson's legendary definition of 1983 treats nation as an "imagined community" in *Imagined Communities: Reflections on the Origin and Spread of Nationalism*, 2nd rev. ed. (London and New York: Verso, 2006. [1991/1983]), 6–7. More recently, Umut Özkýrýmlý collates various recent approaches on the topic in *Contemporary Debates on Nationalism: A Critical Engagement* (Palgrave Macmillan, 2005). Already in 1913, in his book *Marxism and the National Question*, (1928 [1913], 303), Joseph Stalin defined 'nation' thus: "A nation is primarily a community, a definite community of people," and further: "a nation is not a racial or tribal but a historically constituted community of people." Nation and history, in a way, are linked together in Stalin's definition given above. Joseph V. Stalin, *Marxism and the National Question*, in J.V. Stalin, *Works*, vol. 2. (Moscow: Foreign Languages Publishing House, 1954), 300–381; available at: <http://www.marx2mao.com/Stalin/MNQ12.html#c1> (visited 20 September, 2010).
2. Zygmunt Bauman, *Identity: Conversations with Benedetto Vecchi* (Cambridge: Polity Press, 2004), 89.
3. For this idea, one may look up Judith Butler and Gayatri Chakravorty Spivak's *Who Sings the Nation-State?* (London: Seagull Books, 2007), 1–16.
4. There is a growing literature on transnationalism and the interrelated dimensions of postcoloniality, cosmopolitanism, and transculturalism, see, e.g., Arjun Appadurai, *Modernity at Large: Cultural Dimensions of Globalization* (New Delhi: Oxford UP, 1997); Inderpal Grewal, *Transnational America: Feminisms, Diasporas, Neoliberalisms*, ser. Next Wave: New Directions in Women's Studies. Durham: Duke UP, 2005; Raymond

Rocco and Fernando J. García (eds.), *Transnationalism: Issues and Perspectives* (Madrid: Editorial de la Universidad Complutense, 2006).

5. Robert Frost. "Mending Wall," in Frost, *The Poetry of Robert Frost: The Collected Poems, Complete and Unabridged*, ed. Edward Connery Lathem (New York: Henry Holt, 1979 [1969]). 33. [Orig. 1914.]
6. The word 'english' is here used in the specific sense put forward by Bill Ashcroft, Gareth Griffiths, and Helen Tiffin in their ground-breaking work *The Empire Writes Back: Post-Colonial Literatures, Theory & Practice* in which they pit standard English against various other forms of 'english' that are not, however, less important (London: Routledge, 1989), 8.
7. Raja Rao, "Foreword" to *Kanthapura* (New York: New Directions, 1963 [1938]), vii–ix.
8. Salman Rushdie, "The Empire Writes Back with a Vengeance," *The Times* (July 3, 1982): 8.
9. Salman Rushdie, "Imaginary Homelands," in Rushdie, *Imaginary Homelands: Essays & Criticism, 1981–1991* (London: Granta Books, 1991), 17.
10. Butler and Spivak, 4–5.
11. For this phrase, see Rushdie, "Imaginary Homelands," 9–21.

Works Cited

Anderson, Benedict. *Imagined Communities: Reflections on the Origin and Spread of Nationalism.* 2nd rev. ed. London and New York: Verso, 2006. [1991/1983].

Appadurai, Arjun. *Modernity at Large: Cultural Dimensions of Globalization.* New Delhi: Oxford UP, 1997.

Ashcroft, Bill, Gareth Griffiths, and Helen Tiffin. *The Empire Writes Back: Post-Colonial Literatures, Theory & Practice.* London: Routledge, 1989.

Bauman, Zygmunt. *Identity: Conversations with Benedetto Vecchi.* Cambridge: Polity Press, 2004.

Butler, Judith and Gayatri Chakravorty Spivak. *Who Sings the Nation-State? Language, Politics, Belonging.* London: Seagull Books, 2007.

Frost, Robert. "Mending Wall." In *The Poetry of Robert Frost: The Collected Poems, Complete and Unabridged.* Ed. Edward Connery Lathem. New York: Henry Holt, 1979 [1969]. 33. [Orig. 1914.]

Grewal, Inderpal. *Transnational America: Feminisms, Diasporas, Neoliberalisms.* Ser. Next Wave: New Directions in Women's Studies. Durham: Duke UP, 2005.

Özkýrýmlý, Umut. *Contemporary Debates on Nationalism: A Critical Engagement.* Basingstoke: Palgrave Macmillan, 2005.

Rao, Raja. "Foreword" to *Kanthapura.* New York: New Directions, 1963 [1938]. vii–ix.

Rocco, Raymond and Fernando J. García (eds.). *Transnationalism: Issues and Perspectives.* Madrid: Editorial de la Universidad Complutense, 2006.

Rushdie, Salman. "The Empire Writes Back with a Vengeance." *The Times* (July 3, 1982): 8.

Rushdie, Salman. "Imaginary Homelands." In Rushdie, *Imaginary Homelands: Essays & Criticism, 1981–1991.* London: Granta Books, 1991. 9–21. [1982.]

Stalin, Joseph V. *Marxism and the National Question.* In J.V. Stalin, *Works,* vol. 2. Moscow: Foreign Languages Publishing House, 1954. 300–381. Available at: <http://www.marx2mao.com/Stalin/MNQ12.html#c1>. (Visited 20 September, 2010.)

1

Postcolonial Somaticism in Kiran Desai's *The Inheritance of Loss*

YANOULA ATHANASSAKIS

Challenging Body

Immigration at its core is about bodies moving across borders. But it is also about subjectivities which are not only housed by these bodies, but deeply impacted by what happens to their corporeal counterparts. For some immigrants, identity formation within foreign borders is an enervating process; one identity must be relinquished or obfuscated in order for another to be realized. Many works of earlier US ethnic literature are almost exclusively understood to be characterized by an assimilationist model of operation.[1] If we think of immigration as a prism, and the most recent manifestations of globalization as rays of light, the resulting patterns and hues created by those who feel their combined force most urgently, are a newer generation of transnational and diasporic writers who rearticulate immigrant subjectivity in terms of the 21st century. The spectrum of colour and light testifies to the rich narrative fabric of works like Kiran Desai's *The Inheritance of Loss* (2006).[2] Authors such as Kiran Desai are "American,"[3] yet their works juxtapose various homelands and do more than what anthropologist Arjun

Appadurai calls "interpretive acts," instances in which non-western societies reappropriate facets of mainstream (often Eurocentric) cultural forms.[4] In Desai, the fluid and multifaceted nature of traversing borders attests to the changing understanding of postcolonial politics in the era of postnational and transnational debates. As a narrative of multidirectional exchange, Desai's novel rearticulates "interpretive acts" and anchors them in the somatic – it is through their bodies that her characters begin to explore the contours of their beliefs and reimagine their communities as participating in larger, trans/national discourses.

With globalization and the increased speed of technology and access to it across class lines, a younger generation of authors explores the stigmata of change and kinetically navigates what literary critic Paul Jay points to as the future of globalized literary studies, the "multidirectionality of cultural flows."[5] The older model of immigration to the US involved a severing of one's roots, a sense of permanence with regard to settlement in the US and perhaps unquestioning aspirations of assimilation – to become wholly Americanized. This has since shifted and Jay proposes that we "reorganize our approach" to "what we have heretofore treated as national literatures" by studying the ways in which authors treat the "historical processes of globalization."[6] What Jay refers to as the "multidirectionality of cultural flows" implicates the physical and emotional movements of this newer generation of hyphenated American authors.[7]

The immigrant body is frequently caught in the crossfire or the nexus between transnational movements and exchange. These exchanges, whether physical or virtual, involve embodiment and disembodiment – they depend on the body. Thus, the immigrant body attests to an alternate, somatic experience. It must be addressed as the vessel in which one's consciousness resides, and in being addressed. The body rubs, chafes, and finally wears down a fixed and disembodied model of global ebbs and flows which might otherwise ignore the often painful processes of psychosomatic border-crossing.

The Inheritance of Loss contains three main narrative strands which weave together into a patchwork that blankets globalization, immigration and postcolonial politics. The novel opens with Sai, an orphaned teenage Indian girl who lives with her grandfather, most often referred to as "the judge." As the novel progresses we find out about the judge's British education, his intense self-colonization and his hatred of all things Indian. Sai comes to live with her grandfather and develops a crush on her Nepali tutor, Gyan. Sai, the judge, and their elderly cook live out their days in Cho Oyu while the cook's son, Biju, immigrates to New York and drifts from one restaurant job to the other. As an illegal immigrant, Biju experiences the worst of the "shadow class" of workers in New York, with no rights and no agency in the face of manipulative bosses and inhuman working conditions. While Biju, Sai, and the judge constitute the three major narrative threads, Gyan's story, (his involvement and complicity in violence) is crucial to exploring Desai's construction of the movements of history and how the newest forms of globalization reschematize the world:

> Books were making her restless. She was beginning to read, faster, more, until she was inside the narrative and the narrative inside her, the pages going by so fast, her heart in her chest – she couldn't stop. In this way she had read *To Kill a Mockingbird*, *Cider with Rosie*, and *Life with Father* from the Gymkhana Club library. And pictures of the chocolaty Amazon, of stark Patagonia in the *National Geographics* [...]. – She found they affected her so much she could often hardly read the accompanying words – the feeling they created was so exquisite, the desire so painful. [...]
>
> Cho Oyu and the judge's habits seemed curtailments to her then. (*IL* 77)

Desai's image of the text entering body and flesh absorbing text is more than a metaphor for Sai's voracious appetite for reading; it speaks to her permeable subjectivity and her narrow but rapidly expanding knowledge of the world. As Sai becomes enraptured in textual and thus mental escapism, the borders of the body are compromised – as are the confines of the mind – and mind and body together consume these narratives of adolescence.[8] Feminist critic Elizabeth Grosz argues that somatophobia, a fear of the body and its functions, has historically dominated western thought.[9] Grosz's dialectic of corporeal feminism asks that we reorganize the traditional schema of mind over body. The mind is the seat of power and the font of knowledge and thus it subordinates, if not elides, the body.[10] Desai's novel challenges a Groszian model because her characters are thoroughly diplopic and exist in the crossroads of East and West, colonial and postcolonial, national and transnational; that is, they (Sai and her grandfather in particular), experience many forms of double vision, somatically and psychically, which ultimately challenge a clear dichotomy between East and West. It is not only their somaticism which challenges hierarchical and hegemonic schematizations of their surroundings; it is also their relationship with the written word. Sai's subjectivity evolves slowly throughout the novel and she begins to recognize the ways in which lived experiences are invaluable to one's narrative. Her discovery of the cook's paltry living quarters, seeing Gyan's poverty-stricken home, her broken heart and unanswered desires, all these shape her in a way that *National Geographic* once did. In *The Inheritance of Loss* it is the lived, everyday experiences of the body moving through global forces, that most impacts and shapes the characters' subjectivities.

Post/-Colonial Contradictions

Desai's historical placement of *The Inheritance of Loss* is a purposeful choice which brings us to a moment in time of raging political and religious unrest, class-based strife and widespread violence – a wrinkle in the normally neatly written accounts of national histories. The early to mid-1980 years in India brought catastrophe after catastrophe, as writer Amitav Ghosh aptly testifies: "There were days in 1984 when it took courage to open the New Delhi papers in the morning."[11] One can imagine that it indeed "took courage" to read about the slow and painful death of many people in Bhopal, or the environmental and personal devastation as a result of the political unrest in West Bengal.

The 1984 Bhopal disaster killed an estimated 22,000 people (the actual death toll is surely higher) and maimed many more.[12] The 1980s also witnessed the founding of the Gorkhaland National Liberation Front (GNLF) in West Bengal and the Duars, chiefly in Darjeeling.[13] Nepali-speaking Indians campaigned for the Darjeeling district to be turned into an independent "Gorkhaland" state. Massive violence erupted from 1986 to 1988, and in addition to lost lives, it led to the closing down of the tourist industry and tea farms, leaving behind economic disaster in its wake. Desai's first chapter involves the invasion of the home and theft of guns by boys who first sneeringly ask Sai and the judge if they speak Nepali, and then exclaim: "Gorkhaland for Gorkhas" (*IL* 5–8). Gyan's sometimes ambivalent and uncritical involvement with the Gorkhas is a direct engagement with a troubling period in India's history.

Perhaps no less disturbing – but equally divisive and violent – was the mass rioting and subsequent slaughter of Sikhs following the assassination of the then Prime Minister, Indira Gandhi. Amitav Ghosh's 1995 essay in *The New Yorker*, "The Ghosts of Mrs Gandhi," gives a chilling account of the days following the assassination and his own evolution from author to activist. Writing eleven years after the assassination, Ghosh reflects on the time it took him to absorb and then act on this historical period which deeply impacted Southeast Asians: "It is when we think of the world the aesthetic of indifference might bring into being that we recognize the urgency of remembering the stories we have not written."[14] Ghosh admits that the act of unveiling blind spots in recorded history is challenging and even painful.

Desai's characters seem less interested in defining themselves through their histories; Sai, however, is intent on reading about the world and finding her place in it through the folds of the pages. One might think that *National Geographic* is a strange choice for Sai. Is this the same Sai who swoons over Gyan as she rereads *Wuthering Heights* with a "wild animal feeling" (*IL* 274)? Yet *National Geographic* is mentioned repeatedly throughout the novel and it serves as Sai's steady companion; it is, in many respects, her guidebook to the cosmos. The iconographic depictions of "exotic" places, "primitive" peoples, and "rare" animals absorb Sai so fully that in her haste to know something beyond her immediate surroundings she "could often hardly read the accompanying words" (*IL* 77). Although Susan Sontag, in her *Regarding the Pain of Others*, is chiefly concerned with ethical viewing practices of wartime photography, she nonetheless offers a critique of the nature of photography as narrative: "Nonstop imagery (television, streaming video, movies) is our surround, but when it comes to remembering, the photograph has the deeper bite. […] The photograph is like a quotation, or a maxim or proverb."[15] The photograph, according to Sontag, accesses the discourse of memory more effectively than other forms of visual rhetoric. We know that Sai-as-spectator is prompted to think of herself and her family, Gyan, and the world at large as she scopophilically absorbs the pages of *National Geographic* – it is the unacknowledged co-author of the story of her life. Anthropologist Catherine A. Lutz and sociologist Jane L. Collins studied *National Geographic* as an institution, especially from the 1960s until the mid 1990s. Lutz and Collins reinforce the value of querying the magazine and its sociohistorical significance: "The photograph can be seen as a cultural artifact because its makers and readers look at the world with an eye that is not universal or natural but tutored."[16] The "tutored" logic of the magazine, the racialized and gendered messages within the photographs are consumed by Sai and countered only by the somatic and lived knowledge which she acquires.

Desai's authorial strategy appears to be intensely invested in prodding the reader to enter into a dynamic relationship with her text; in so far as Sai becomes an increasingly savvier consumer of scopic and textual regimes, so too the reader absorbs her shifting register of transnational reimagining of colonial politics. Sai is a protagonist whose visuality informs much of the narrative thread which strings the reader along; we experience the book through her scopophilic and occularcentric apprehension of her surroundings. In *Reading National Geographic*, Lutz and Collins are fundamentally concerned with "how to imagine and value difference."[17] What is Sai learning about the value and place of "primitive" peoples, and "rare" animals, and how does she position herself in relation to them? If we think of *National Geographic* as a commentary *not* on the exotic locales it covers, but as revealing an Americanized production of the Other then Sai's location as reader is complicated and opaque. Furthermore, if *National Geographic* contains the rhetoric of hardening – a linear, hierarchical, and universal code for systematizing nature – this rhetoric stands in opposition to the corporeal knowledge that Sai gains. *National Geographic* is part of the skewed visual regime which Sai is in part introduced to by her grandfather.

Inherent in Lutz and Collins' concern with "how to imagine and value difference" is a global perspective on bodies which questions visual ideologies. The complex meeting of gazes in Sai's consumption of the photographs in *National Geographic* is fascinating.[18] Sai occupies a uniquely conflicted position as consumer. Lutz and Collins aptly state: “we become aware that it is not simply a captured view of the *other*, but rather a dynamic site at which many gazes or viewpoints intersect.”[19] Lisa Bloom points out that even if this intersection of gazes becomes less Eurocentric, the effect on the reader/viewer remains the same because the magazine continues to offer a “national identity that is white and male through the mass circulation of images of the colonial ‘other’ (brown bodies), but, oddly enough, this identity still remains unproblematically white even as American women and men of color are now incorporated.”[20] Sai’s rampant curiosity about the world and how it works, her newfound feelings of love and desire and the sociopolitical unrest she witnesses, all these factors constitute a malleable subjectivity in search of meaning. Perhaps in her unique position as a foreign reader of *National Geographic*, the images she consumes spur her to action. In fact, as the novel crescendos in violence and injustice, Sai increasingly feels that she “must escape” (*IL* 355). Her mind expands its consciousness and she considers the intricate and delicate global connections that dominate the world: “She thought of her father and the space program and she thought of all the *National Geographics* and the books she had read. Of the judge’s journey, of the cook’s journey, of Biju’s. Of the globe twirling on its axis” (*IL* 355). Fittingly, in this narrative of global networks and connections, Sai’s final thoughts are of the movement of the earth in time and space.

Skin: The Porous Boundary

Diasporic South Asian literature is often about immigration, exile and displacement; history has demonstrated that the movement of people is inextricably linked with violent disjuncture and cleavage and this motivates reinvention. With the new awareness of globalization and the fluidity of borders, how has American-made ethnicity changed and how does one define one’s cultural heritage in US diasporic communities?[21] When nations are collectively traumatized by natural disasters or war, or mass emigration, the imagined community often rebuilds a sense of shared goals and aspirations by turning to cultural artefacts and objects. This dialectic is pressured and troubled when immigrants are confronted with visual and written representations of national identity from both their past and current nations. The deterritorialized community rubs up against the grain of national agendas and destabilizes hegemonic blueprints that are often taken for granted. *The Inheritance of Loss* moves us through tumultuous historical moments and identifies what might be thought of as convulsions in the seemingly serene and relaxed musculature of the historical body.

In Desai, political, social and personal changes are firmly bonded and move together as a unit. Gyan's at times unwitting involvement with the Gorkhaland movement crescendos in mass rioting and police violence: "This was how history moved, the slow build, the quick burn, and in an incoherence, the leaping both backward and forward, swallowing the young into old hate. The space between life and death, in the end, too small to measure" (*IL* 303). The narrator's personification of history as a living being swallowing its young, and "leaping" in space embeds a critique of traditional understandings of historical movements, especially as related to the often untold stories of those that are literally swallowed into history books. The oversexed (often female) immigrant body is linked to the formation of national imperialist narratives of superiority. In works such as *The Inheritance of Loss*, the body is unabashedly present and in its corporeal presence we find alternate histories and questionings of hegemonic discourse.

Desai's opening section encapsulates the tension between lived and learned knowledge. The first sentence brings the reader's attention to a prominent and frequent trope in the novel, liquid and solid forms of moisture: "All day, the colors had been those of dusk, mist moving like a water creature across the great flanks of mountains possessed of ocean shadows and depths. Briefly visible above the vapor, Kanchenjunga was a far peak [...]" (*IL* 1). Mist, vapor, fog, rain, moisture, and condensation are personified and take on a life of their own. As Sai reads an old copy of *National Geographic* and learns about giant squid, nature envelops her and overshadows human activity (the scorpion's nest distracts the cook, the stone that keeps the house cold, and the mountain range dominates the view). The mist, vapour, and smoke dominate this first section and the narrator describes a pseudo-erotic interaction between Sai and the mist: "The caress of the mist through her hair seemed human, and when she held her fingers out, the vapor took them gently into its mouth. She thought of Gyan [...]" (*IL* 2). The mist prompts Sai to think of her mathematics tutor's impending arrival. Because of the mist, her physical body leads her train of thought towards her blossoming feelings of desire.

Nothing is safe from the penetrating vapours, much less the judge's house, a decaying symbol of colonial rule. Jemu's house is an ode to colonial times and as such remains a relic of imperial and colonial attitudes: "The house had been built long ago by a Scotsman, passionate reader of the accounts of that period: *The Indian Alps and How We Crossed Them*, by a Lady Pioneer" (*IL* 13, original italics). The Scotsman "refused to be denied the right to adventure" and builds Cho Oyu on the backs of others (*IL* 13). The narrator underscores the Orientalist connotations of the Scotsman's house by describing the physical toll it took on those that built it: "Porters had carried boulders from the riverbed – legs growing bandy, ribs curving into caves, backs into U's, faces being bent slowly to look always at the ground–[...]" (*IL* 13). The view and the height come at the price of constant moisture and the home is slowly invaded by the outside: "Up through the chimney and out, the smoke mingled with the mist that was gathering speed, sweeping in thicker and thicker [...]. Gradually the vapor replaced everything with itself, solid objects with shadow, and nothing remained that did not seem molded from or inspired by it" (*IL* 2).

The elements and inhabitants of the house must come into sometimes violent contact with the outside world. Although the house is "contained by stone walls several feet deep" the passage of time, the past, and memories of the past in particular, can no longer be kept at bay. The vapour is powerfully described as having gradually "replaced everything with itself"; a metaphor for the British Empire's blanketing of itself across the Indian continent. The duality of colonizer and colonized is nowhere more apparent than in the form of the mist, which occurs when two different temperatures and entities come into contact with one another. "The gray had permeated inside," and the domestic and internal space is colonized by the thickening mist which allows Sai to leave "a perfectly formed film star kiss" on a mirror. She catches a "glimpse of herself being smothered" by it, but it is through the mist (and her body) that she mimics a Westernized cinematic moment and expresses her nervous excitement over Gyan's arrival. The collision course between Cho Oyu and the outside world speeds along with the same sense of urgency as Sai's kiss.

Sai's scene with the mirror is momentarily interrupted by her thoughts about the giant squid in *National Geographic*. Specifically, Sai imagines what it might mean for them to live a solitary existence and never meet other beings like themselves: "The melancholy of this situation washed over Sai" (*IL* 3). The progression is as follows: body to mind, back to body. The knowledge of solitude "washes over" her and she muses on the differences between loss and fulfillment: "Romantically she decided that love must surely reside in the gap between desire and fulfillment, in the lack [...]" (*IL* 3). At the beginning of her romance with Gyan Sai believes that love is the absence and ache of something that was; it is a spectral existence that depends on there having once been something or someone.

Chapter one begins and ends in the thickening of the mist, in the realm of fluidity and change. The mist returns at the close of chapter one, bringing the narrative full circle. The narrator motions towards the arbitrary yet violent nature of borders: "Darjeeling stolen from here, Kalimpong plucked from there – despite, ah, despite the mist charging down like a dragon, dissolving, undoing, making ridiculous the drawing of borders" (*IL* 10). The mist does not discern between countries, ethnicities, lands or bodies/people. The mist mixes with Sai's breath and effectively relies upon her breath for its own visibility, it permeates the body and mind in unexpected ways.

Corporeally speaking, Sai can no longer exist as an individual container that remains untouched by other things and beings. The mist is the connection between inside and outside, it is the dynamism of water that moves between the body and its surroundings. Elizabeth Grosz identifies two somatic disorders (the phantom limb and agnosia) which exemplify the overlapping echelons of biology and psychology, or to speak reductively, of body and mind. The phantom limb is a disorder in which a patient still reports sensation and pain in the location of an amputated limb, while agnosia is the failure of the senses to recognize a body part.[22] Using phenomenological philosopher Maurice Marleau-Ponty's work on memory and the body, Grosz takes the evolution of his work on corporeal perception and suggests a revision of subject-object relations.[23] Grosz notes that whereas the divide between subject and object was clear in Marleau-Ponty's earlier work, in his later work it becomes a porous boundary in which the skin becomes the fold between interiority and exteriority, between subject as subjectivity and subject as phenomena: "Neither subject nor object can be conceived as cores, atoms, or nuggets of being, pure presence; not bounded entities, they 'interpenetrate,' mingle."[24] The human becomes coextensive with the world at large and with both biological beings and inanimate objects.

Global Embodiment

If we recognize that knowledge resides in the body and that the senses are connected to memory, embodiment becomes a complex and multi-faceted process. What might "global embodiment" feel like and how does the lived global body's everyday experience differ from a non-global body's experiences? Sociologist Michael Burawoy, who has done extensive work on globalization "from below," suggests that lived experiences of globalization often bring pressure to bear on hegemonic powers that might otherwise remain unchallenged. Burawoy points to the manner in which one might ultimately – and somatically – feel the force of the global, of "the lived experience of globalization – the way global forces, global connections, and global imaginations uphold, accommodate, resist, or contest the existing order."[25] Global forces are felt internally and externally. Not only does one embody a narrative as it unfolds (i.e., you react physically and emotionally to words on the page), but cultural memories are often embodied and experiences are written on the body. Grosz interestingly links the biological disorder of the phantom limb to memory: "It is the refusal of an experience to enter into the past; it illustrates the tenacity of a present that remains immutable."[26] The search for an history, an exploration of one's lost origins, is the very foundation of the protagonists in many immigrant and diasporic narratives. They feel that they must first understand their histories to understand themselves.

The notion that the body does not exist on its own, that it is both permeable and permeating, that it immigrates and emigrates in and out of its husk (the skin), is especially relevant to Desai's construction of Biju and Jemubhai's experiences as immigrants.[27] Sai's arrival causes the judge to engage in a "revisitation of his past" and as his memories dislodge and flood his mind, he recalls his boat trip to Cambridge by way of Liverpool (*IL* 42). Jemubhai's mother packs him a banana that rots and he throws it overboard; the putrid banana is the first of many representations of the judge's self-hatred and self-colonization. He remembers the banana as a sign of "Undignified love, Indian love, stinking, unaesthetic love–" (*IL* 43). Ethnicity, food, smell, and shame are all projected onto one object, which is quickly dispensed into the ocean below. The judge's multisensory hatred of all things Indian reveals the motivations behind his encompassing and absorbing spiteful sentiments towards himself, the cook, and his surrounding at Cho Oyu.

The immigrant body and the ways in which it signifies difference become increasingly problematic for the judge as he spends more time at Cambridge. Stinging remarks from English girls that "he stinks of curry!" lend Jemubhai no respite from his own growing feelings of insecurity. He begins to despise his smell, his skin, his body: "he grew stranger to himself than he was to those around him, found his own skin odd-colored, his own accent peculiar [...]. He began to wash obsessively, concerned he would be accused of smelling [...]" (*IL* 45). Because he repudiates all signs of himself and his body, the judge becomes so far removed from society that he feels inhuman: "Eventually he felt barely human at all, leaped when touched on the arm as if from an unbearable intimacy [...]" (*IL* 46). The judge's failing humanity – his emotional and physical alienation as he tries to avoid all other people – manifests itself as pure hatred. His obsession with his skin and his wish to lighten and remove its oiliness sets up one of the most disturbing scenes of the book, when Jemubhai forces Nimi (his bride) to have sex with him. When the judge returns to India he insists on powdering his skin, and Nimi, oblivious to the importance of the "powder puff" stuffs it down her dress as she goes through his things. Her rape comes on the heels of Jemubhai's discovery that she has taken his "puff," and fueled by shame, "with rage, blundering" Jemubhai forces himself on her (*IL* 186). But just as Sai can no longer live as an individual vessel, untouched by others, so too the judge's past haunts him in these moments of remembrance. His terror at the thought of his own body betraying him grows into such a strong hatred of Nimi that he eventually kills her. The judge is aware of the ways in which he and Sai represent the Anglicized elite, the mantle of colonial power in India. As he pieces together his memories, he is overwhelmed by the feeling that "the present changes the past" (*IL* 227), and that "the truth und[oes] you" (*IL* 229).

The judge's obsession with his body resonates with Biju's experiences decades later in New York. As the son of a poor cook, he knows his chances of monetary success in Cho Oyu are slim to none, and he dreams the classic American immigrant dream – work hard, make money, create a better future, and perhaps never return home. Emblematic of the conflicting feelings involved in the immigrant experience is Biju's boss at the Gandhi Café, Harish-Harry: "the two names, Biju was learning, indicated a deep rift that he hadn't suspected [...]. He tried to keep on the right side of power, tried to be loyal to so many things that he himself couldn't tell which one of his selves was authentic, if any" (*IL* 164). Harish-Harry's Gandhi Café is Biju's last workplace. It is the final stop on his journey of self-realization, when he begins to question the paradigm of wealth bringing happiness, of whiteness as superior to darkness.

While Biju is not as obsessed with lightening his skin, he is acutely aware of the power of smell and how it permeates the body. It is not just the smell of food that draws him to the café, it is the recognition of a certain type of smell: "His country called him again. He smelled his fate. Drawn, despite himself, by his nose, around a corner, he saw the first letter of the sign, *G*, then an *AN*. His soul anticipated the rest: *DHI*. As he approached the Gandhi Café, the air gradually grew solid" (*IL* 154). The fragmented text indicates the lack of unity inhabiting the space of the Gandhi Café. It is here that immigrants and foreign students, or those of mixed Indian-American heritage come to dine: "Confusion was rampant among the '*haalf 'n' haf*' crowd (*IL* 164). The myth of the American dream and the promises of happiness and assimilation are encapsulated in the broken text. In a poststructural textual model the signified object-world and the signifying letters do not align and Biju is left with the "unbudgeable" smell emanating from the café.

The Gandhi Café represents any number of restaurants where the dirty underbelly of quasi-indentured labour depends on the steady influx of desperate immigrants. As the narrator shares: "It was horrible what happened to Indians abroad and nobody knew but other Indians abroad. It was a dirty little [...] secret" (*IL* 154). Biju sleeps in the kitchen and his wages are docked because of his housing arrangement. The description of the café marks it as a place of dingy sin: "In the Gandhi Café, the lights were kept low, the better to hide the stains. It was a long journey from here to the fusion trend [...]. This was the real thing, generic Indian [...] one stop on the subway line or even on the phone: gilt and red chair, plastic roses on the table with synthetic dewdrops [...]" (*IL* 161). The synthetic dew drops are reminiscent of the mist of Cho Oyu, but here they have been hardened and plasticized – a simulacrum of authenticity.

The oils and smells from the Gandhi Café are synecdochic of the relationship between Biju and the US (between immigrant and host country). Just as the moisture of Cho Oyu moves freely in and out of the body, so too smell permeates and clings to the body, and also emanates from it. Metropoles have become a space for cultural fusion and sensory experiences which are different from those of the past. Cultural regimes of knowledge are challenged when one regime meets another, and evermore so when the body and its senses offer often intangible modes of understanding and knowledge-making.

Smell requires a meeting of two things; one's olfactory senses come into contact with a smell which emanates from someone or something else. Subject and object are collapsed and both participate in the exchange. Grosz's revision of subject-object relations creates a schematic in which the human is co-extensive with the echelon of non-human objects. The skin is the membrane which supposedly separates inner and outer, but with the simultaneous absorption and creation of fluids and scents, even the role of skin is pressured. If we acknowledge that memory is intricately linked to the body and its experiences, then might we think of the body as capable of remembering when the mind and our ocularcentric *modus operandi* elude the past? Grosz's ideas of the body require that one thinks of subjectivity and the corporeal experiences as acephalous; one's vision, for example, is on equal footing with taste, smell, hearing, and touch.

The smell of his various workplaces remains with Biju as he switches jobs (Chinese, American, Indian) and in running from the stench of impurity he finds at the Gandhi Café. Later Biju realizes that Harish-Harry inhabits a moral vacuum and that he in fact signifies a lacuna of integrity: "Would he [Biju], like Harish-Harry manufacture a fake version of himself and using what he had created as clues, understand himself backward?" (*IL* 293). Biju muses that his body is devoid of meaning and has instead become a place-holder which simply takes up space: "in a space that should have included family, friends, he was the only one displacing the air" (*IL* 293). Biju's body-as-matter disturbs him because it lacks the expanding consciousness (though he notes his increased "self-consciousness") that he had considered being innate to the immigrant experience.

Biju does something which contradicts the assimilationist model of the immigrant's journey in the US – he returns home. *En route* to Cho Oyu, Biju is robbed of all of his money and the men strip him down to his underwear. Taking a lady's dressing gown for cover, hounded by dogs and dragging his injured leg, Biju arrives at Cho Oyu and cries out for his father, the cook, "*Pitaji*?" (*IL* 357). Against the backdrop of violence (as the judge beats the cook), the reader learns the cook's name on the last page of the novel. This is the scene to which Biju returns, and yet the reader may somehow still feel as if he has made the right choice; as if, in fact, he is much more "conscious" than he thinks he is. Kiran Desai acknowledges the ambiguity of her ending: "I think there's a moment of hope with Biju's returning home, and even with the young girl Sai realizing that hers is not going to be a mean life. [...] I think it had to be a complex ending and somewhat hopeful maybe, but also somewhat shadowy."[28]

The Politics of the Body and the Body Politic

As globalization and the speed of communication have been widely discussed in recent years, so has the threat of cultural homogenization. Globalization theorist and literary critic Giles Gunn points to the increasing anxiety over the sentiment that globalization will lead to the *elision* of diversity: "the erasure of local differences and the integration of more and more of the world's people, as well as of entire sovereign states, into a geopolitical system that inevitably erodes their ability to shape their own destinies."[29] Yet literary critics and artists propose that it is sometimes in the moments of cultural transference and appropriation that "third world" communities and individuals redefine and express themselves.[30] Ghanaian philosopher and cultural critic Kwame Anthony Appiah fears that globalization "contaminates" local cultures and challenges local homogeneity: "People who complain about homogeneity as a product of globalization often fail to notice that globalization is, equally, a threat to homogeneity."[31] While Appiah praises globalization's cross-cultural contamination (especially if it might lead to increasing understanding from culture to culture), he is not convinced that the human interactions and meetings are any more valuable than the connection one feels to historical and ancestral objects. Appiah understands the imaginary connection one feels to the Benjamin-like aura attached to a cultural artifact as equal in value to the "real" connection of physical contact in real time.[32] Interestingly, what Appadurai, Appiah and Gunn all motion towards is agency in the realm of the symbolic.

Yet not all critics see globalization as a process of empowerment for what sociologist Zygmunt Bauman terms the "locals" (versus the "globals"). In *Globalization: The Human Consequences*, Bauman points to the ways in which capital stratifies and separates the locals and the globals: "Some of us become fully and truly 'global'; some are fixed in their 'locality' – a predicament neither pleasurable nor endurable in the world in which the 'globals' set the tone and compose the rules of the life-game."[33] In *The Inheritance of Loss* the body not only serves as a unifying common denominator between the different characters, it also embodies labouring flesh and national traumas. In Desai, bodies are forever on the move. They are in high states of expansive mobility both internally and externally, but they do not operate according to the same rules. As Bauman reminds us, capital allows one freedom to travel in space and time because there "are no 'natural borders' any more, neither are there obvious places to occupy."[34] He adds that people of the first world "travel at will," while those of the "second travel surreptitiously, often illegally."[35] In Desai we see the repeated collision of first and second world global travellers; and ironically, although they depend on their corporeal presence more than others, labouring bodies are often left unexamined because they are the very "natural boundaries" that Bauman claims do not exist. As much as we can theorize and talk about the body as a social construction, we cannot deny the powerful experiences of embodied subjectivity and our limitations as biological beings.

The face of the immigrant diasporic experience has changed and asserting agency in the shifting territory of one's ethnic identity is possible in many respects because of the evermore fluid nature of today's borders.[36] In her 2004 American Studies Association presidential address, Shelley Fisher Fishkin called for the "transnational turn" in American Studies and she offered that the "United States is and has always been a transnational crossroads of cultures."[37] Indeed, many diasporic authors have found themselves writing about the experience of coming, leaving, and returning to their homelands, and/or to the United States. Desai's work methodically explodes this bipolar sensibility and interweaves it with the colonial and postcolonial history of India and its relation to Britain and the US. The transnational nature of Desai's imaginative writing demonstrates that the politics of the body are not only inseparable from the body politic, but that one in fact relies on the other and in the shifting landscape of globalization, as our spatiotemporal relationship to the body changes, so too, subjects begin to think differently of their national allegiances.

Notes

1. Werner Sollors avers that ethnic literature has in general been read as narratives of descent in which "ethnic-group membership" is considered the defining driving force. Sollors says: "Instead of understanding their texts as codes for socialization into ethnic groups and into America, readers have overemphasized and exaggerated the (frequently exoticized) ethnic particularity of the works – even if they were published in English by major American publishing houses,"

Beyond Ethnicity: Consent and Descent in American Culture (New York: Oxford UP, 1986), 11.

2. Kiran Desai, *The Inheritance of Loss* (New York: Grove Press, 2006); references to the novel are to this edition and will be given parenthetically, preceded by *IL*.
3. At the time of publication of this article, Kiran Desai is a permanent resident of the United States of America and a citizen of India.
4. Arjun Appadurai, *Modernity at Large: Cultural Dimensions of Globalization* (Minneapolis: University of Minnesota Press, 1996), 84.
5. Paul Jay, "Beyond Discipline? Globalization and the Future of English," *PMLA: Publications of the Modern Language Association of America* 116.1 (2001): 42.
6. Jay, 33.
7. "Hyphenated" is also a term that has caused friction among transnational South Asian authors. Bharati Mukherjee refused, in a 1997 *Mother Jones* piece to be known as "hyphenated," while Jhumpa Lahiri wrote a powerful *Newsweek* article entitled "My Hyphenated Identity," (2006) but this was renamed in subsequent reprintings as "My Two Lives."
8. The books that Sai reads are versions of the classic *Bildungsroman;* Harper Lee's *To Kill a Mockingbird* (1960) is perhaps the most well known to a US audience. Laurie Lee's *Cider with Rosie* (1959) is a British literary biography about growing up in the countryside after World War I. *Life with Father* (1936) is an autobiographical collection of stories by American author Clarence Day Jr. The stories are for the most part based on his family and his father, who bears eerie similarities to Sai's grandfather.
9. Elizabeth Grosz's introductory chapter briefly outlines a definition of somatophobia, *Volatile Bodies* (Bloomington: Indiana UP, 1994), 5. She argues that Western philosophy, working from a Cartesian mind/body duality, has regarded the body as a type of threat to reason.
10. See Grosz's Chapter 4, "Lived Bodies: Phenomenology and the Flesh." Here Grosz takes French existentialist/psychologist Maurice Merleau-Ponty's work in *Phenomenology of Perception* and revises Western conceptions of knowledge and the body; she specifically argues that lived bodies and perceptual experiences are equally important to knowledge-formation.
11. Amitav Ghosh, "The Ghosts of Mrs Gandhi," *The New Yorker* July 17 (1995): 36.
12. On December 13, 1984, Union Carbide's factory in Bhopal leaked deadly methyl isocyanate gas and marked what is reportedly one of the worst industrial disasters in history. Anthropologist Kim Fortun's

Advocacy After Bhopal (Chicago: U of Chicago P, 2001) is a comprehensive resource on the Bhopal disaster and its larger implications. Based in part on Fortun's fieldwork in Bhopal six years after the disaster, her work is also a critique of modernity and a study of time. Also, see Margaret E. Keck and Kathryn Sikkink, *Activists Beyond Borders*, (Ithaca and London: Cornell UP, 1998) for their pioneering work on transnational advocacy networks as related to Bhopal.

13. As political scientist Rajat Ganguly comments, "the violence drove a deep wedge between the majority Bengali and the minority Gorkha communities in West Bengal," Ganguly, "Poverty, Malgovernance and Ethnopolitical Mobilization: Gorkha Nationalism and the Gorkhaland Agitation in India," *Nationalism and Ethnic Politics* 11.4 (2005): 468. See the article for more on the GNLF movement, past and present.
14. Ghosh, 35.
15. Susan Sontag, *Regarding the Pain of Others* (New York: Picador, 2004), 22.
16. Catherine A. Lutz and Jane L. Collins, *Reading National Geographic* (Chicago: U of Chicago P, 1993), xiii.
17. Lutz and Collins xiii.
18. Lutz and Collins, in a subsection of their book entitled "Erasing the Colonizer," discuss how the presence of Westerners in *National Geographic's* photos decreased with pre- and post-colonial unrest (Lutz and Collins, 39). The writers became aware of the loaded political messages encoded in a white explorer's body as he or she stands among, for example, naked and disenfranchised native African tribal people.
19. Lutz and Collins, 187.
20. Lisa Bloom, "Constructing Whiteness: Popular Science and *National Geographic* in the Age of Multiculturalism," *Configurations* 2 (1994): 19.
21. In the mid 1980s, Werner Sollors rightly pointed out that "American-made ethnicity" had garnered little attention from critics, and while I admit that in part due to his work this is less true now, works about immigration still seem non-canonical or novel, Sollors *Beyond Ethnicity: Consent and Descent in American Literature* (New York: Oxford UP, 1986),11.
22. Grosz, 89.
23. The section on which Grosz focuses regarding biological disorders is in large part from Merleau-Ponty's work on neurological matters. Grosz is clear, however, that Marleau-Ponty's writings rely on Goldstein and Gelb's "case study of the brain-damaged aphasic Schneider" (Grosz, 87).

24. Grosz, 96.
25. Michael Burawoy, *Global Ethnography: Forces, Connections, and Imaginations in a Postmodern World* (Berkeley: U of California P, 2000), 344.
26. Grosz, 89.
27. As Grosz suggests, the corpus is never something that exists purely on its own terms, "Bodies themselves, in their materialities, are never self-present, given things, immediate, certain self-evidences because embodiment, corporeality, insist on alterity [...]. Alterity is the very possibility and process of embodiment [...]" (Grosz, 209).
28. Desai, *Brick* interview 106.
29. Giles B. Gunn, "Introduction: Globalizing Literary Studies," *PMLA: Publications of the Modern Language Association of America* 116.1 (2001): 19.
30. Appadurai puts forward the argument that "[...] the consumption of the mass media throughout the world often provokes resistance, irony, selectivity, and, in general, *agency*" (Appadurai, 7). He is quick to point out, however, that there is a difference between agency and freedom, and that the possibility of freedom sits in what he calls the "collective imagination" of a given community (7). Appadurai's claim that "The imagination is now central to all forms of agency, is itself a social fact, and is the key component of the new global order" (31) suggests some of the ways in which the various nodes of cultural interaction and transference in contemporary US fiction must be examined in order to understand both US and global shifting literary landscapes.
31. Kwame Anthony Appiah, *Cosmopolitanism: Ethics in a World of Strangers*, Issues of Our Time (New York: W.W. Norton, 2006), 101.
32. Appiah, 134–135.
33. Zygmunt Bauman, "Tourists and Vagabonds," in Bauman, *Globalization: The Human Consequences* (New York: Columbia UP, 1998), 2. While I agree with Bauman's explication that the freedom to travel across space – specifically, one's fixity of position – largely depends on one's access to capital, I am not as convinced that there is a clear divide between "locals" and "globals." While those that are not free to move are certainly less apt to traverse the globe and are thus localized, they also have agency in that they can speak back to "globals" and participate or initiate exchanges and contact between the two.
34. Bauman, 77.
35. Bauman, 89.
36. I acknowledge the troubling nature of the term, "diaspora," which has been freely used for the "Asian" experience at large. See Shirley Geok-lin Lim's work for an extensive study of the issues at stake in

terming the Asian-American, or Indo-American experience as a diaspora. In short, she argues that the term connotes a perpetual longing for a geopolitical space that ceases to exist once one has left, Shirley Geok-lin Lim, "Immigration and Diaspora," in *An Interethnic Companion to Asian American Literature*, ed. King-Kok Cheung, (Cambridge: Cambridge UP, 1997), 289–311.

37. Shelley Fisher Fishkin, "Crossroads of Cultures: The Transnational Turn in American Studies – Presidential Address to the American Studies Association, November 12, 2004," *American Quarterly* 57.1 (Mar 2005): 43.

Works Cited

Appadurai, Arjun. *Modernity at Large: Cultural Dimensions of Globalization.* Minneapolis: U of Minnesota P, 1996.

Appiah, Kwame Anthony. Issues of Our Time. *Cosmopolitanism: Ethics in a World of Strangers.* New York: W.W. Norton, 2006.

Bauman, Zygmunt. "Tourists and Vagabonds." In Bauman, *Globalization: The Human Consequences.* New York: Columbia UP, 1998. 77–102.

Bloom, Lisa. "Constructing Whiteness: Popular Science and *National Geographic* in the Age of Multiculturalism." *Configurations* 2 (1994): 15–32.

Burawoy, Michael. *Global Ethnography: Forces, Connections, and Imaginations in a Postmodern World.* Berkeley: U of California P, 2000.

Desai, Kiran. *The Inheritance of Loss.* New York: Grove Press, 2006.

Desai, Kiran. "An Interview with Kiran Desai." By Eleanor Wachtel. *Brick* 79 (Summer 2007): 89–108.

Fishkin, Shelley Fisher. "Crossroads of Cultures: The Transnational Turn in American Studies – Presidential Address to the American Studies Association, November 12, 2004." *American Quarterly* 57.1 (Mar 2005): 17–57.

Fortun, Kim. *Advocacy After Bhopal: Environmentalism, Disaster, New Global Orders.* Chicago: U of Chicago P, 2001.

Ganguly, Rajat. "Poverty, Malgovernance and Ethnopolitical Mobilization: Gorkha Nationalism and the Gorkhaland Agitation in India." *Nationalism and Ethnic Politics* 11.4 (2005). 467–502.

Ghosh, Amitav. "The Ghosts of Mrs Gandhi." *The New Yorker* 17 July (1995): 35–41.

Grosz, Elizabeth. *Volatile Bodies: Towards a Corporeal Feminism.* Bloomington: Indiana UP, 1994.

Gunn, Giles B. "Introduction: Globalizing Literary Studies." *PMLA: Publications of the Modern Language Association of America* 116.1 (2001): 16–31.

Jay, Paul. "Beyond Discipline? Globalization and the Future of English." *PMLA: Publications of the Modern Language Association of America* 116.1 (2001): 32–47.

Keck, Margaret E. and Kathryn Sikkink. *Activists Beyond Borders: Advocacy Networks in International Politics.* Ithaca and London: Cornell UP, 1998.

Lim, Shirley Geok-lin. "Immigration and Diaspora." In *An Interethnic Companion to Asian American Literature.* Ed. King-Kok Cheung. Cambridge: Cambridge UP, 1997. 289–311.

Lutz, Catherine A. and Jane L. Collins. *Reading National Geographic.* Chicago: U of Chicago P, 1993.

Sollors, Werner. *Beyond Ethnicity: Consent and Descent in American Literature.* New York: Oxford UP, 1986.

Sontag, Susan. *Regarding the Pain of Others.* New York: Picador, 2004.

2

Partition, Private Lives and Co-Wives

Women, Modernity and Nation in Shauna Singh Baldwin's *What the Body Remembers* and Manju Kapur's *Difficult Daughters*

CHRISTINE VOGT-WILLIAM

Possible Metaphors for the Divided Nation

A common denominator in Shauna Singh Baldwin's *What the Body Remembers* (2000) and Manju Kapur's *Difficult Daughters* (1999) is their focus on Partition as a significant influence on the formation of India's postcolonial national imaginary, as read and filtered through the gendered private arenas of the home.[1] Post-independent nations are ineluctably defined by heteronormative indigenous male authority (often located in the socially elite classes), which prescribes official public identities, citizenship ideals and regulates public discourse.[2] In these two women-centred narratives, Singh Baldwin and Kapur problematize and contribute to destabilizing the national imaginary through their focus on maternal genealogies and female sexuality.[3] Singh Baldwin and Kapur commemorate the Indian independence movement and Partition by gendering cultural memory, nationalism and narrative through the embodied experiences and private desires of their female protagonists; thus gender roles and expectations are imbricated in negotiations of modernity and tradition. Hence, Singh Baldwin and Kapur's approaches serve to reconfigure the ostensibly homogenous spaces and knowledge mapped out by traditional masculine authority (both the indigenous and the imperialist), by examining possible sites of official selfhood, belonging and agency for women during India's struggles for independence in the 1930s and 1940s.

In her discussion of South African and Indian women writers of the 1990s, Elleke Boehmer discusses Frederic Jameson's definition of the problematically designated "Third World novel" as the embodiment of the post-independence nation and its process of coming into being.[4] Remarking that the masculine ways of knowing underlying this process, imply exclusively Western cultural worldviews, Boehmer advocates breaching such exclusivity. She cites Gillian Rose's assertion of the importance of other hitherto marginalized axes of social identity: "by exploring the relationships between them, by looking at various permutations and imbrications of alternative identity."[5] These articulations across degrees of difference, beyond accepted dualistic traditions, acknowledge that difference operates within and among supposedly homogenous spaces and subject positions, allowing for the voices of those who have hitherto been silenced.

Taking Jameson's definition of "national allegory" as the site where the individual story and experience ultimately involves the story of the collectivity itself as a point of departure,[6] I read the novels' focus on culturally sanctioned polygamy as possible metaphors for the divided nation. In a 2002 interview, Singh Baldwin draws the connection between Partition and polygamy[7] in *What the Body Remembers*:

> I [...] found that the central conflict of the polygamous marriage was an allegory for what was happening to the whole country. So the tension in the story built naturally to 1947 and the transformational event for my characters became Partition/Independence, just as it was for 17 million displaced people on the subcontinent.[8]

The allegory of the polygamous marriage is also applicable to Kapur's narrative, since it also focuses on the developments and destinies of a pair of co-wives, who, to all intents and purposes embody India's negotiation of modernity and tradition in its fledgling attempts to cull a new national identity from its colonial past.[9]

What the Body Remembers is the story of Roop, a young Sikh girl from a village near Rawalpindi, who agrees to become the second wife to Sardarji, an older wealthy man of higher social class and caste (he is an engineer employed by the British colonial administration). In return, she is prepared to bear his children and be educated by him to suit his Anglophile lifestyle. The senior wife Satya commits suicide when she realizes that her husband is lost to her. Roop and Sardarji are soon caught up in the tumult of Partition and escape to Delhi to begin new lives in a newly independent India.

Difficult Daughters tells the story of Virmati, the eldest daughter of a goldsmith's family, who prefers education to an arranged marriage. While pursuing her studies at the university, she falls in love with a professor of English literature named Harish, who is married to an uneducated woman, Ganga. Harish finally marries Virmati after a five-year love affair; she becomes his second wife to fulfil his needs for intellectual companionship. Virmati and Harish set up their new home in Delhi after the Partition and Harish forbids Ganga to return to him, banishing her and her children from his life.

One notes that Singh Baldwin and Kapur set their narratives in the cultural contexts of the Sikh and Hindu communities respectively. The Muslim cultural perspective recedes into the background and is marginally (and not necessarily positively) addressed.[10]

A House Divided: Modern Wives for a New Nation

The narratives of co-wives living in family constellations, which are not congruent with the ideals of the modern nuclear family unit, can be instrumentalized to articulate alternative familial experiences. These then could contribute to reconceptualizing the domestic sphere of the home as flexible and diversified alternatives to the (hetero)normative masculine circumscribed idea of home as identifying with "a conventional national framework, classically constructed with reference to the West."[11] This domestic ideal is constituted through the monogamous marriage contract as the central organizing principle of the nuclear family that forms the basic building block of the nation. While polygamy in the two novels may proffer a peculiarly indigenous strategy in conceptualizing alternative domestic contexts for envisioning the new nation,[12] these domestic situations are far from providing safe environments for the female protagonists. Rather, one notes the blatant disregard for the feelings, desires and individualities of both sets of co-wives, all of whom evince losses in diverse forms, in order to promulgate the more masculine codified agendas of cultural preservation, decolonization and nation building. At the same time, one notes that the younger co-wives are not helpless victims of tradition; they are able to exercise some form of agency in that they choose to marry the men of their choice.

The male protagonists had been part of the elite academic Indian diasporic groups in England and returned to India on the verge of Independence. These Anglophile "Oxford-returned" men are savvy in western (read: modern) ways of thinking and enjoy elevated social reputations.[13] They marry a second time, in order to fill certain gaps in their lives to satisfy their desires for progeny, social status and intellectual companionship. By choosing to marry and educate younger women, while supplanting their first wives, these men stake their claim in the newly independent India as nation builders with suitable life partners, who then produce new national subjects.[14] Hence, the strategy of bigamy is used in the novels to illustrate a particular discourse of nationalism that emerged in the second half of nineteenth century India,[15] where, as observed by Partha Chatterjee: "the attempt was made to define the social and moral principles for locating the position of women in the 'modern' world of the nation."[16]

Thus, while striving to build the new nation in accordance with the knowledges gained by the social elite from their western education and socialization, one notes that women were still closely monitored and policed: "their bodies, behaviours and roles are objects of national concern."[17] Chatterjee describes this ambivalence in the greater nation-building project with regard to negotiations and evaluations between modern and traditional perceptions, delineated by gendered spaces:

> The discourse of nationalism shows that the material/spiritual distinction was condensed into an analogous, but ideologically far more powerful dichotomy: that between the outer and the inner. [...] a separation of social space into [...] the home and the world. The world is the external, the domain of the material; the home represents our inner spiritual self, our true identity. The world is a treacherous terrain of the pursuit of material interests, where practical considerations reign supreme. [...] The home in its essence must remain unaffected by the profane activities of the material world – and woman is its representation [...] Once we match this new meaning of the home/world dichotomy with the identification of social roles by gender, we get the ideological framework within which nationalism answered the women's question.[18]

Thus, while the desire to be considered modern, and hence fit for self-rule, was uppermost in the minds of most Indian elite with some access to political agency at the time of the independence struggle, the domestic space of home – a designated female space – was where the core of cultural authenticity was meant to be preserved by women. Here, modern views and practices, coded as western, were often declared impermissible among women for fear of contamination and hence weakening of the nationalist cause. However, in her reading of Chatterjee's dichotomy, Jill Didur cautions that "while the 'spiritual' or private domain is constructed as a place free from colonial cultural influence, it is not considered above the need for reform."[19] Deniz Kandiyoti further remarks that simplified ethnocentric definitions of public and private spheres of gendered action bear reflection, since "the boundaries of the so-called private domain are in fact structured by the state," whereby these boundaries are fluid and subject to realignment.[20] Thus, Sardarji and Harish's education of their second wives, while ostensibly meant to be understood as emancipation, is soon revealed to be new and refined modes of subordination in the interest of nation-building.

In the interests of social reform with regard to women's issues, Indian women from all walks of life were active participants in the anti-colonial struggles, which in turn set the scene for the emergence of women's movements[21] in India. Modernizing efforts in pre-Partition India (and immediately afterwards) consisted of social reform measures with regard to age of marriage, polygamy, property rights, women's education, treatment of widows (*sati* and remarriage) and so on. While attempting to improve women's lives, in response to western criticisms of Indian society, these efforts were not always successful in ameliorating women's subjugation within and outside the family. Gradually rising awareness of such subjugation instigated women's resistance to both indigenous and imperialist patriarchal structures.[22]

Jyoti Puri links women's involvement in the nationalist cause with the perception of progressive thinking in the treatment of women in society: "That the status of women was the litmus test of societies was the result of the encounter between the colonial state and official anti-colonial nationalism."[23] The second wives in the novels – young malleable women desiring social advancement – are thus the perfect templates for (re-)education in accordance with the husbands' desires for intellectually compatible companions with social aptitudes befitting the husbands' cosmopolitan attitudes and social circles. Thus, their educational advancement could be read superficially at least as an attempt to confer autonomy on them, making them 'modern'. However, as Kumari Jayawardena astutely observes: "'[m]odernity' meant educated women, but educated to uphold the system of the nuclear patriarchal family."[24] Hence social reform was not necessarily a clear-cut project with a view to improving women's status in education and circumstances in life, as well as their potential as equal citizens in the new nation. This is borne out by Chatterjee's observation that "the nationalist paradigm in fact supplied an ideological principle of selection. It was not a dismissal of modernity; the attempt was rather to make modernity consistent with the nationalist project."[25] It follows then that the social reform envisioned was meant to ensure that women's roles and place in society, while 'modernized' conditionally, were to remain essentially the same – those of wife and mother, albeit educated.

Homi K. Bhabha points out the ambivalence and double standards pertaining to perceptions of modernity in national space: "The problematic boundaries of modernity are enacted in these ambivalent temporalities of the national space. The language of culture and community is poised on the fissures of the present becoming the rhetorical figures of a national past."[26] I read these 'problematic boundaries of modernity' in the husbands' choice of the culturally accepted tradition of polygamy to overturn yet another cultural tradition – that of the arranged child marriages that they themselves had been subjected to as young boys (*WBR* 159; *DD* 103). These fissures are apparent in both novels through the justification of polygamy by these 'modern' Indian men in order to ameliorate their personal dissatisfactions with their first wives. This subversion of the cultural dictum imposed on them by the tradition of child marriage thus articulates their own intellectualized criticism of this particular indigenous tradition from their perspectives as colonized subjects, while subscribing to 'Western' value systems. While both men are advocates for the modern nation-state, one notes that their private cultural observances seem to adhere to certain perceptions of cultural tradition that acquire social advantages for them devoid of the censure of the community, because of their caste and their socio-economic background.

The plots of the novels bear certain congruencies to the greater drama of the Partition of India and the concomitant tensions between perceptions of modernity and tradition, which then may be particularly seductive in their tidiness, prompting allegorical readings. However, Boehmer cautions against reading these texts merely as nationally symbolic, since such a one-dimensional reading strategy proves to be of disservice to the obvious centring of women's experience in the narratives, which deploy more modest, local and intimate modes of representation.[27] Indeed on careful reading, one notes that the grand narrative of the national imaginary, though important, is not the main focus; rather it takes on secondary, even peripheral dimensions in favour of the messy excess, the rootlessness and ambivalence of the women's private, hidden lives. The perspectives of the two sets of co-wives in the novels will trace how their private lives contribute to particularly feminine perceptions of the effects of the politics of the day.

First Wives' Club

The senior wives in both novels, Satya and Ganga, seem to adhere to more traditional roles expected of women in pre-Partition India: both women were married to their respective husbands as children, both run their households and see to their husbands' creature comforts – both are in love with their husbands. While they are accorded respect as wives by society for fulfilling their duties, both Satya and Ganga are considered lacking in certain qualities by their husbands. Their knowledge and services are devalued as archaic, backward and uneducated, thus rendering them abject and unattractive to these men. Their consciousness of their own subjugated gendered positions also contribute to their inability to articulate their own desires as autonomous sexual beings, which in turn also deflates their value as desirable sexual partners in their husbands' eyes.

Bari-Sardarni Satya

Roop's senior co-wife, Satya seems to be a contradiction in terms of traditional Indian womanhood, in that she combines devotion to her husband's well-being along with an acerbic independence of thought and open criticism of the British as well as of patriarchy. Described as "a woman who had come into this world with her eyes wide open and so could never lower them before a man" (*WBR* 325), Satya is not submissive to any man, nor does she condone subservience in women. She confronts Sardarji about his second marriage, refusing to keep silent in the face of the indignity of being replaced in her husband's affections:

> 'I tell you, I am so tired of your shouting.'
>
> 'Tired of my shouting? You don't want me because I tell you what you have become. I tell you what I see inside you, that's why you throw me away.'
>
> Sardar Kushal Singh raised his voice. 'Collect your wits, Satya! You have brought this upon yourself with your quarrelling.'
>
> Then Satya screamed so loud the djinns might hear. (*WBR* 26)

Satya's articulacy in voicing her rebellion against Sardarji's decision depicts her as a complex woman, who could be read as a herald of a possible new feminist stance in post-independence, post-Partition India. She confounds more docile, old-fashioned stereotypes of the subservient domestic goddess, who caters to every whim and need of the family without any thought for herself. Despite her consciousness of her gendered role, Satya still retains her individuality and speaks out against her husband's patriarchally sanctioned manipulation of tradition to fulfil his desires, which negate her own. She is derisive of his attempts to educate Roop in keeping with his ambitions of joining the post-independence Indian elite in heralding a modern nation. She reads Roop's pliancy and uneducated naivetè as strategies to usurp her husband's affections:

> Satya cannot deny her love, but she will not flutter her eyelashes like Roop and pretend stupidity and incompetence to win his love. How can she pretend, she whose very name means Truth. [...] Roop may be able to sit on chairs, she may have learned to eat with knife and fork, [...] But unlike Satya, she will not know how to mock the words she does not know and carry her ignorance like a badge of nationalist honour. (*WBR* 346–347)

Here Satya interprets and deploys her own ignorance of the English language and customs favoured by Sardarji, as a means to demarcate her own loyalties as an Indian nationalist who subscribes to an indigenous cultural authority, informed by her ethnic affiliation, her caste and social class. This chosen ignorance and refusal to be educated and moulded into one of Macaulay's "brown memsahibs" is thus an exercise in agency – a form of resistance as a colonized female subject. In turn Satya reads both Sardarji and Roop as as being traitors to the nationalist cause, conflating her husband's betrayal of her with his ostensible betrayal of India.

Finding herself cast off because she is barren, Satya does not remain passively inactive; she exacts her revenge by insidiously terrorizing Roop, but keeping within the bounds of expected propriety. She indulges in her jealousy of Roop's youth, beauty and fecundity, by making Roop uncomfortably aware of her lower class village origins and her lack of urbane sophistication. She exacerbates her cruelty to the younger woman, by manipulating Sardarji into giving her Roop's first two babies at birth; an arrangement that Sardarji agrees to, in order to gain some respite from Satya's constant reproaches of infidelity (*WBR* 199–201). Satya's intention is to raise Sardarji's offspring as befitting their social status, while attempting to expunge Roop's lowly origins in them, and by extension eradicating Roop herself. Here Satya acts ostensibly in her husband's interest, while instrumentalizing Roop to satisfy Sardarji's (and her own) personal desires for children.

Satya soon realizes that her efforts are fruitless; seeing that her husband has fallen in love with Roop. Desperate, Satya contemplates suicide; driven by sheer rage, shame at her abandonment, and helplessness in the face of her husband's authority, Satya effects her demise through rather unorthodox means. During a pilgrimage, she kisses her cousin Mumta, who is suffering from tuberculosis in order to contract the disease:

> Pleading, first, then fiercely, tasting the harshness of Mumta's shock, but permitting no pulling back. Not in Mumta. Not in herself. She parts Mumta's lips, takes her poison by a European kiss, and she is thinking of Sardarji as her lips touch Mumta's, remembering how he taught her this when he returned from England, taught her to kiss. [...] Mumta jerks away, her eyes wide with horror, a hand cupped over her mouth. "Satya!" She covers her head. [...] [S]he coughs and spits blood. A smile of triumph stretches Satya's lips. She trembles with daring. There is a long, long moment till a mixture of pity, sorrow and understanding dawns in Mumta's eyes. (*WBR* 369–370)

Satya thus engineers her own demise through a western expression of love taught her by her erstwhile husband. However, in exacting her drastic revenge, Satya's rebellious self-destruction can be subjected to a queer reading, in that she performs an act of same-sex desire (while not actively entertaining any form of sexual desire for her cousin) in order to challenge patriarchal dictates that require her to quiescently accept her fate as a displaced wife. In this sense, Satya can indeed be read as a harbinger of a potential new feminist consciousness that actively challenges socio-cultural expectations of women to condone degradation in the interests of upholding the heteronormative ideal of women's reproductive capabilities and by extension the heteronormative family unit of the new nation. Here too one sees how Satya implements what is ostensibly a western expression of sexual desire through a homosexual act (in itself often read as an imported cultural orientation from western contexts)[28] in order to articulate her resistance against indigenous and imperialist patriarchal agendas. Satya voices her objections to a post-independence society which still advocates the subjugation of women, by physically annihilating herself, thus stating her unwillingness to be complicit in the same.

However, at the moment of Satya's death, she is not completely eradicated; her spirit transmigrates into Roop – the younger woman literally breathes her in:[29]

> And in that breath, Satya joins the virulence of her unremitting anger to Roop's hope. For the one long moment that Roop feels the smoulder of Satya's anger, the open wound of Satya's humiliation passes past flesh, past bone, past breath. For that moment Satya's desires flame within Roop [...] because Roop felt that one single moment [...] Satya will live on in Roop [...] Roop will be Satya's vessel, bearing Satya's anger, pride and ambition forward from this minute. She will contain her woman within woman [...]. (*WBR* 378)

Thus, as Satya departs this life, in a seeming final change of heart she bestows her own strength on Roop to serve her husband; however one is not quite sure whether Satya's "possession" of Roop has altruistic purposes, as might initially be supposed. Jealous of Roop's fecundity, Satya might have actually rejoiced in finally inhabiting a "perfect" female body, thus enabling her to vicariously share Sardarji.

While Satya lived, both these female bodies were rivals for respect, attention and visibility. J. Edward Mallot observes: "The battle for respect within Sardarji's household and room within his heart was very much one of body politics, Satya's 'this body was Sardarji's first' claim competing with Roop's 'this body will bring Sardarji children' response."[30] However, when Sardarji's family is sundered through Satya's violence towards herself, Roop gains in substance, as it were, in order to prepare her to be more than just a procreative machine. Satya infuses Roop with her strength of will and determination, thus engendering a potential composite new woman of independent India. At the same time, Roop reconstitutes Satya, in that the older woman's past, her feelings and personality are re-inscribed on the younger body, thus rendering Satya more acceptable, less abject than when inhabiting her former barren, enraged and thus "imperfect" body. Thus this new body is used as the site for re-aligning certain elements of the old order of womanhood, perhaps allowing the same potential for subversive challenging of women's subjugation.[31] Roop one day comes into her own, through her remembrance of Satya's past as well as her own; her body serves as the template on which to conceive of a new nation. One notes however despite the linkages of private dreams and desires with the greater national narrative, independence is not the direct cause of Roop's newfound strength – an important aspect which will be taken up in the later section on the junior wives.

Ganga: Domestic Goddess Interrupted

In contrast to Satya in Singh Baldwin's narrative, Ganga the senior wife in Kapur's novel, silently caters to her husband's every need and whim, adhering to more traditional Hindu ideals of husband worship.[32] She is uneducated, has given Harish two children and has never felt the necessity to acquire the education ostensibly befitting a professor's wife.[33]

Although Ganga is put out by her husband's affair with Virmati she grimly continues with her domestic responsibilities, while trying to win him back with her subservience. Despite her efforts to reconnect with her estranged husband, Ganga is shocked and humiliated to find him returning with Virmati one day, married in secret (*DD* 208–212). Like Satya in *What the Body Remembers*, Ganga uses every possible means to make her new co-wife feel like a polluting influence in her home, all the while resenting her husband's obvious preference of the younger educated woman. After much conflict, when Virmati leaves Harish and his family in Amritsar to study philosophy in Lahore, Ganga is goaded into further resentment because of what she perceives as the unnecessary spending of the family's meagre finances to pander to her co-wife's whims:

> The resolution concerning Virmati's further learning had been preceded by bitterness, because the family money was limited, and why should it be wasted unnecessarily on the higher education of a married woman? Ganga who couldn't wait for Virmati to leave, resented her studying the most. She couldn't

> read, and Virmati was to do an MA! If that much attention had been given to her, she would not be in the position she was today. She had taken her duties as a wife seriously, looked after the house, children, in-laws, and husband's salary, but she had got no recognition for her hard work and years of sacrifice. (*DD* 250)

Ganga considers this a personal affront, since she has never been rewarded for her constancy to her husband; in addition she feels neglected by her husband's lack of interest in her personal development. While she envies her co-wife, Ganga nevertheless is of the opinion that a married woman does not require more education than being able to manage a household (an opinion held by Virmati's own mother, with whom Ganga shared common characteristics); here she evinces "a straightforward defence of 'tradition' and outright rejection of the new."[34] Ganga thus reads Virmati as being a westernized woman who was disinterested in the 'proper' duties of a wife (i.e., caring for the wellbeing of the home), who relishes useless luxuries.[35] Here Ganga's resentment also underlines her consciousness of putative class differences engendered in her own family and domestic space through her husband's bigamous activities. While Virmati embodies a higher social class due to the education she has enjoyed, Ganga is relegated to the status of a lower class menial. Thus Virmati is the desirable New Woman, to be contrasted with Ganga, who embodies the "degenerate condition of women which nationalism claimed it would reform."[36] In marrying Virmati, Harish of course is desirous of his disassociation with this degeneracy, hence proving himself a viable modern national subject.

Despite this, Ganga tries to rebuild her home and family around her husband, in an attempt to reassert her wifely rights in Virmati's absence. This however proves in vain as history intervenes; when the violence of Partition begins, Ganga leaves Amritsar with her children, her mother-in-law and her sister-in-law. Virmati leaves the university in Lahore for the same reasons and returns to Harish in Amritsar, where she reorganizes her home, now devoid of her rival:

> Ganga's leaving home, in the pressures and tensions of the moment, was meant to be a temporary affair. However she could never return. She wept, begged and stormed indirectly through

> her mother-in-law, but circumstances did not favour her. After Independence, Harish was offered a principalship in one of the new colleges of Delhi University. Amritsar had become a place to leave, rather than stay in, and the couple moved to Delhi and a much smaller house. (*DD* 278)

Thus, Ganga, the disturbing factor in the professor and Virmati's lives, is removed without any consideration of her needs and rights as a wife. Unlike Satya, whose spirit lives on in Roop and is hence still present despite her physical absence, Ganga is completely silenced, never to be heard from again. Although she pleads with Harish to allow her to return to him after the political turbulence of Partition, Ganga is exiled by her husband to Kanpur with her children. Robbed of the respectability that her husband's presence could have conferred on her, Ganga is unable to claim any form of agency that could have afforded her some compensation for the losses and indignities she suffers, nor is she to experience the new India as part of an intact family unit. Rather Virmati is to be the companion and helpmate of Harish's future in the post-Independence metropolis of Delhi, while Ganga seems relegated to a distant, pastoral past in a more suburban setting.

On reflection, the callousness with which the first wives are treated by their erstwhile husbands is troubling. Indeed, why do these men elect to keep their first wives in the marriages? Was it the prestige of being able to afford two wives and thus being able to adhere to acceptable tradition, while ascribing to modern cultural tenets? Was it to avoid scandal, out of a sense of duty and perhaps a modicum of affection for these wives of their youth? Was it for altruistic reasons, since abandoned wives would not be able to fend for themselves? Since exploring such questions at this time would exceed the scope of this article, I will turn to an analysis of the junior co-wives in both narratives with a view to elucidating how they negotiate the impending changes in their own lives in the light of Indian independence.

Traditional New Women: The Junior Wives

The junior wives in both novels have different priorities: Roop yearns for marriage to a rich and powerful man who will fulfil her material desires, while Virmati acquires the formal education she desires and also gains a husband of her own choosing. Yet, despite being potential agents of modernity, both these young wives share traditional outlooks with their senior co-wives, as regards wifehood and women's domestic roles. At the same time, the husbands demonstrate a Pygmalion complex in the education of their respective second wives, which requires these young women to be conversant with their husbands' more Anglophile pursuits while adhering to the traditional subservience expected of Indian wives. Thus, I read the junior wives' beauty, feminine decorum, intellectual and social aptitudes as well as the expected progeny as prerequisites in defining Indian (heteronormative) masculinity.

Choti-Sardarni Roop

While Roop is grateful for Sardarji's attention and her elevation in social standing through her marriage to him, she ponders on her function as the bearer of his sons as well as being a decorative feature in his home to impress his Indian and British friends. She fulfils her role admirably, by maintaining her traditionally circumscribed position as Sardarji's subordinate, unquestioning of his dictates and authority. Bereft of her mother in early childhood, Roop adheres to the rules taught her by the other women in her extended family:

> Rule number one: You want to make a good marriage; you must be more graceful, more pleasing to your elders. [...] Rule number two: speak softly, always softly. [...] Rule number three: never feel angry, never, never. No matter what happens, or what your husband says, never feel angry. You might be hurt, but never feel angry. (*WBR* 97–98)

These injunctions, which serve as the basis of a woman's education to fulfil her duties as a wife and a homemaker, also form a cornerstone of gendered expectations in Indian cultural traditions. Although Roop has been of an enquiring and independent turn of mind as a child, she soon conforms to what is expected of her, thus paving the way for her future marriage. The young woman chooses to marry the much older Sardarji, believing that it is her chance to acquire social prestige – Roop's desires pertain to social advancement and financial security that she did not have at her father's house. Her adherence to the aforementioned rules allows her to develop an amiable relationship with her husband, which make her a pleasing companion who eschews criticism, dissent and disagreement, unlike her senior co-wife Satya.

Indeed, confronted with Satya's independent and aggressive stance, Roop is surprised and critical of Satya's demands for her husband's love and loyalty: "Satya's difficulty has always been that she wanted love and marriage to go hand-in-hand. What a thing to want! It is the cause of all her troubles, even this" (*WBR* 375)! Love[37] and personal sexual desire had never been motivating factors for Roop; her quiescence to Sardarji's will is founded on her inculcated respect for male authority and cultural tradition, as well as a desire not to jeopardize the financial security that she has acquired through her marriage. Roop cannot conceive of love as an element in the relationship between a husband and a wife, neither can she conceive of a woman having expectations of a man, as Satya does. Despite such reservations and her initial ineptitude, Roop's natural sweetness of character and her willingness to please Sardarji, ultimately make him fall in love with her.

While Roop's presence seems to rejuvenate Sardarji's conjugal life, through her ability to produce his heirs, thus reinvigorating his enthusiastic planning for his role in an independent India, the young woman is also an element of disharmony in his household. Intimidated by Satya's capability and self-confidence, Roop does not question her authority, despite noting the older woman's obvious resentment of her. She is puzzled by Satya's hostility; Roop had hoped to form a friendship with the older woman, even wanting to see a surrogate mother in her, since she had been deprived of her own mother at a young age. Thus, just as Satya suffers because of her husband's vagaries, Roop too has to bear the consequences of Sardarji's bigamy.

When she loses her children to Satya soon after their births, Roop finally decides to take action. Conditioned not to make outright demands, Roop resorts to a passive form of aggression by depriving Sardarji of her company. She travels to her father's home under the pretext of a family visit and stays there till Sardarji comes for her. Telling her father and her older brother of the situation at Sardarji's home, she displaces her rebellion onto the two men in her family, who then undertake to negotiate with Sardarji for better treatment of Roop (*WBR* 303–337). Confronted with her family's displeasure, Sardarji undertakes to move to a new home with Roop and her children, leaving Satya in the old house.[38] Here Roop wins a significant victory, devised within her own understanding of the rules for culturally acceptable feminine behaviour.

Roop's passive resistance of Satya's tyranny and Sardarji's thoughtless implementation of his authority is reminiscent of the *satyagraha* advocated by Gandhi against colonial attempts to curb nationalist fervour for self-rule. However, Roop's quiet strategy also lays the groundwork for the family's own partition, Satya's abandonment and the subsequent violence the older woman commits towards herself. Thus, within the confines of a domestic setting, the new order – the New Woman – as embodied by Roop, is empowered by Sardarji's patriarchal authority in order to consolidate his own reputation and cultural *izzat*. In the next section I will proceed to read this form of empowerment in Roop's personal development, as a site of reflection and remembering, in the greater context of Partition violence where discourses of power were literally inscribed on women's bodies at the time.

Roop and Gendered Violence during Partition

Singh Baldwin's text locates Partition on the margins of her narrative, where two specific scenes of violence towards women cast their shadows over the main text. Deniz Kandiyoti observes that nationalist rhetoric is reaffirmed consciously "where the nation itself is represented as a woman to be protected or less consciously, in an intense preoccupation with women's appropriate sexual conduct."[39] Women's sexuality is the currency with which cultural validation was affirmed, preserved or negated, with regard to nationalist sentiments and cultural authentification (read: *izzat* or cultural honour, which is equated with male honour). Yet, there are different extents to which the exercise of cultural validation is carried out since, as Nira Yuval-Davis Floya and Anthias observe: "Women are divided along class, ethnic and life-cycle lines and in most societies different strategies are directed at different groups of women."[40] Along these lines of rumination, one notes that both sets of co-wives appear exempt from the kind of overt gendered violence during Partition depicted in the novels, as being perpetrated on the bodies of women from more rural and uneducated backgrounds (e.g., Kusum and Roop's Muslim maid Jorimon). These co-wives appear to enjoy certain immunities through their social standing, protection afforded by their husbands and extended households as well as their own ability to avoid or manage potentially violent situations at the height of the tumult of Partition. Such literary depictions of course may not be in line with actual reports of violence that were perpetrated on women in general, regardless of class or caste backgrounds.[41]

The forms of violence committed against women involved abduction, rape, forced marriage and religious conversion, mutilation and murder of women by men of opposing religious convictions. Ritu Menon and Kamla Bhasin posit:

> the dramatic episodes of violence against women during communal riots bring to the surface, savagely and explicitly familiar forms of sexual violence – now charged with symbolic meaning that serves as an indicator of the place that women's sexuality occupies an all-male, patriarchal arrangement of gender relations, between and within religious or ethnic communities [...] In the context of Partition, it engraved the division of India into India and Pakistan on the women of both religious communities in a way that they became the respective countries, indelibly imprinted by the Other.[42]

Thus, women's bodies were sites where Muslim, Sikh and Hindu patriarchal authorities were inscribed and debated, in order to establish the superiority of the one or the other ethnicity and religion. Against this backdrop, Menon and Bhasin also point out that during Partition, women were often murdered by the men of their own families and communities to prevent debasement of their female bodies by members of rival ethnic groups, in order to "preserve chastity and protect individual, family and community honour."[43]

In *What the Body Remembers*, this particular brand of violence is graphically described by Roop's father Bachan Singh who kills his son's wife Kusum, (Roop's sister-in-law), to prevent her denigration by the Muslim mob about to enter the village, during the Partition riots:

> "I said to myself: Kusum was entrusted to me by Jeevan, she is young, still of child-bearing age. I cannot even endure the possibility that some Muslim might put his hands upon her. Every day I had been hearing that the seeds of a foreign religion were being planted in Sikh women's wombs. No, I said: I must do my duty." [...] Roop knows because Papaji's story cannot be so very different from other men who see their women from the corner of their eyes, who know their women as bearers of blood, to do what women are for. [...] Bachan Singh's telling falters [...]. "I raised my kirpan high above her head [...] it came down. Her lips still moved, as mine did, 'Vaheguru, Vaheguru," as her head rolled from my stroke." [...] Roop knows [...] that she will have to tell Jeevan's sons one day: that their mother went to her death just as she was offered it, baring her neck to Papaji's *kirpan*, willingly Papaji said, for the *izzat* of her quom. (*WBR* 520–521)

Mindful of her own privileged standing as the wife of a rich upper class Sikh as well as of her own immunity against such violence from her husband, Roop undertakes to remember Kusum and tell her story to her nephews, while reflecting on how women are subject to the honour of their families and clans (*quoms*). Pondering Kusum's violent demise at her father-in-law's hands, Roop reflects on her own place in her husband's life in relation to her value as a woman in the newly formed India born in the blood of Partition, whereby Sikh manhood and the continuance of family lines through women's bodies form the crux of cultural honour.

Having narrowly escaped rape and murder herself at the hands of Muslim sepoys patrolling the newly defined border regions, even as she saves her Muslim maidservant and her children from the same, Roop becomes aware of her own potential to actively resist male oppression to survive (*WBR* 481–485). Grateful at being reunited with her husband in Delhi after their recent transnational migration across the newly drawn border, Roop ponders on the uncertain position of women in the new nations of Pakistan and India:

> So many Sikh, Hindu and Muslim women did not survive that journey. [...] But a kind of calm is falling, after all the dislocation Again everyone must worry who is higher-up and who is lower-down and what-will-people-say. Women and children are

> being sorted between the two countries [...] The sorting baskets are the old ones: religion, class, caste, *quom*. (*WBR* 528–529)

Here, the young woman realizes that despite the prospect of building a new India, after the acquisition of independence from the British colonial powers, women of all ethnic groups will still have to contend with religious, class and caste differences; legacies which survived Partition border crossings and were not lost in that particular geographical and cultural translation. Although the work of nation building and belonging lay ahead, ostensibly based on more modern ideas of nationalist thinking propagated by Anglophile colonial intellectuals like her husband,[44] certain perceptions will still be bound by past beliefs seemingly grounded in tradition, where women will again have to conform and comply.

In the meantime, Roop is grateful for surviving the actual event of Partition and the ensuing life changes which allow her to exercise her confidence and resourcefulness – a legacy left to her by the deceased Satya, the co-wife:

> She reaches, arms above her head, hands stretched out to the sky. Thankfulness surges within her – she survived. She is in Delhi, with Sardarji. [...] [A]n answering djinn soft touch, brushes her fingertips. Now there is no Bari-Sardarni, no Choti-Sardarni, no senior wife, no junior wife. Few people remain who remember Satya now [...] Now, there is only one Sardarni. (*WBR* 528)

Since Satya's death, Roop feels more secure in her role as Sardarji's wife and the mother of his children. And yet, Roop's public image as Sardarji's wife is still not quite what she had envisioned (*WBR* 395). As a second wife, who has progressed to the position of the only wife, Roop is able to command resources that she had lacked before, but is still perceived as an interloper in Sardarji's community, which is thus a constant reminder of her tenuous position (*WBR* 395). Alongside this and her precarious sense of security during her post-Partition reunion with Sardarji, Roop entertains a childish fear that her husband could still reject her based on a physical imperfection – she is deaf in one ear.[45] Despite her successful reinvention as an upper class colonized intellectual's wife, Roop is concerned that her new identity is built on her being able to heed and obey her husband; the afflicted ear (an imperfection that can be read as a sign of her individuality) could thus jeopardize her present happiness. Roop fears that she will suffer a fate similar to Satya's due to her imperfection, mirrored in Satya's barrenness and inability to be subservient.

Thus wary of her own individuality, Roop reflects on her new identity in a new India, realizing that she is still subject to her husband's (good)will and that certain traditional values remain unchanged. Roop's self-perception is still very much predicated on a negotiation between old and new value systems, requiring constant vigilance. Thus, as stated earlier, Indian independence cannot be read as a direct cause for Roop's new self-image; rather independence and the concomitant Partition has contributed to making it even more precariously ambivalent, in the face of new reconceptualizations of gender expectations and the potential of individual choice *vs.* communal loyalties to tradition.

Virmati: Galatea Remembered

While acknowledging the politically volatile atmosphere evident immediately before Partition and during the event, Kapur's novel does not provide immediate graphic descriptions of the violence perpetrated against women.[46] Rather it considers the protagonist's articulation of her self-definition through education against a changing socio-political background. At the same time, Kapur also addresses the fledgling feminist movement of the 1930s in India, congruent with the anti-colonial nationalist campaign, and its significance in Virmati's personal negotiations of desire and agency.

Virmati seems to equate the agency acquired through education, with the choice of a life-partner. Indeed one is tempted to read Virmati as being in love with the idea of being able to choose her lover, rather than actually being in love with him. As a school-going adolescent, Virmati dares to dream of a different future, spurred on by the example of a beloved older cousin, Shakuntala, a graduate student at the University of Lahore. Here I read Virmati's initial impetus for pursuing higher education as a yearning for autonomy where she sees herself liberated from the dependent humdrum existence led by her mother; indeed she desires a point of access to modern cosmopolitan life.

Flattered by the attentions of Harish Chandra, the charismatic Oxford-returned English professor, when he notices her hunger for knowledge as well as her youthful beauty, Virmati redoubles her efforts to go in for higher education, rather than subject herself to an arranged marriage as expected by her family. Confronted with Virmati's stubborn resistance to her family's expectations, her parents finally send her to the university in Lahore, where she meets other intellectual young women, like her college roommate Swarna Lata. Despite Shakuntala's and Swarna Lata's encouragements and attempts to involve her in revolutionary feminist political activism in pre-Partition Lahore, Virmati draws a boundary between her own academic ambition and other forms of self-definition advocated by her more emancipated contemporaries who aspire to other destinies besides those espoused by cultural tradition. Partha Chatterjee links the nationalist project and Indian women's autonomy: "the nationalist construct of the new woman derived its ideological strength from the fact that it was able to make the goal of cultural refinement through education a personal challenge for every woman, thus opening up a domain where woman was an autonomous subject."[47] Virmati's agenda however was not necessarily congruent with her contemporaries' political efforts to acquire equal citizenship and a claim to India's nation building process through cultural refinement and education, as propounded by Chatterjee's observation here. Despite this as well as her knowledge of her own father and grandfather's Arya Samaji efforts for the nationalist cause, Virmati's approach to higher education does not allow for her own involvement in the political activities of the greater feminist and nationalist agendas as advocated by her cousin and her peers.[48] Rather, she has difficulty with the kind of autonomy and raucous political outspokenness that her college mates exhibit. Virmati's conflict is demonstrated through her attraction to the kind of independence lived by these young women, as well as her love affair with the professor.

Lahore also offers the professor and Virmati the opportunity to continue their secret trysts, where Virmati is taught by the professor to appreciate the finer things in life such as art and literature, outside the university context. While engaged in her academic pursuits, Virmati is thus also preoccupied with her own sexual education, i.e., giving and receiving sexual gratification and taking charge of her own body in the process. At the same time, one notes that Virmati is in thrall to the professor's demands, which preclude any involvement in the greater politics of the time: "And what was she doing going to women's meetings anyway. She was in Lahore to study, not fritter away her energies" (*DD* 136). Obviously, while indulging in Virmati's academic interests, the professor does not want Virmati to elude his proprietory grasp and develop an independence of spirit like her compatriots. In this the professor depicts feminist political activity as a waste of time and effort that she could better invest in her studies.

After five years of indecision, they get married and Harish achieves his dream of finally having a wife with an intellectual capacity comparable to his, but someone he can mould according to his preferences: "The Professor looked upon her with the eyes of a Pygmalion. My Galatea, he thought" (*DD* 126). Virmati is captivated by the new perspectives he introduces her to: "Of course, all that the Professor was saying must be true, he was older and so much more refined and civilized. He knew" (*DD* 130). Here, Virmati's usual critical stance towards social observances seems to diminish in the face of Harish's intellectual superiority while being dazzled by the more cosmopolitan influences he teaches her to appreciate. However, when she attempts to take up her role as a homemaker, Harish admonishes Virmati:

> 'Why bother yourself with these things?' replied Harish impatiently. 'You are a thinking girl. Let those others handle the housework.' [...]
>
> As your wife, am I to do nothing for you? Just be in your bed?'
>
> Harish looked upset. 'You are my other self. Let her wash my clothes if she feels like it. It has nothing to do with me. I don't want a washerwoman. I want a companion.' (*DD* 217)

Here, as Harish openly relegates Ganga to the position of a servant, he also dictates Virmati's role in his life: that of a partner for whom he entertains sexual desire, informed by their intellectual compatibility. Despite the obvious compliment that Harish is trying to confer on Virmati, she does not feel that she is a true wife unless she is able to serve her husband, in accordance with her cultural socialization. In chasing her dream of higher education, in order to be free of a life full of children and household cares, Virmati has traded in her freedom for another kind of thraldom: she is now Harish's trophy designed to enhance his public intellectual image:

> For him it was a joy to have her waiting when he came home, to have her eat with him, sleep with him, move with him in his rhythms through the day. He reflected how wisely he had acted. There was no more tension, no more indecision. Even the social opprobrium was not expressed openly. He glanced fondly at his wife as she lay [...] next to him on the bed. [...] "[N]ow I have a wife I can be proud of." "A woman's happiness lies in giving her husband happiness," remarked Virmati, in a language she had learned long ago. (*DD* 226–227)

Virmati uses Ganga's own wifely principle here ironically to describe her own efforts to fulfil what Harish expects of her. She is convinced that she can aspire to education and refinement while fulfilling her homemaker and caretaker responsibilities. Here Virmati experiences a considerable disconnect between her desires, her learned perception of traditional conjugal relations and social perceptions of modernity and tradition.

Worn out by a miscarriage, the deaths of her father and grandfather, her own family's expulsion of her and the constant animosity from Ganga, Virmati withdraws into apathy. Harish sends her to study in Lahore, in the hope that their romance will be rekindled with a change of scenery. Finding a new sense of purpose and acceptance in the university community, despite Harish's dissatisfaction with her other activities besides study, Virmati resorts to a form of passive resistance: she builds up her own circle of friends and carves out a space for herself. Refusing to subject herself to her co-wife's continued hostility, she forces Harish to make a decision: "Direct action was needed. She refused to fight Ganga with cunning, guile or seduction. If Harish's love for her wasn't strong enough to survive an MA, it certainly wasn't going to survive a lifetime" (*DD* 262). Here, like Roop, Virmati uses the resources she has to effect the desired change, i.e., she is unwilling to tolerate his enjoyment of his male privileges at the expense of both wives. A significant difference however is that Virmati does not require anyone else to speak on her behalf as was the case with Roop.

Kapur allows the grand narrative of Partition struggles to take the stage, alongside Virmati's private dilemma towards the end of the novel. She finds her problematic relationship with the professor trivial, when compared with the violence taking place around her: "I fret about my petty domestic matters, at a time when the nation is on trial. I too must take a stand. I have tried adjustment and compromise. Now I will try non-cooperation" (*DD* 239). In this particular rumination, Kapur aligns Virmati's private domestic struggles in the polygamous relationship alongside the national dissension against the British and the conflicts between the ethnic communities. This is taken further, when Partition turbulence begins, and the professor's bigamous family structure is dissolved. When Virmati hears that Ganga and her children have left Amritsar, she contemplates returning:

> Virmati heard of their departure with mixed feelings. Harish was there in an empty house, waiting. She knew [...] that he had chosen to stay behind for her. On the other hand, they had been married for three years, and somewhere along the way, the prize had tarnished. For the moment however, the most practical solution was to go home to Amritsar and her husband. She left Lahore the next morning to start her new life as a housewife. She had not been happy studying the second time. Perhaps things will be different later, she thought as she left. (*DD* 265)

Thus, just as it was an arena of Partition violence, the border city of Amritsar was also the site of conflict and territorial claims between the Professor's two wives. That all the parties involved in the struggle suffered loss is also mirrored in Ganga and Virmati's subsequent lives: Ganga loses her husband and her model Hindu family, while Virmati loses her own sense of ambition and independence, which her education was meant to foster. Here allegorical possibilities seem to exhaust themselves, while private female perspectives of the ambivalent realization of personal desires emerge.

Having internalized her mother's injunction that "[a] woman without her own home and family is a woman without moorings" (*DD* 111), Virmati decides that she requires the husband of her choice and a family, to find a modicum of self-respect and belonging in a country rocked by political instability. Knowing that she has won an ambivalent victory through her own circumvention of traditional demands on her as a woman, she comes full circle to a fate that she has mapped out herself. Here, as Jandial observes: "one cannot undermine the role of the two main factors, which can give a woman some semblance of freedom and the ability to assert herself – education and economic independence. But to be able to strike independent roots and grow requires much more. What is necessary is to break the patriarchal mould [...]."[49] Cultivating the kind of independence advocated by Indian feminists thus requires a radical re-setting of cultural perceptions of established gender roles – an herculean exercise, already rife with conflict and ambiguity, exacerbated during political upheaval of nationalist struggles in the 1940s. Virmati's character shows development by the end of the novel, in accordance with the prevailing social conditions and changes of the time, while exhibiting a measure of assertion allowed by her circumstances.

Conclusion: Uneasy Belongings

Despite the allegorical readings undertaken here, these narratives should be considered feminist both in content and intent, where the gendered issues of agency and the female body are paramount in their interrogations of the public/private dyad as well as the roles of culture and memory in India's postcolonial national imaginary at the time of Partition and Independence. Thus women negotiate inequalities that imbricate the nation in the definition of gender roles and social expectations, often as instruments deployed in the interest of supporting more the public patriarchal interests of cultural and national authority and viability.

As transnational and transcultural subjects, due to their return to India from previous diasporic contexts in England, the husbands' cultural identities undergo an extent of hybridization which requires a new order for them to function as nation builders, social critics and intellectuals who could be considered the Macaulayan caste of "brown sahibs". This consciousness (and their newly minted young wives) allows them to traverse the cultural boundaries between their affiliations with postcolonial India and the former British empire. At the same time the forced migration that they undergo across newly established geographical borders dividing greater India into post-independence Pakistan and India, allows them to readjust their allegiance to the new nation-state, inculcating new loyalties and contributing to reshaping the national consciousness. It is apparent in both narratives that both sets of co-wives have been significant elements in these transcultural negotiations, as well as in the husbands' own reinventions of themselves in postcolonial India.

A significant indignity addressed in both novels, is the disregard and abandonment of the senior wives by the husbands. These women are removed from the narratives to accommodate the younger wives at India's independence. Thus, the senior co-wives can be read as an archaic order of Indian womanhood, being pushed aside in favour of the 'new woman' of post-independence India. The younger co-wives in the texts embody versions of the new woman, where "[f]ormal education became not only acceptable, but in fact a requirement for the new [...] respectable woman, when it was demonstrated that it was possible for a woman to acquire the cultural refinements afforded by modern education without jeopardizing her place at home."[50] Thus, after Partition, both younger co-wives unit traditional expectations of the subservient wife and the fecund mother, with a more modern (read: nationalistically prescribed) feminine ideal. This ideal resonates with a brand of worldly sophistication required by their upper class husbands for the reconstitution of post-independence Indian society.

Despite this modicum of success in establishing new homes in post-Partition India, both wives are ambivalent about their new subject positions, especially with regard to how post-independence Indian society perceives them. These young women also realize that they are still subject to traditional gender expectations concomitant with Indian cultural sensibilities of the time. Although the new political context marks them as Indian national subjects, it confers an uneasy belonging, whereby both women are conscious of their complicity in upholding the same gender expectations that while consolidating the Indian nationalist enterprise, it still promulgates certain forms of gender inequality. Thus the kind of citizenship conferred on these women under their husbands' aegis does not really instil comfort or security in their self-perceptions; rather the elements of loss and self-vigilance are constant companions informing their post-independence worldviews.

Notes

1. Shauna Singh Baldwin, *What the Body Remembers* (London: Anchor, 2000) and Manju Kapur, *Difficult Daughters* (London: Faber & Faber, 1999); references to these will be given parenthetically in the text, preceded by *WBR* and *DD* respectively.
2. Elleke Boehmer, "Without the West: 1990s Southern African and Indian Women Writers: A Conversation?" *African Studies* 58.2 (1999): 161–162; see also Partha Chatterjee, "The National Resolution of the Women's Question," in *Recasting Women: Essays in Colonial History*, eds. Kumkum Sangari and Sudesh Vaid (New Delhi: Kali for Women, 1989), 233–253.
3. Both authors undertake the project from their different perspectives: Baldwin as a South Asian Canadian diasporic writer and Kapur as a South Asian subcontinental writer; hence the cultural memory of Indian history has significance for both contemporary diasporic and subcontinental imaginaries. A recent novel focusing on the relevance of Partition memories for South Asian diasporic subjects is South Asian Canadian author Anita Rau Badami's *Can You Hear the Nightbird Call?* (Viking Penguin India, 2006), whereby South Asian Canadian diasporic experience plays a key role.
4. See Boehmer.
5. Boehmer 162; see also Gillian Rose, *Feminism and Geography: The Limits of Geographical Knowledge* (Oxford: Polity Press, 1996).
6. Frederic Jameson, "Third World Literature in the Era of Multinational Capitalism," *Social Text* 15 (Fall, 1986): 69.
7. Polygamy has valency in the Hindu cultural context, as is illustrated by legends of polygamous marriages among Hindu gods and goddesses. These Hindu legends show that co-wives, even amongst the gods, make for uncomfortable domestic situations, despite the husbands' obvious sexual satisfaction and affirmation of their patriarchal authority, see Devdutt Pattanaik, *The Goddess in India* (Rochester: Inner Traditions International, 2008), 34–36. Chatterjee cites Vidyasagar's campaign to abolish Kulin (Bengali Brahmin) polygamy during early and mid-19th century social reform debates in Bengal. (Chatterjee, 233). These

debates later contributed to subsequent efforts of the Indian nationalist agenda for Indian independence.

8. Nupur Sinha, Interview with Shauna Singh Baldwin, *The Statesman* (18 Mar. 2002): 1, available at: <http://www.sawnet.org/books/writing/ssb_031802.html> (visited 1 July, 2009). Baldwin notes that her interest in the issue of polygamy was based on her grandmother's experience as a second wife, thus showing how the author's perception of her maternal genealogy influences her own diasporic engagement with cultural and personal memory in her fiction. Similarly Kapur reveals her own preoccupation with her maternal genealogy, remarking that *Difficult Daughters* was the result of her own problematic personal relationship with her mother, according to Gur Pyari Jandial, "Evolving a Feminist Tradition: The Novels of Shashi Deshpande and Manju Kapur," *The Atlantic Literary Review* 4.3 (July–September 2003): 124.
9. Marriage used as a plot in nationalist allegory has been applied by Katie Trumpener in her consideration of English, Irish and Scottish political relations during the 1700s, see Katie Trumpener, *Bardic Nationalism* (Princeton: Princeton UP, 1997). Reading Jonathan Swift's *The Story of an Injured Lady, Being a True Picture of Scotch Perfidy, Irish Poverty and English Partiality* (1748), Trumpener makes observations on Irish jealousy at Scotland being favoured to enter a political union with England:

   matters of state are presented as private, familial and sentimental problems. [...] What is surprising is that she had not joined forces with her rival; the most inexplicable part of this story is that two women betrayed by the same scoundrel should continue to compete with one another for a man who "pretended honourable love to us both" and deserves neither (Trumpener, 133).

   Baldwin and Kapur's narratives, while bearing similarities to Trumpener's reading, however, raises the question of the smooth applicability of the Irish and Scottish historical paradigms and relations to England, to the Indian nationalist agenda during the struggle for independence from British colonial rule. Indeed both sets of co-wives cannot form alliances of solidarity against an oppressive indigenous patriarchy, however there are strong social forces in the South Asian context that influence such behaviour, e.g., generational differences gender expectations, class and caste.

   Yet one does not discount that the familial conflicts engendered by the husbands' bigamous actions are echoes of the painful state of the Indian nation at the time, Ralph J. Crane, "More than a Partition Novel," *CRNLE Journal*, NS1 (2000): 141. This conflict is succinctly described in

What the Body Remembers: "Satya was Sardaji's tool, the instrument by which he tortured Roop, then stood back complaining how his women fought [...] never giving him any peace. But so too was Roop the instrument by which he tortured Satya" (*WBR* 378). In *Difficult Daughters*, Harish complacently makes observations on his wives' hostilities and obvious distress: "In his experience these troubles that women had with each other generally sorted themselves" (*DD* 222). These attitudes are of course mirrored in the context of impending Partition and independence of India and Pakistan, which was marked by British indifference to the distress caused by the dissension between the Hindu, Sikh and Muslim communities, each of which feared the other was being favoured by the patriarchal condescension of the Raj.

10. In Kapur's narrative, Virmati's younger sister describes Muslim violence towards Hindus: "The Mussulmans chopped our people's heads, raped our women, cut off their breasts, all of which they claimed was in retaliation for what the Hindus were doing to them" (*DD* 270). In Baldwin's novel, Roop, her children and her Muslim maid Jorimon are interrogated and almost attacked near the new Indo-Pakistani border by Muslim soldiers, on their way to Delhi. Roop's presence of mind and resolve, (along with Satya's disembodied support), bring them through the encounter unscathed (*WBR* 481–485). Thus both novels implicitly depict Muslims as the aggressors and hence unfit to be part of the Indian national narrative, which seems to be underscored with a distinct Hindu sensibility.
11. Boehmer 162.
12. Rosemary George observes of the concept of home in colonial texts by Indian subcontinental and African writers of the postcolonial era: " Hence we are led to believe that the absence of a 'self/home' that resembles the 'self/home' born of western individualism signals the absence of alternative notions of subjecthood" (Rosemary Marangoly George, *The Politics of Home* (Cambridge: Cambridge UP, 1996), 24.
13. In both narratives, both men offer privileged, modern and westernized perspectives on the political climate of India on the brink of independence in public contexts, while embracing more traditional cultural tenets in their domestic establishments. The men's social status empowers them to acquire brides in keeping with their taste, while leaving them free of blame. Another factor that could have influenced this resorting to bigamy is their anticipated enjoyment of the culturally inculcated acquiescence the two young women Roop and Virmati show towards their husbands' male cultural authority and experience.
14. See Nira Yuval Davis and Floya Anthias, *Women, Nation, State* (Basingstoke and London: Macmillan, 1989), 7; see also Jyoti Puri,

Encountering Nationalisms (Oxford: Blackwell, 2004), 114. Puri synthesizes the connections between women and nations drawn up by Nira Yuval Davis and Floya Anthias in their 1989 seminal text *Woman, Nation, State*, as follows: "women as reproducers of nations, women as vessels of cultural nationalism, and women as markers of internal and external boundaries of nations/ethnic groups" (Puri, 114).

15. Jill Didur, *Unsettling Partition: Literature, Gender, Memory* (Toronto: U of Toronto P, 2006), 23.
16. Chatterjee 241. Chatterjee points out the concerns of 19th century Indian literature on women, which focused on the threatened westernization of Bengali women (Chatterjee, 240). In his discussion of the Indian nationalist project and the "New Woman" question, Chatterjee accesses the 19th century Bengali Hindu cultural context in addressing the social reform measures to emancipate and educate Indian women in keeping with the Indian nationalist agenda. While one could question its relevance for other ethnic communities like the Sikhs and other Hindu communities, it is to be supposed that since the Bengali middle class often furnished cultural translators for interaction between the British colonial government and the other Indian social strata, this particular ethnic community provided a pan-Indian framework with regard to the New Indian woman model as a nationalist instrument.
17. Puri, 115.
18. Chatterjee 238–239. Jill Didur observes that the gendering of the home (*ghar*) and the world (*bahir*) as feminine and masculine respectively has its foundations in colonial patriarchal structures that used to govern Hindu Bengali (*bhadralok*) communities. Didur further remarks that Chatterjee's material/spiritual dichotomy is significant in the discussions of how patriarchal nationalist interests locate women as the repositories of recalibrated ideas of tradition in the nation building project, whereby "[t]hough the feminized subject is pushed to the margins of this scene, she is still tethered to its production" (Didur, 22–23).
19. Didur, 23.
20. Deniz Kandiyoti, "Identity and Its Discontents: Women and the Nation," in *Colonial Discourse and Post-Colonial Theory: A Reader*, eds. Patrick Williams and Laura Chrisman (Harlow: Pearson Education, 1994), 377–378.
21. For the intricate connections between the histories of anti-colonial nationalist and feminist movements in India, see Kumari Jayawardena, *Feminism and Nationalism in the Third World* (New Delhi: Kali for

Women, 1986), especially Introduction and Chapter 6 "Women, Social Reform and Nationalism in India."

22. Puri, 125.
23. Puri, 125.
24. Jayawardena, 16–17.
25. Chatterjee, 240.
26. Homi K. Bhabha, *The Location of Culture* (London: Routledge, 1994), 203.
27. Boehmer, 167.
28. Ruth Vanita remarks that sexual categories, e.g., heterosexuality and homosexuality, have long been extant in South Asian contexts although they may not operate in similar ways as in Euro-American socio-cultural matrices (see Puri 146; see also Ruth Vanita's Introduction in her *Queering India: Same-Sex Love and Eroticism in Indian Culture and Society* (London: Routledge, 2002), 1–11.
29. This element of magical realism shows how Roop's body commits Satya to body memory. Interspersed throughout the narrative, Satya's spirit lurks in the penumbral shadows of the spirit world of the djinns, in the liminal in-between spaces, on the margins of history, waiting for her reincarnation in a post-independent India. She does however stay close to Roop, literally haunting her with strength and cunning when the younger woman needs it most.
30. J. Edward Mallot, "Body Politics and the Body Politic," *Interventions* 8.2 (2006): 166.
31. See also Mallot, 172.
32. See Judith Walsh's discussion of Nagendrabala's descriptions of *pativrata* in *Women's Dharma* (1900): "Her husband is a woman's god" (Judith Walsh, *Domesticity in Colonial India: What Women Learned When Men Gave Them Advice* (New York: Rowman & Littlefield Publishers, 2004), 151–153. The concept of *pativrata* is underpinned by the idea that: "the dharma of women, the central purpose and meaning of their lives, is their devotion to their husbands" (Walsh 151). Susan Wadley explains the roles of women in Hindu tradition, where 'a woman by being a true and devoted wife (*pativrat*, literally "one who fasts for her husband"), increases her '*sakti*' (Susan Wadley, "Women and Hindu Tradition," in *Women in Indian Society: A Reader*, ed. Rehanna Ghadially (London: Sage, 1988), 25. '*Sakti*' or '*shakti*', according to Wadley, is defined as follows: "The female is first of all *sakti* (energy/power), the energizing principle of the universe" (ibid.). Thus the role of the wife is one of complete subordination, duty and devotion to her husband, regardless of the circumstances – an attitude that Ganga subscribes to

wholeheartedly and which ultimately leads to her silencing in the narrative. In the epilogue, the last impression of Ganga that the reader gets is as follows: "Her husband continued to be Ganga's public statement of selfhood. Her *bindi* and her bangles, her toe rings and her *mangalsutra*, all managed to suggest that he was still her god" (*DD* 278).

33. Ganga first encourages the friendship between the professor and Virmati, when the professor and his family move into the neighbourhood, where Virmati's family lived (*DD* 38–44). One notes that Ganga is referred to as "the wife" through most of the narrative, while Virmati's character is more three-dimensional. It is Virmati, who first refers to Ganga by her name in a letter to Harish (*DD* 104). In this it becomes apparent that Ganga is signified mainly through her function as a wife, who doubles as a domestic servant and is considered as such by her husband.
34. Chatterjee, 241.
35. See also Chatterjee, 240–241.
36. Chatterjee, 245.
37. Wadley remarks: "The theme of love between a husband and a wife is minor in the classical written literature, whether Sanskrit or vernacular; rather devotion and dutifulness dominate" (Wadley 32).
38. Sardarji justifies his treatment of Satya: "Perhaps in a few years if Satya comes to him ready to touch his feet, with eyes down cast, with the words 'sorry' repeating itself on her lips and a sweeter tongue, Sardarji might take her in and give her the keys to his household again" (*WBR* 356). Here Sardarji uses Satya's outspokenness as his excuse for her abandonment, stipulating her possible return on the condition that she assumes the role of the reformed and subservient wife. One notes however that the intended reward is her relegation to the role of housekeeper in Sardarji's home.
39. Kandiyoti, 377.
40. Yuval-Davis and Anthias 7.
41. See Ritu Menon and Kamla Bhasin, *Borders and Boundaries: How Women Experienced the Partition of India* (New Brunswick: Rutgers UP, 1998).
42. Menon and Bhasin 41 and 43.
43. Menon and Bhasin, 42.
44. In his *The Wretched of the Earth*, Franz Fanon observes: "this passionate quest for a national culture prior to the colonial era can be justified by the colonized intellectuals' shared interest in stepping back and taking a hard look at the Western culture in which they risk becoming ensnared. Fully aware they are in the process of losing themselves and conse-

quently of being lost to their people, these men work away with raging heart and furious mind to renew contact with their people's oldest, inner essence, the farthest removed from colonial times," Frantz Fanon, *The Wretched of the Earth*, trans. Richard Philcox (New York: Grove Press, 2004 [orig. 1963]), 148). This inner conflict is best illustrated by Sardarji, who has returned to India from England and has taken up a government job, working alongside British officials in preparation for independence.

He wrangles with his British alter-ego Cunningham, who haunts him from his Oxford days, convinced that India cannot get on without the British, Sardarji is bent on proving that Indian colonial intellectuals are every bit as qualified and invested in building the new nation, based on their own understandings and affiliations with their former British colonial masters. In contrast to Satya's haunting of Roop's mind and body, Cunningham's haunting of Sardarji is a purely cerebral exercise, extolling the virtues of English value systems as propounded by the Raj administration and Sardarji's Oxford education. Thus, these inner conversations evince alternating moments of assent and disagreement with his domineering alter-ego, demonstrating his ambivalence in his cultural loyalties, while attempting to consolidate his position as an intellectual working towards Indian independence.

45. Mary Conde links metaphorical deafness among the three main ethnic groups – the Sikhs, Muslims and Hindus – and the Indian politicians during Partition, with the actual physical deafness that Roop suffers from typhoid (see *WBR* 92–93). Conde further remarks on: "actual deafness which also becomes metaphorical, since Roop is taught that to listen is to obey, she later realizes, punning on 'bad', that 'I have one bad ear that does not listen. So sometimes, it cannot obey' (276)," Mary Conde, "A Feminist View of Partition: Shauna Singh Baldwin's *What the Body Remembers*," *The Atlantic Literary Review* 2.1 (January–March 2001): 51.
46. Jandial observes that Partition violence is related through the lives of minor characters by Kapur: 'how women lost their brothers and husbands and how men found their women brutally raped and murdered' (Jandial, 126). See the testimonial descriptions of Partition violence from Virmati's siblings, friends and relatives close to the end of the novel (*DD* 267–273).
47. Chatterjee, 1989: 246.
48. See also Jandial 124–125. Deniz Kandiyoti observes that women participants in nationalist movements often justified their active involvement outside their narrowly prescribed 'private' roles in the name of patriotic self-sacrifice for the ideals of the nation (Kandiyoti, 379). It is to be

inferred then that many women were not necessarily invested in a feminist agenda *per se*, and their involvements might often have been temporary instances of political outspokenness as advocates of an independent India freed from the British Raj.

49. Jandial, 126.

50. Chatterjee, 246.

Works Cited

Boehmer, Elleke. "Without the West: 1990s Southern African and Indian Women Writers: A Conversation?" *African Studies* 58.2 (1999): 157–170.

Bhabha, Homi K. *The Location of Culture*. London: Routledge, 1994.

Chatterjee, Partha. "The National Resolution of the Women's Question." In *Recasting Women: Essays in Colonial History*. Eds. Kumkum Sangari and Sudesh Vaid. New Delhi: Kali for Women, 1989. 233–253.

Conde, Mary. "A Feminist View of Partition: Shauna Singh Baldwin's *What the Body Remembers*." *The Atlantic Literary Review* 2.1 (January–March 2001): 50–63.

Crane, Ralph J. "More than a Partition Novel." *CRNLE Journal*, NS 1 (2000): 141–142.

Didur, Jill. *Unsettling Partition: Literature, Gender, Memory*. Toronto: U of Toronto P, 2006.

George, Rosemary Marangoly. *The Politics of Home*. Cambridge: Cambridge UP, 1996.

Fanon, Frantz. *The Wretched of the Earth*. Trans. Richard Philcox. New York: Grove Press, 2004 [orig. 1963].

Jameson, Frederic. "Third World Literature in the Era of Multinational Capitalism." *Social Text* 15 (Fall, 1986): 65–88.

Jandial, Gur Pyari. "Evolving a Feminist Tradition: The Novels of Shashi Deshpande and Manju Kapur." *The Atlantic Literary Review* 4.3 (July–September 2003): 108–128.

Jayawardena, Kumari. *Feminism and Nationalism in the Third World*. New Delhi: Kali for Women, 1986.

Kandiyoti, Deniz. "Identity and Its Discontents: Women and the Nation." In *Colonial Discourse and Post-Colonial Theory: A Reader*. Eds. Patrick Williams and Laura Chrisman. Harlow: Pearson Education, 1994. 376–391.

Kapur, Manju. *Difficult Daughters*. London: Faber & Faber, 1999.

Mallot, J. Edward. "Body Politics and the Body Politic." *Interventions* 8.2 (2006): 165–177.

Menon, Ritu and Kamla Bhasin. *Borders and Boundaries: How Women Experienced the Partition of India.* New Brunswick: Rutgers UP, 1998.

Pattanaik, Devdutt. *The Goddess in India.* Rochester: Inner Traditions International, 2008.

Puri, Jyoti. *Encountering Nationalisms.* Oxford: Blackwell, 2004.

Rose, Gillian. *Feminism and Geography: The Limits of Geographical Knowledge.* Oxford: Polity Press, 1996.

Salvador, Dora Sales and Christopher Rollason. "Critical Commentary on Manju Kapur: Excerpts from a Work in Progress (with Bibliography)." *The Atlantic Literary Review* 4.4 (October–December 2003): 219–248.

Singh Baldwin, Shauna. *What the Body Remembers.* London: Anchor, 2000.

Sinha, Nupur. Interview with Shauna Singh Baldwin. *The Statesman* (18 Mar. 2002): 1–2. Available at: <http://www.sawnet.org/books/writing/ssb_031802.html>. (Visited 1 July, 2009.)

Trumpener, Katie. *Bardic Nationalism.* Princeton: Princeton UP, 1997.

Vanita, Ruth. *Queering India: Same-Sex Love and Eroticism in Indian Culture and Society.* London: Routledge, 2002.

Wadley, Susan. "Women and Hindu Tradition." In *Women in Indian Society: A Reader.* Ed. Rehanna Ghadially. London: Sage, 1988. 23–43.

Walsh, Judith. *Domesticity in Colonial India: What Women Learned When Men Gave Them Advice.* New York: Rowman & Littlefield Publishers, 2004.

Yuval Davis, Nira and Floya Anthias. *Women, Nation, State.* Basingstoke and London: Macmillan, 1989.

3

"The Cane Is Singing"

South African Indian Literature on Indenture

DEVARAKSHANAM [BETTY] GOVINDEN

> Everyone lives in a story ... they all lived in stories, because stories are all there are to live in, it was just a question of which story ...
>
> – Amitav Ghosh, *The Shadow Lines*[1]

> The cane is singing. All along it is singing: to the left, from where I am sitting in this train on my way to the big city to visit my children, to the rolling land where the sea begins, and to my right, into the interior where the sun sets. The cane is singing, but it is a sad refrain that the cane is singing … . For us only the bitter notes of this sad song, this soul-searing song that the cane is singing
>
> – Narain Aiyer, "The Cane Is Singing"[2]

Introduction: A Time of Memory

South Africa is going through a "time of memory." One of the most interesting features of the post-apartheid political scene is the way memory is negotiated, produced and inscribed. It mirrors the way in which the nation itself is being negotiated, produced and inscribed, reminding us that "nations are narrations."[3] The work of the Truth and Reconciliation Commission (TRC) after South Africa's first democratic elections in 1994 was described as an attempt at "healing the wounds of history."[4] The TRC was specifically concerned with narratives of the atrocities committed under apartheid, and these dealt largely with state-sponsored violence, with emphasis on the work of the security police. It was an attempt at reconciliation through truth, a reckoning with the actors of apartheid.[5]

Alongside the formal project of the TRC there has been much need to recount the suppressed histories of the past. A "refusal of amnesia" is as important as some of the more material changes that are taking place in the reconstruction of our new democracy. This memory work includes narratives of the experiences of prisoners on Robben Island, with *Mandela's Long Walk to Freedom* (1994) being a definitive text here, narratives of daily lives lived under the oppressiveness of apartheid, of the humiliation and injustices of the Group Areas Act and of the difficulties of life in exile. These writings have been produced by a broad spectrum of writers living in South Africa.[6]

In this context, South African Indian writing comprises a significant body of work engaged in re-imagining the past in the present. Since 1994 South African Indian writing in every genre has blossomed and a wide diversity is evident in poetry, fiction and autobiographical writings.

Amidst this broader "memory work," the history of Indian indenture in South Africa has emerged as an especially potent archive for local writers. This history is being reclaimed from the margins and rightly seen as an intrinsic component of the South African national narrative. The title of Uma Dhupelia-Mesthrie's book *From Canefields to Freedom: A Chronicle of Indian South African Life* (2000) sums up this trajectory very aptly, and shows how the "canefields" is claimed as a defining, originary trope for Indian history in South Africa.

In this article, I shall present a survey of writings on the theme of indenture and then provide critical reflections on the broader value and implications of indenture writing.

History: The Indentured Experience

The history of the main wave of Indian migration since 1860 has been well surveyed by South African historians such as Bridgelal Pachai, Joy Brain, Surendra Bhana and Goolam Vahed. A recent attempt at taking an indepth look at the history of Indian indenture is Ashwin Desai and Goolam Vahed's work, *Inside Indenture* (2007). Among other things, Desai and Vahed point to the casteism that returning migrants experienced in India: crossing the *kala pani*, or black waters, was seen as a desecration – "the enigma of arrival." Their intensive archival research reveals the appalling racism they experienced on the sugar cane plantations. The style of writing of *Inside Indenture*, with its numerous biographical sketches produced from extensive archival research, resembles the narrative texture of literary writing. In this genre it is similar to Fatima Meer's trail-blazer *Portrait of Indian South Africans* (1969) that contains imaginatively composed stories of indenture in Natal.[7]

The world of the mid-19th century was entering a new phase in history. Slavery had been abolished, but other forms of labour had to be found to maintain the infrastructure of trade and expansion for the European nations, especially Britain. P.S. Joshi argues that indentured labour was a new form of slavery and was inaugurated in India from 1830.[8] Similarly, in her article "And They Christened It Indenture," Agnes Sam writes of how slavery was cunningly transmuted into indenture.[9] In 1857 the East India Company was abolished and the Indian subcontinent came under the direct rule of the British Crown. British subjugation of India initiated the Indian diaspora, which led to the dispersal of Indians into the far-flung parts of the British Empire. A pattern of indentured labour had already been established in the movement of Indians to Mauritius in 1833, to British Guinea in 1938, as well as Trinidad and Jamaica around the same time.[10]

It was at this time that colonial eyes were being turned to the East Coast of Natal in South Africa, where the soil was fertile and the prospects seemed promising for sugar farming. Wherever white British colonists settled they required labour, and colonized subjects in the colonies such as India, as Surendra Bhana and J. Brain record, became the logical transportable "commodity."[11] Gandhi was to draw attention to the plight of indentured Indians not only in South Africa but in Fiji, East Africa and British Guyana, referring to the indentured workers as "the pariahs of the Empire." Elleke Boehmer has observed that:

> it is often forgotten that millions of people, both colonized and colonizing, who were identified with or unconcerned about

colonization formed part of the British Empire, in the sense of responding to it, having to deal with it, and in many millions of cases surviving through it.[12]

Mahadai Das, in her poem "They Came in Ships," writing of her Guyanese experience, captures this well:

From across the seas, they came,

Britain colonising India,
Transposing her chains ...

Wooden missions of imperialist design.
Human victims of her majesty's history.

They came in fleets.
They came in droves.
Like cattle
Brown like cattle
Eyes limpid, like cattle ...[13]

The first "batch" of Indians, a total of 341 labourers, mainly from Madras (now Chennai), came to Natal on the *SS Truro* on 16 November 1860. A few years later, in 1870, apart from the indentured Indians, there came "Passenger" Indians – entrepreneurs, mainly from Bombay and other parts of the west coast of India. By 1866, a total of 6 445 indentured immigrants had arrived in South Africa. By 1911, 152 184 indentured migrants from India had arrived in Natal, as had an estimated 30,000 Passenger Indians.[14]

All indentured labourers endured abject working conditions. Indentured workers, referred to as "coolies" – a derogatory word at the time – came in accordance with an agreement (they called it *girmit*) or contract concerning their stay and they were referred to as *girmityas.* They worked for sugar farmers in Natal – farmers who were mainly English. A near-feudal system of labour operated, with the indentured labourers being recruited to work for a particular employer and being bound by contract to live on the estate of the employer for a stipulated period of time. This is seen by many historians, as pointed out earlier, as not unlike slavery which was, as defined by Ronald Takaki, a "system of bonded black labour."[15] This is why sugar was a commodity, but also a metaphor of servitude,[16] as the Trinidadian writer Sam Selvon suggests in his novel, *Cane is Bitter* (1957), or as Narain Aiyer illustrates in the vignette, "The Cane is Singing," included here as part of the epigraph and as the Epilogue; and as is further indicated by Brij V. Lal's choice of title for Indo-Fijian stories of *girmityas*: *Bittersweet: The Indo-Fijian Experience* (2004).

It is sometimes stated that Indians came to work on the sugar cane plantations because the "Africans were lazy." Keletso E Atkins questions this stereotype and, in a well-documented research on the subject, gives an important alternative view:

> Natal Africans were themselves experiencing an unprecedented socio-economic crisis; and both private and governmental agencies had already invested time and energy designed to mould blacks into a European ideal of what workers ought to be like. From the beginning, however, the results of their efforts were discouraging. Finally, the European recognized that only by a complete immersion in western culture – that is, only after a prolonged process of acculturation – would the pre-industrial African worker be transformed into a model based on the Protestant capitalist work ethic, itself a contested area in nineteenth century Europe.[17]

African men were being thrown into a wage economy and the emergence of colonial capitalism at this time in the development of South Africa led to their increasing proletarization during the rest of the century. This was a time of major changes on many fronts, amounting to an "upheaval" of considerable magnitude. Cheryl Walker points out that there were

> massive changes in the economic, political and social life, from pre-capitalist to capitalist relations of production, from African political independence to subjugation, from rural to urban forms of social and spatial organization, and from white co-existence with indigenous societies [and Indian settlers] to white supremacy within a new, racially structured state.[18]

The introduction of Indian indentured labour was to change the racial composition of Natal, and introduce a new pattern of racial diversity in South Africa. We have to reflect on how British political appropriation of the colony, and subsequent apartheid policies, resulted in cultural appropriation as well. Both the indigenous and indentured peoples were seen as foreigners and outsiders, and were systematically "othered." The history of the past century has been a struggle to change that perception – to ensure that Indians, Africans and Coloureds belong to South Africa as much as the English and Afrikaners did. Both white groups were a powerful minority who had the power to define South African culture.

Literature: The Indentured Experience

An interesting development is the way this early history of indenture has provided the background directly or indirectly for autobiographical and fictional writings in South Africa. This trend is similar to writers in other parts of the Indian diaspora, who have given expression to the indentured expression in imaginative ways, with V.S. Naipaul and Salman Rushdie being the most famous.

Agnes Sam frames her short story cycle, *Jesus Is Indian and Other Stories* (1989), by providing a vivid, critical description of the Indian indentured experience. In 1990 we had the publication of the well-known autobiography, *Coolie Doctor* (1990) by Dr Goonam whose work in the Passive Resistance and Defiance Campaigns was exemplary. Other examples are Jay Naidoo's *Coolie Location* (1990), and Rèshard Gool's *Cape Town Coolie* (1990). These are just a few of the numerous examples of the way the word "coolie" has been reclaimed and re-defined.[19] M.K. Gandhi records in his book, *An Autobiography, or The Story of My Experiments with Truth*, that he was referred to as the "Coolie Barrister."[20] When we are looking at "plantation" literature we should not forget that Gandhi's sojourn in South Africa includes the period of indenture, which ended officially in 1911, and that he has woven narratives of the indentured experiences in his writings.

It was through the example of Gandhi and others like the three eminent "coolies" mentioned above – Dr Goonam, Jay Naidoo and Rèshard Gool – that Indians were seen not only as victims of discrimination, but actors in history, as subjects. It is through such an engagement that the derogatory term "coolie" was redefined as a symbol of resistance. It was Gandhi who made the telling statement, in "Satyagraha in South Africa," that the steamers "which carried those labourers to Natal carried with them the seeds of the great Satyagraha movement."[21]

The resistance ethos of the indentured labourers is reminiscent of the implacable spirit of that other plantation history in the United States, where slaves such as Nat Turner, Frederick Douglass,[22] Harriet Tubman and Sojourner Truth, as well as post-slavery freedom fighters such as Martin Luther King Jr. – who, as we know, was directly influenced by Satyagraha – and Rosa Parks, rose to the challenge of shaking off their shackles.[23]

Since the first democratic elections we see a further flourishing of the theme of indenture in literary writings by South African Indians. The presence of "*girmitya*" or "coolie" texts points to the way the history of indenture continues to shape the psyche of Indians in South Africa.

Imraan Coovadia, in his novel *The Wedding* (2001), shows the way in which South Africa during the indentured period was portrayed as a paradise, in contrast to India, which was seen as decaying.[24] That Coovadia's narrator presents his grandparents, of passenger class, as arriving in Natal on the *SS Truro* in 1860, the first ship that brought indentured Indians, shows his intentionally conflating indentured and passenger history.[25] *The Wedding* also shows that the lives of passenger Indians in the colony were not necessarily more luxurious than those of their indentured counterparts. While the novel does not deal with indenture *per se*, it is set in this period, and considers the efforts of the new migrants to claim a stake in the land of their adoption at the turn of the 20th century.

Song of the Atman (2006), by Ronnie Govender, presents the indentured narrative as a founding history, on which succeeding events are built. As a family saga fans out more broadly in different directions, Ronnie Govender paints "an evocative portrait of five generations of descendants of former indentured Indian labourers and their struggle to build an identity in an emerging South Africa."[26] Himself a second generation descendant of indentured Indians, Ronnie Govender presents, through the texture of the writing and resonant evocations of the Tamil language, the atmosphere of the coolie era and shows how indentured life was part of a continuum of struggle for Indians in South Africa through the better part of the 20th century.

In following the life of Chin Govender, *Song of the Atman* traverses the physical and political landscape of South Africa, with its beginnings in Cato Manor, where some of the indentured labourers settled after their *girmits* had expired. The novel captures the lives of the Indian settlers, the subsequent forced removals they endured, and their struggles to get a social and economic footing in a country where setbacks are experienced at every turn. Ronnie Govender creates many instances where he is able to paint portraits that hark back to the founding days of indenture. Of Mr Baijnath, Chin Govender's employer in Durban, he writes:

> The father had come to South Africa from Bihar in India, where he and others like him had been fed stories of gold nuggets being picked up on the streets of Durban. It was a different story, of course, when they arrived, aching to get away from an India impoverished by waves of Arab and British imperialism. The word "indenture," as he and his fellows were to discover, was a politics word for slavery. Baijnath's father had saved enough to pay a small deposit on a piece of land in Cato Manor, practically mortgaging himself for life. He'd started a market garden and had built up a steady trade selling vegetables to the housewives on the Berea. He'd hoped that his son would follow him. But the time Baijnath was a grown man, the land would be free.[27]

Against this background, the novel charts a wide trajectory, of movement from Durban to Maritzburg, to Richmond, to East London, to Port Elizabeth, to Cape Town. The novel works as a wide-ranging building across time and place, charting a life filled with vicissitudes in the social and political landscape of 20th Century South Africa, but beginning in the indentured experience.

The same is true of Riason Naidoo's *The Indian in Drum Magazine in the 1950s* (2008) which includes a photograph of indentured labourers, although the compendium is concerned with a later history. This photograph is similar to the one used on the cover of *Inside Indenture*, referred to already. The first section, "Meet the Indian in South Africa" begins appropriately with images from indentured history:

> In a collage of identity photos of indentured labourers from the nineteenth century, twelve naked torso-length portraits of Indian males, some not yet adults, face the viewer, each holding up his identification number. Rib cages protrude from beneath some of

> the men's skins and sunken eyes tell of grueling voyages. The figures are replicated like patterned wallpaper, suggesting a continuity, an infinite number of other labourers beyond the borders of the image, while also underlining their presence in the colony as mere numbers – commodities in the sugar industry.[28]

Riason Naidoo then presents various successive images of Indians in different roles and capacities reflecting apartheid, liberation histories, gangsters, and social and cultural activities that characterized Indian life in South Africa, as represented in *Drum Magazine*.

Using the background of indenture, Praba Moodley has produced historical fiction similar to Daphne Rooke's *Ratoons* (1953).[29] In her novel, *The Heart Knows No Colour* (2003), Praba Moodley, who dedicates her book "to my forefathers," develops a narrative of family life and the familiar theme of transgressive love relations on a sugar cane plantation in Verulam, Natal, at the turn of the century.[30] The theme of "intimacy" has been posited by cultural critics in South Africa[31] where the emphasis is not so much on separation than on interaction and "intimacy" between the different race groups during colonial and apartheid times. "Intimacy" is illustrated well in Moodley's novel, with the unequal relations between master and servant, as well as forbidden love across the colour line.

Fiona Khan's novel, *Reeds of Wrath* (2009), is also situated in the history of indenture.[32] Similar to many of the other writings in this *genre*, it is referred to as *faction* – fiction based on facts – of indentured labour in South Africa. *Reeds of Wrath*, which straddles the Mogul era in India and Indian indentured history in South Africa, is a historical romance similar to Praba Moodley's novels. The Orientalist exoticism of these novels notwithstanding, the genre of popular fiction is a legitimate field of study, as Terry Eagleton reminds us, with possibilities for comparative study in a variety of directions.[33] It is worth noting that there are interesting examples of this genre in other parts of the Indian diaspora. Among these are the Mauritian novels such as Arthur Martial's *La Poupee de Chair* (1931) and *Sphinx de Bronze* (1935), and Loys Masson's *Mutins* (1951), which all deal with love relationships across class and race.[34]

Pat Poovalingam's novel, *Anand* (2003), another "period piece," merges the colonial and apartheid eras.[35] Poovalingam's narrative is set against the power and privilege of whites, and shows solidarity among the colonized. *Anand*, the novel, is about a young lawyer who is the "grandson of a coolie indentured immigrant labourer," and much of the action is set against the background of sugar cane farm relations in Umhlali on Natal's North Coast. Anand, the central character, is the grandson of an Indian coolie woman and a white sugar planter and is being tried for treason against the apartheid government. It is similar to *The Madonna of Excelsior*, by Zakes Mda (2002), which shows a preoccupation with the apartheid past and transgressions of the Immorality Act in particular.[36] Vijay Mishra sees *Anand* as an example of "the master-slave dialectic that has led to writers using plantation narratives to write either about the legacy of apartheid … or about liberation struggles in the country."[37]

An interesting variation of the indenture theme is Rubendra Govender's *Sugar Cane Boy* (2008), where the indentured history of the Murugappas, a third generation indentured family, who live at the foothills of Inanda on the North Coast of Natal, provides the background for the drama between Indian and African workers and their families. The author draws from his own experiences of growing up on a sugar estate. The novel is set in 1972, during the heyday of apartheid, but the sugar cane plantation culture is ubiquitously present. The protagonist takes naturally to working the sugar cane fields. As he says, "I am a Sugar Cane Boy, just like my forefathers."[38] And the juxtaposing of the old diaspora history with that of apartheid history is tacitly achieved, with the challenges of new oppressions that confront both Africans and Indians, as well as internal prejudices within communities. Rubendra Govender is concerned with a "politics of memory," where reconciliation between variously oppressed groups may be sought. He shows that "Africanness" and "Indianness" are part of fluid, shared, syncretic identities, and portrays the goodwill of all ethnic groups.

This is similar to Ronnie Govender's *Lahnee's Pleasure*, originally a play and published in 2008 as a novel, the story of a working class man in the sugar cane fields. As Ronnie Govender writes: "North of the city, plonked amidst rolling hills of sugar cane lay Mt

Edgecombe. But for the occasional grunts of the workers digging and clearing the soil or cutting the cane and the cranking and farting of the old sugar mill, it was just another somnolent little village."[39]

Neelan Govender's *Girrmit Tales* (2008), a recent text in the plantation genre, is a collection of interesting and unusual stories of Indian indentured labourers in Natal, drawn from random and informal oral testimonies.[40] It comprises stories of many individuals who came into contact with the author, whose profession as a medical doctor allowed him access to a wide variety of experiences, recounted with great animation and theatricality. More than a mere "interpreter of maladies,"[41] the author shows great empathy as a social historian and evokes tellingly an age that is past.

Neelan Govender, who is aware of the vast canvas against which the individual stories are narrated, also shows how slavery became transmuted into indentured labour. He locates the immigration scheme to Natal in South Africa in the wider context of the diasporic imaginary of the old India diaspora, connecting different parts of the world, such as Fiji, the Caribbean, Mauritius, Seychelles and East Africa. He shows how indenture was a bald and soulless contract between employer and employee, which basically ensured that the labourer received 10 shillings and rations of dhal and rice per month. Apart from this the agreement included details about the stipulated period of indenture, nature of labour, number of days the migrants were required to work and details about the passage back home. What is interesting is the way the words "*girmit*" and "*girmitya*" have been reclaimed as an important part of the lexicon of indenture, becoming a metaphor or metonym for it, with the very words encapsulating one of the darkest episodes in all of human history.

Girrmit Tales also draws attention to the fact that the history of the indentured Indians did not begin with the arrival of the *SS Truro* in 1860, but long before that, and the lives of the labourers when they were still in India are described. A remarkable element of the narratives in the collection, *Girrmit Tales,* is that there is a close connection between India and South Africa in the lives recounted. We are told of the immigrants' journey in India to the port cities from whence they would continue their journeys to distant lands.

We are also given important information about their arrival in South Africa and their holding places before they were distributed as chattel. Sometimes the life of struggle in India continues seamlessly on foreign soil. For people like Juta, for example, in the short story, "Juta," scraping a living through many odd jobs in Durban, "little had changed in ... life or circumstance. It seemed not so long ago that he was a mere starving youth seeking sanctuary at the temples of Kancheepuram."[42]

India is evoked as much in fact as in memory and dream, as incidents in the new spaces trigger off memories of similar happenings in the place of their birth. The migrants long for their homeland, seeing their indenture as a mere sojourn. V.S. Naipaul, in *A House for Mr Biswas*, speaks of a "familiar temporariness" that characterized their life.[43] It is no wonder they worked like automatons in the new abode, keeping their souls alive by the memories of life lived in another place, another time. For Vengetapathy, for example, in the short story, "Wrought by Prayer,"

> his mind seemed to enter a time-top in reverse gear; he seemed oblivious of the present. His mind was reaching back to a long time ago, as if to gain strength from the past. Sirdar Vengetapathy was once more in his native land [...] his mind projected thus to his ancestors, seven generations away [...].[44]

Ben Okri suggests that this may be the scripting of a new kind of history:

> [S]ometimes we find ourselves living in the dreams of the dead. Who knows the destination of a dream? How many worlds do we live in at the same time? When we sleep do we wake up in another world, in another time? When we sleep in that other world do we wake up here, in this world? Is history the converging of dreams of many millions of people, living or dead?[45]

Aziz Hassim's novel, *Revenge of Kali* (2009), is the newest addition to local plantation literature.[46] The novel is divided into three parts, the Canefields of Natal, the Duchene and the Casbah of Durban, and all three are connected through the life of the central character, Thiru. It is around the 1970s, when Thiru lives in Riverside, having moved from the Duchene and the Casbah, and he expresses a longing to know of his past. He plans to go to the chilly canefields to reconnect with the stories of his forebears.

Hassim refers to Thiru's quest as "a coolie odyssey," thereby invoking similar narratives in other Indian diasporic contexts, such as David Dabydeen's poetry collection, *The Coolie Odyssey* (1988), and Marina Carter and Khal Torabally's *Coolitude: An Anthology of the Indian Labour Diaspora* (2002), which begins with a description of "The Coolie Odyssey, a voyage in time and space."[47] The plantation experience in Natal is part of a shared history of the old Indian diaspora,[48] which includes Fiji, South Africa, the West Indies and the Indian Ocean Islands. In 2005 the well-known South African actor Rajesh Gopie wrote and directed *Coolie Odyssey*, a successful stage production. The play recounted the indentured history of South African Indians from a novel perspective, where an old labourer returns reincarnated as a monkey[49] and writes his story. Gopie was inspired by Vikram Chandra's *Red Earth and Pouring Rain* (1995).[50]

In *Revenge of Kali*, Thiru's desire to find his past takes him to the Canefields outside Durban where he is transported in time and listens to the stories of his forebears – indentured labourers on the sugar cane fields of Natal. The sugar cane fields reveal their dark secrets and blend of history and fantasy. The stories of Thiru's ancestors echo through the canefields. *The cane is singing.* It is a hundred years after they had lived there, and the spirits of the dead answer Thiru's call. He becomes aware of spectral voices speaking in soft whispers. Indeed, Thiru is surrounded by ghosts from the past. The gentle murmurs of the ancestors through the canefields hold him in thrall and this experience becomes part of a homecoming, a return to his roots. Thiru's passionate need to know of his 'story' finds echoes, for me, in Lebogang Mashile's poem, "Tell your story":

Tell your story
Let it nourish you,
Sustain you
And claim you
Tell your story
Let it feed you,
Heal you

And release you
Tell your story
Let it twist and remix your shattered heart
Tell your story
Until your past stops tearing your present apart.[51]

Hassim eschews linear history; he ingeniously reconstructs a collective plantation memory through fictional oral testimony. There is a sense of "lived experience," of "lived history," a "history from below," that is conveyed, as Thiru listens to the stories of his grandfather, and submerged voices seem to rise from the very canefields themselves. Hassim is also concerned with a "politics of memory," where the social and cultural meanings of memory produce an identity located in (subaltern) history. As Miki Flockemann points out: "Memory is the cornerstone of identity."[52]

Oral history also underlines the work of Alleyn Diesel, whose work, *Shakti: Stories of South African Indian Women* (2007) is a compendium of stories, drawing from a cross section of women from Pietermaritzburg.[53] Raaz Pillay's story, "Grandmother's Feet," with which the collection begins, draws on the grand narrative of the arrival in South Africa of Indian indentured labourers.[54] Instead of the impersonal recounting of textbook history this is a flesh and blood narrative, recreating a lost life originating in India. The family sit around the *bowla* and listen intently as the grandmother narrates her experiences of leaving India and coming to work in the coal mines in Newcastle. Indeed, this and the other texts mentioned remind us that the past century and a half is resonant with countless indenture tales recited orally and passed on from generation to generation. So many of these rich oral renditions are lost to posterity, which makes writings such as these surveyed here invaluable.

A recent autobiographical work, *Salt Water Runs in My Veins* (unpublished manuscript, 2009) by Pritz Dullay recounts a life in the struggle both in South Africa and in exile and alludes to Dullay's connection with the history of indenture.[55] Dullay recalls the harsh world of indentured labour of his grandparents' time.

All these writings, with their "imaginary coherence"[56] of the plantation experience, conjure up in their different ways a past era in all its granular realism, straddling a thin line between fictional, ethnographic and historical writing. Indenture has become an important element of the iconography of memory in post-apartheid writings among Indian South African writers. It seems to act as a template for memory – a memory of suffering, of endurance, of struggle and survival, of quintessential subaltern experience. That this writing has developed largely after 1994 and particularly in the last decade, shows how Indian identity is constructed against the "detritus of indenture," to use Mishra's phrase,[57] in order to legitimatize national belonging.

The writers show the way in which indenture seamlessly merged with the life under colonialism and apartheid. Against the larger backdrop of writing on indenture, crossing the *kala pani*, and living under Empire and colonialism, is the writing of post-indenture life under apartheid, which was also described as a kind of "internal colonialism."[58] The coolies or *girmityas* continued to live as outsiders in apartheid South Africa. After the initial displacement from their homeland, they were subjected to further displacement in the land of their adoption, and for succeeding generations, in the land of their birth. The writings serve as an extended TRC project, where indenture is presented, like slavery, as an epic struggle. They remind us that history is a palimpsest: it has layers and layers of memory, private and collective, imagined and mythologised, but no less palpable.

What is the Significance of Indentured Writing?

What is the significance of this rehearsal and performance of indentured history? Amartya Sen argues against the "miniaturization" of Indian history and experience and, similarly, with respect to indentured experience, what are the consequences of taking a broad, expansive view?[59]

By insisting on the ongoing recuperation and insertion of indentured history, historians and writers are revisioning South African historiography and colonial historicism. The genealogy, indeed, the historicity, of institutional history, with its homogenizing tendencies, is laid bare, when local histories and local memories of indenture are brought to the fore, and "life worlds" – the everyday worlds in which people live and work – are highlighted.[60] Subjugated knowledges, through a "history from below," become part of the corpus of official history. Thus historians and writers are contributing not only ontologically and aesthetically, but epistemologically as well. Certainly, a consideration of South African Indian writings on indenture gives a different trajectory to western modernity with its high nodes being the Renaissance, Reformation and the Enlightenment, and takes in other nodes of world history and culture, such as slavery and indenture. It also participates in a literature of the diasporic imaginary beyond the traditional western canon, and the writings become allegories of the diasporic writer and his or her relationship with colonization. Here, V.S. Naipaul's *A House for Mr Biswas* is a paradigmatic text.[61]

We need to see indenture not in a compartmentalized way, but as part of the long exploitation of all black people in this country for economic gain, as part of a long history of colonial capital. Agnes Sam puts this succinctly when she writes:

> Indentured labour replaced slavery. Migrant labour replaced indentured labour. The Bantustans will replace migrant labour. The difference between these four forms of labour may have been only in the letter of the law. The labourers – slaves, indentured labourers, migrant workers and the people in the Bantustans – shared the status of foreigners in South Africa.[62]

Writings on indenture have expanded the literary universe, pushing South African literary criticism beyond its conventional boundaries. Our scholarship in South Africa is propelled horizontally, across spaces, and temporally, across periods. The problem with an exclusivist approach, when the corpus is approached solely through one perspective, is that it misses the way the writing moves centripetally as much as centrifugally. The formulation of literatures as exemplifying *roots and routes* shows that the two processes are intertwined, focusing on circulation and flows as well as on origins and places of ancestry. Andrew MacDonald rightly points to "the zones of contact occasioned by the economics of modernity," and that we need to wake up to the fact that "the identity of our species is shaped by diasporic and transnational imaginaries of long gestation."[63]

The notion of "contact zones" – a well-known trope in postcolonial literature – is a useful way of considering the many different types of spaces of interaction that may be attributed to any individual or group and these zones may be found in multiple spaces, given the history of Empire. Multiple, multi-directional impulses can co-exist and critical readings should open up the literature to show how different strands are intertwined and intermeshed. The challenge is not to lose the specificity of the South African Indian experiences as reflected in the writings, or of the South African context as a whole but, at the same time, not to be bound parochially to it.

Plantation literature of, what has been termed, the "*girmit* diaspora," expands the canvas of South African literatures transculturally and transnationally, away from the way it is conventionally imagined and, in the process, expands thinking on the South African nation. Indenture literature situates South Africa and South African literary writing beyond narrow confines. It is an inextricable part of the body of "struggle" literatures of colonialism and of postcolonialism, both of the African continent, of the African and Indian diasporas and beyond.

Transculturally, an expansive view would make us realize that the boundaries around "our" histories are porous and imagined. The arrival of Chinese indentured labourers, also referred to as "coolies," to work in the gold mines, occurred during the period when Indian indenture was proceeding apace.[64] Khal Torabully, the Mauritian poet, has developed the concept of coolitude that is similar to negritude; it is an inclusive term that depicts the coolie/indentured history, and is not restricted to the Indian experience. He proposes a bridge between negritude and coolitude, as an encounter between two *imaginaires*, two poetics.[65]

Transnationally, in the history of Empire, this writing inevitably intersects with other literatures and writings in South Africa, the rest of Africa – Indian indentured labourers came to East Africa to work on the construction of the railways from 1985 to 1914, with India in particular and with post-colonies elsewhere.

A broad re-focussing on indenture prompts us to appreciate more fully our strong links to current transnational investigations of an Indian Ocean map of South/South interaction. Emerging comparative literary criticism has seen the development of the category of "Indian Ocean literatures" where Africa, Indian Ocean Islands (such as Madagascar, Mauritius and Seychelles), South

Africa and India are considered, and with South African writings – of which Indian writings are an inextricable part – being seen as an important component of such study.[66]

Stephen Gray, in his anthology *Invitation to a Voyage: French Language Poetry of the Indian Ocean African Islands* (2008), shows how the Indian Ocean has been linked to South Africa for the past 400 years, highlighting the slavery of the 18th century, the sugar industry of the 19th, and Socialism in the 20th century.[67] While there has been scholarship on The Middle Passage of the Atlantic slave trade, attention has now been directed to the Indian Ocean, which was a globalized workspace for centuries. It is necessary to see this not in exclusivist ways but as an interrogation of the "important spaces between terra-centric polities,"[68] and as part of the same history.

Amitav Ghosh, in his novel *A Sea of Poppies* (2008), illustrates this well.[69] The novel, which is set in the context of the opium trade between India and China, a trade mediated by the British Empire, shows the criss-crossing of peoples in a cosmopolitanism that was quite normal in the 19th century. Colonial experiences of empire, slavery and indenture induce a consideration not only of the themes of exile, migration and identity in postcolonial literary criticism, but of oppression and struggles for liberation. Ghosh, working on a global scale, rewrites the history of indenture, and shows how it is interfaced with that of slavery, as he re-narrativizes it in his novel. He paints a wide canvas, spatially and temporally, with actors linked to the slave trade, indenture, colonial and imperial trade history and economies and its aftermath. His depiction of the "lascars" who were from a range and mixture of countries shows the border crossing that was common in our history for a long time. Ghosh clearly moves us beyond a dualistic logic, a logic which "is unproductive in understanding the intertwinings of a world marked by the aftermaths of slavery, colonialism and globalization."[70]

Further scholarship, which highlights the overlapping of histories, is important and necessary and is being prompted by the focus on indenture. The work of critics, such as that of Brinda Mehta, whose germinal work, *Diasporic (Dis) Locations: Indo-Caribbean Women Writers Negotiate the Kala Pani* (2004), showing the points of intersection between the Indian and African diasporas globally, is worth invoking here.[71] Mehta speaks of "rhizomatic spatiality" between and across the *kala pani* or the black waters of the Atlantic (and not only of the Indian Ocean) and draws from Caribbean and Mauritian writers to develop her argument.

Similarly, Hershini Bhana Young widens the scope of her literary and critical gaze by connecting with the history of slavery in the African diaspora in her book, *Haunting Capital: Memory, Text and the Black Diasporic Body* (2006), against the background of her own experiences as a young Indian woman growing up in South Africa and of her ancestors who came from India to South Africa.[72] The debates in South African literary criticism on "national literature," "cosmopolitanism," and "world literature" are certainly mapped out differently when the theme of plantation literature is considered.

An interesting historical account that shows this pushing of the conventional borders of Indian indenture in South Africa is contained in Ashwin Desai and Goolam Vahed's book, *Inside Indenture* (2007). It is an account of Goordeen Bhagoo and his wife Golaba Lalsa, who arrived in colonial Natal in 1890. While they were from Lucknow, they were listed as residents of Guadeloupe, in the eastern Caribbean Sea.[73] Khal Torabully, a Mauritian writer – whose father was Trinidadian and mother from India and Malaysia – also maps a wide and far-flung canvas when he writes using the sea – a coral imaginary – to suggest the flow and movement across spaces:

> And I anchored in Durban, Dina Morgabine,
> Singapore, Fiji, the West Indies, in the dust of waves.
> To be scattered in the gales of continents.
> In the currents of colonies.[74]

The notion of a "coral imaginary" suggests this mosaic of shared identities that ultimately embraces an inclusive subaltern experience. It brings into play the metaphor of the rhizome, as used by Edouard Glissant, the West Indian theorist of creolization.[75] This certainly expands the understanding of South African identities, beyond considerations of an ethnocentric, or even a nationalistic, one. It gives new meaning to the notion of "*Shared Histories*"... "*Words on Water.*"

Most importantly, recounting the indentured experience comes with a responsibility for writer, literary critic and reader to the present moment. Recalling this earlier history of oppression under indenture, of personal and collective trauma, makes us mindful of new oppressions in the post-apartheid state and elsewhere and the need to continue to work for an egalitarian society and world. If suffering and trauma were defining elements of the old diaspora of indenture as we know it, we have to ask how "our memorial practices … foster the work of remembrance as part of the work of freedom, the ultimate ethical frontier."[76] We need this "re-membering" to effect not only a restorative justice for the past but for the present as well, for South Africa and for the rest of our world.

Conclusion: Imagined Memories

I would like to conclude on a personal note, with reference to my own grandparents who came as indentured labourers to Natal. This is an excerpt from a larger narrative I have written on my maternal grandmother, who came to South Africa from India at the age of eight:

> Indian women worked very hard. My grandmother worked in the Hulett tea plantations in Kearsney from the time she arrived up to her marriage. I have now learnt that the "most intensive use of women's labour on plantations was made by tea estates in the Stanger district on the North Coast" (Beall, 1990: 153). Young women were seen to be particularly suited for this job as they were considered to have small deft fingers, as Munsamy points out (1997: 29). My grandmother worked for a shilling a month. When she moved to work in the nearby mill, her work included scaling and packing the tea that was brought by ox-wagon from the outlying fields. The bags were hoisted up to the second floor of the mill, where they were spread out to dry. My grandmother's job involved turning the leaves on the shelves lined with hessian and then packing them for transportation by train to Durban *via* Stanger; ships then took this cargo to India. In India the leaves were processed and blended with "Ceylon tea" and exported to different parts of the world. My grandmother was thus a small participant in the larger capitalist enterprise for the "mother country," Great Britain.[77]

My grandmother died in January 1948, six months after India's independence. Never tasting freedom, she died in the land of her adoption at a time when the stranglehold of apartheid was beginning to tighten. My mother died in South Africa, the land of her birth, in 1993, a year before the country would have its first democratic elections.

My poem, "Memory of Snow and Dust," written after reading Breyten Bretenbach's novel of the same name, connects Africa and India, and reflects my own imagined memories of indentured experience. The following is an excerpt:

> I too sat at fireplaces
> on my father's lap
> listening to tales of kings and kingdoms
> of wrestlers and gatekeepers
> of lovers beyond their reach
> wily grandmothers
> temples and human snakes
>
> time collapses
> dream and reality
> stories of Ramayana and Soundiata
> words on water
>
> my grandfather held his mother's hand
> severing memory
> time of lion and tiger
> elephant and demons and stars
>
> castaways
> tilling in coolie canefields sighing
> toiling for tea for empire
> stonebodies in compounds.[78]

Epilogue

"The Cane Is Singing"

> The cane is singing. All along it is singing: to the left, from where I am sitting in this train on my way to the big city to visit my children, to the rolling land where the sea begins, and to my right, into the interior where the sun sets. The cane is singing, but it is a sad refrain that the cane is singing.
>
> They first landed on these shores in 1860. Some were eager to come. Others were eagerly brought. That is why the cane is singing now. The mills are grinding and the sugar is pouring down the chutes, the quota increasing and on its return from Durban this train will have many men from the Transkei in its many bellies coming to this singing sugar-cane land. The

chairman of the Board reports a net profit after tax of two comma five. Sweet melody to the shareholders. No shares for me, for my father and his father before him and my children and their children after them. For us only the bitter notes of this sad song, this soul-searing song that the cane is singing … .[79]

Notes

1. Amitav Ghosh, *The Shadow Lines* (New Delhi: Ravi Dayal Publisher, 1988), 184.
2. Narain Aiyer, "The Cane Is Singing," *Staffrider* 3.4 (1980/1981): 82–87. Aiyer is a descendant of indentured labourers, who came to work in the sugar plantations in the North Coast of Natal in 1892. He was a highly respected teacher of English and played a leading role in the English Society of the Teachers' Association of South Africa [TASA]. He was a political activist in TASA; he died in 1997.
3. See Homi Bhabha (ed.), *Nation and Narration* (London: Routledge, 1990).
4. In Rob Nixon, "Aftermaths: South African Literature Today," in *Transition: An International Review* 6.4 (72) (Winter, 1997): 74.
5. See Sarah Nuttall and Carli Coetzee (eds.), *Negotiating the Past: The Making of Memory in South Africa* (Oxford: Oxford UP, 2002 [1998]): 2.
6. See Devarakshanam Govinden, *A Time of Memory: Reflections on Recent South African Writings* (Durban: Solo Collective, 2008).
7. Fatima Meer, *Portrait of Indian South Africans* (Durban: Avon House, 1969).
8. P.S. Joshi, *The Tyranny of Colour: A Study of the Indian Problem in South Africa* (Durban: E.P. & Commercial Printing, 1942), 44.
9. Agnes Sam, "And They Christened It Indenture," in Sam, *Jesus Is Indian, and Other Stories* (Oxford: Heinemann, 1989), 129–131.
10. Joshi, 41.
11. Surendra Bhana and Joy B. Brain, *Setting down Roots: Indian Migrants in South Africa 1860–1911* (Johannesburg: Witwatersrand UP, 1990), 15.
12. Elleke Boehmer, *Empire Writing: An Anthology of Colonial Literature 1870–1918* (Oxford: Oxford UP, 1998), xviii.
13. Mahadai Das, "They Came in Ships," in *India in the Caribbean*, eds. David Dabydeen and Brinsley Samaroo (London: Hansib Publishing, 1987), 288–289.
14. Bhana and Brain, 15 and 36.
15. Ronald Takaki, *A Different Mirror: A History of Multicultural America* (Boston: Little Brown & Co., 1993), 7.
16. See Vijay Mishra, "Voices from the Diaspora," in *The Encyclopedia of the Indian Diaspora*, ed. Brij V. Lal (Singapore, Kuala Lumpur, Paris: Editions Didier Millet, 2006), 120.

17. Keletso E. Atkins, *The Moon is Dead! Give Us Our Money!: The Cultural Origins of an African Work Ethic, Natal, South Africa, 1843–1900* (Portsmouth, NH: Heinemann and London: James Currey, 1993), 2.
18. Cheryl Walker, "Women and Gender in Southern Africa to 1945: An Overview," in *Women and Gender in Southern Africa to 1945*, ed. Cheryl Walker (Cape Town: David Philip, 1990), 1.
19. Dr K. Goonam, *Coolie Doctor* (Durban: Madiba Press, 1990), Jay Naidoo, *Coolie Location* (London: SA Writers, 1990), Rèshard Gool, *Cape Town Coolie* (Oxford: Heinernann, 1990).
20. M.K. Gandhi, *An Autobiography, or The Story of My Experiments with Truth* (Ahmedabad: Navijan Publishing, 2006 [1925]).
21. Gandhi, 24.
22. In 1852, eight years before the *SS Truro* arrived in South Africa, Frederick Douglass made a "4th of July" speech in upstate New York. This is an excerpt:

    "For it is not light that is needed, but fire;
    It is not the gentle shower, but thunder.
    We need the storm, the whirlwind and the earthquake.
    The feeling of the nation must be quickened;
    The conscience of the nation must be roused;
    The propriety of the nation must be startled;
    The hypocrisy of the nation must be exposed;
    And the cries against God and man must be proclaimed
    And denounced …."

    Frederick Douglass, "What to the Slave Is the Fourth of July?" extract from an Oration, at Rochester, July 5, 1852, available at: <http://www.gutenberg.org/files/202/202.txt> (visited 7 January, 2010).
23. See Olive Gilbert, *Narrative of Sojourner Truth* (Mineola, NY: Dover Publication, 1997), iii; Johan U. Jacobs, "Life Writing (South Africa): Autobiography," in *Encyclopaedia of Post-Colonial Literatures in English*, vol. 1, eds. Eugene Benson and Leonard W. Connolly (London: Routledge, 1994), 878–882.
24. Imraan Coovadia, *The Wedding* (New York: Picador USA, 2001).
25. Gandhi incidentally points out that the merchants were known as "coolie merchants" (Gandhi, 121).
26. Ronnie Govender, *Song of the Atman* (Johannesburg: Jacana Media, 2006), back cover notes.
27. Ronnie Govender, *Song*, 19–20.
28. Riason Naidoo, *Indian Ink: The Indian in Drum* (Cape Town: Bell-Roberts Publishing, 2008), 12.
29. Daphne Rooke, *Ratoons* (London: Gollancz and Boston: Houghton Mifflin, 1953).

30. Praba Moodley, *The Heart Knows No Colour* (Cape Town: Kwela Books, 2003).
31. Sarah Nuttall and Cheryl-Ann Michael (eds.), *Senses of Culture: South African Cultural Studies* (Cape Town: Oxford UP, 2000).
32. Fiona M. Khan, *Reeds of Wrath* (Durban: Washesha Publications, 2009).
33. Terry Eagleton, *After Theory* (London: Penguin, 2004), 4.
34. Arthur Martial, *La Poupee de Chair: Récit de l'Ile Maurice* (Port Louis: General Printing and Stationnery, 1931) and *Sphinx de Bronze* (Port Louis: General Printing and Stationery, 1935); Loys Masson, *Mutins* (Paris: Editions de la paix, 1951).
35. Pat Poovalingum, *Anand* (Durban: Madiba Press, 2003).
36. Zakes Mda, *Madonna of Excelsior* (Oxford: Oxford UP, 2002).
37. In Mishra, "Voices," 123.
38. Rubendra Govender, *Sugar Cane Boy* (Durban: Bambata Publishing, 2008), 51
39. Ronnie Govender, *Lahnee's Pleasure* (Johannesburg: Jacana Media, 2008), 1.
40. Neelan Govender, *Girrmit Tales* (Durban: Rebel Rabble, 2008).
41. An allusion to Jhumpa Lahiri's 1999 collection of short stories by the same name.
42. Neelan Govender, 100.
43. V.S. Naipaul, *A House for Mr Biswas* (Harmondsworth: Penguin, 1961), 164.
44. Naipaul, *A House.*
45. Ben Okri, *Infinite Riches* (London: Phoenix House, 1998), 6.
46. Aziz Hassim, *Revenge of Kali* (Johannesburg: STE Publishers, 2009).
47. David Dabydeen, *The Coolie Odyssey* (London: Hansib Publishing & Mundelstrup: Dangaroo Press, 1988); Marina Carter and Khal Torabully, *Coolitude: An Anthology the Indian Labour Diaspora* (London: Anthem Press, 2002).
48. Vijay Mishra distinguishes between the old and new diasporas, where the former was dictated by the labour needs of colonial powers in the 19th century, and the latter, by contemporary dispersion due to globalization and voluntary migration since the mid-20th century, see Mishra, *The Literature of the Indian Diaspora: Theorising the Diasporic Imaginary* (Oxford and New York: Routledge, 2007).
49. What I have referred to as " the signifying monkey," from the title of a book by Henry Louis Gates, Jr.
50. Vikram Chandra, *Red Earth and Pouring Rain* (New Delhi: Penguin/India, 1995).
51. Lebogang Mashile, "Tell your story," in Mashile, *In a Ribbon of Rhythm* (Johannesburg: Mutloase Arts Heritage Trust and Cape Town: Oshun, 2005), 46.

52. Miki Flockemann, "Memory, Madness and Whiteness in Julia Blackburn's *The Book of Colour* and Rachel Zadok's *Gem Squash Tokoloshe*," *English Academy Review* 25.2 (2008): 6. Aziz Hassim is similar to other diasporic writers, such as Cyril Dabydeen, who have addressed the problems of delocalization of identities and cultural loss, see Marina Carter and Khal Torabully, *Coolitude: An Anthology of the Indian Labour Diaspora* (London: Anthem Press, 2002), 139.
53. Alleyn Diesel (comp.), *Shakti: Stories of Indian Women in South Africa* (Johannesburg: Witwatersrand UP, 2007).
54. Pillay, Raaz. "Grandmother's Feet," in Alleyn Diesel (comp.) *Shakti: Stories of Indian Women in South Africa* (Johannesburg: Witwatersrand UP, 2007), 9–20.
55. Pritiraj Dullay, *Salt Water Runs in My Veins* (unpublished manuscript, 2009).
56. From Brij V. Lal, "Introduction," in *The Encyclopedia of the Indian Diaspora*, ed. Brij V. Lal (Singapore, Kuala Lumpur, Paris: Editions Didier Millet, 2006), 14.
57. Mishra, *Literature*, xvii.
58. Ronit Frenkel, *Reconsiderations: South African Indian Fiction and the Making of Race in Postcolonial Culture*, Phd Dissertation, University of Arizona, 2009 (in press), 2.
59. Amartya Sen, *The Argumentative Indian: Writings on Indian History, Culture, and Identity* (New York: Farrar, Straus & Giroux, 2005).
60. See Mishra, "Voices," 126.
61. See Mishra, "Voices," 127.
62. Agnes Sam, "Introduction," in Sam, *Jesus Is Indian, and Other Stories* (Oxford: Heinemann, 1989), 9.
63. Andrew MacDonald, "In a Littoral Sense," *Mail and Guardian* (26 November, 2008), 2; available at: <http://www.mg.co.za/article/2008-11-26-in-a-littoral-sense> (visited 7 January, 2010).
64. See Darryl Accone's autobiographical fiction, *All Under Heaven: The story of a Chinese Family in South Africa* (Cape Town: David Philip, 2004).
65. See Carter and Torabully 151.
66. See John Hawley (ed.), *India in Africa, Africa in India: Indian Ocean Cosmopolitanisms* (Bloomington: Indiana UP, 2008).
67. Stephen Gray (ed.), *Invitation to a Voyage: French Language Poetry of the Indian Ocean African Islands* (Pretoria: Protea, 2008).
68. MacDonald 2.
69. Amitav Ghosh, *Sea of Poppies* (London: John Murray, 2008).
70. Frenkel 4.
71. Brinda Mehta, *Diasporic (Dis)Locations: Indo-Caribbean Women Writers Negotiate the Kala Pani* (Kingston, Jamaica: U of West Indies P, 2004).

72. Hershini Bhana Young, *Haunting Capital: Memory, Text and the Black Diasporic Body* (Hanover: Dartmouth College Press, 2006).
73. Ashwin Desai and Goolam Vahed, *Inside Indenture: A South African Story, 1860–1914* (Durban: Madiba Publishers, 2007), 49.
74. Khal Torabully, *Cale d'etoiles Coolitude* (Reunion: Editions Azalees, 1992).
75. See Carter and Torabully 152.
76. Achille Mbembe, "On the Postcolony," interview with Christian Hoeller, *Springerin* 3 (2002), reissued in English in *Chimurenga.*, available online at: <http://www.chimurenga.co.za/page-56.html> (visited 7 January, 2010).
77. Devarakshanam Govinden, *Sister Outsiders: Representation and Identity in Selected Writings by South African Indian Women* (Pretoria: Unisa Press, 2008), 75.
78. See Govinden, *Sister.*
79. Aiyer 82–87.

Works Cited

Accone, Darryl. *All Under Heaven: The Story of a Chinese Family in South Africa.* Cape Town: David Philip, 2004.

Aiyer, Narain. "The Cane Is Singing." *Staffrider* 3.4 (1980/1981): 82–87.

Atkins, Keletso E. *The Moon is Dead! Give Us Our Money!: The Cultural Origins of an African Work Ethic, Natal, South Africa, 1843–1900.* Portsmouth: Heinemann and London: James Currey, 1993.

Beall, Jo. "Women under Indentured Labour in Colonial Natal 1860–1911." In *Women and Gender in Southern Africa to 1945.* Ed. Cheryl Walker. Cape Town: David Philip, 1990. 146–167.

Bhabha, Homi (ed.). *Nation and Narration.* London: Routledge, 1990.

Bhana, Surendra and Joy B. Brain. *Setting down Roots: Indian Migrants in South Africa 1860–1911.* Johannesburg: Witwatersrand UP, 1990.

Boehmer, Elleke. *Empire Writing: An Anthology of Colonial Literature 1870–1918.* Oxford: Oxford UP, 1998.

Carter, Marina and Khal Torabully. *Coolitude: An Anthology of the Indian Labour Diaspora.* London: Anthem Press, 2002.

Chandra, Vikram. *Red Earth and Pouring Rain.* New Delhi: Penguin/India, 1995.

Coovadia, Imraan. *The Wedding.* New York: PicadorUSA, 2001

Dabydeen, David. *The Coolie Odyssey.* London: Hansib Publishing & Mundelstrup: Dangaroo Press, 1988.

Das, Mahadai. "They Came in Ships." In *India in the Caribbean.* Eds. David Dabydeen and Brinsley Samaroo. London: Hansib Publishing, 1987. 288–289.

Desai, Ashwin and Goolam Vahed. *Inside Indenture: A South African Story, 1860–1914*. Durban: Madiba Publishers, 2007.

Diesel, Alleyn (comp.). *Shakti: Stories of Indian Women in South Africa*. Johannesburg: Witwatersrand UP, 2007.

Douglass, Frederick. "What to the Slave Is the Fourth of July?" Extract from an Oration, at Rochester, July 5, 1852. Available at: <http://www.gutenberg.org/files/202/202.txt>. (Visited 7 January, 2010.)

Dullay, Pritiraj. *Salt Water Runs in My Veins*. Unpublished manuscript. 2009.

Eagleton, Terry. *After Theory*. London: Penguin, 2004.

Flockemann, Miki. "Memory, Madness and Whiteness in Julia Blackburn's *The Book of Colour* and Rachel Zadok's *Gem Squash Tokoloshe*." *English Academy Review* 25.2 (2008): 4–19.

Frenkel, Ronit. *Reconsiderations: South African Indian Fiction and the Making of Race in Postcolonial Culture*. Phd Dissertation. University of Arizona, 2009. [In press].

Gandhi, M.K. *An Autobiography, or The Story of My Experiments with Truth*. Ahmedabad: Navijan Publishing, 2006 [1925].

Ghosh, Amitav. *Sea of Poppies*. London: John Murray, 2008.

Ghosh, Amitav. *The Shadow Lines*. New Delhi: Ravi Dayal Publisher, 1988.

Gilbert, Olive. *Narrative of Sojourner Truth*. Mineola, NY: Dover Publication, 1997.

Gool, Rèshard. *Cape Town Coolie*. Oxford: Heinernann, 1990.

Goonam, Dr K. *Coolie Doctor*. Durban: Madiba Press, 1990.

Govender, Neelan. *Girrmit Tales*. Durban: Rebel Rabble, 2008.

Govender, Ronnie. *Song of the Atman*. Johannesburg: Jacana Media, 2006.

Govender, Ronnie. *Lahnee's Pleasure*. Johannesburg: Jacana Media, 2008.

Govender, Rubendra. *Sugar Cane Boy*. Durban: Bambata Publishing, 2008.

Govinden, Devarakshanam. *Sister Outsiders: Representation and Identity in Selected Writings by South African Indian Women*. Imagined South Africa, 14. Pretoria: Unisa Press, 2008.

Govinden, Devarakshanam. *A Time of Memory: Reflections on Recent South African Writings*. Durban: Solo Collective, 2008.

Gray, Stephen (ed.). *Invitation to a Voyage: French Language Poetry of the Indian Ocean African Islands*. Pretoria: Protea, 2008.

Hassim, Aziz. *Revenge of Kali*. Johannesburg: STE Publishers, 2009.

Hawley, John (ed.). *India in Africa, Africa in India: Indian Ocean Cosmopolitanisms*. Bloomington: Indiana UP, 2008.

Jacobs, Johan U. "Life Writing (South Africa): Autobiography." In *Encyclopaedia of Post-Colonial Literatures in English*, Vol. 1. Eds. Eugene Benson and Leonard W. Connolly. London: Routledge, 1994. 878–882.

Joshi, P.S. *The Tyranny of Colour: A Study of the Indian Problem in South Africa.* Durban: E.P. & Commercial Printing, 1942.

Khan, Fiona M. *Reeds of Wrath.* Durban: Washesha Publications, 2009.

Lal, Brij V. "Introduction." In *The Encyclopedia of the Indian Diaspora.* Ed. Brij V. Lal. Singapore, Kuala Lumpur, Paris: Editions Didier Millet, 2006. 10–15.

MacDonald, Andrew. "In a Littoral Sense." In *Mail and Guardian* (26 November, 2008): 2. Available online at: <http://www.mg.co.za/article/2008-11-26-in-a-littoral-sense>. (Visited 7 January, 2010.)

Martial, Arthur. *La Poupee de Chair: Récit de l'Ile Maurice.* Port Louis: General Printing and Stationnery, 1931.

Martial, Arthur. *Sphinx de Bronze.* Port Louis: General Printing and Stationery, 1935.

Mashile, Lebogang. "Tell your story." In Mashile, *In a Ribbon of Rhythm.* Johannesburg: Mutloase Arts Heritage Trust and Cape Town: Oshun, 2005. 46.

Masson, Loys. *Mutins.* Paris: Editions de la paix, 1951.

Mbembe, Achille. "On the Postcolony" Interview with Christian Hoeller. *Springerin* 3 (2002). Reissued in English in *Chimurenga.* Available online at: <http://www.chimurenga.co.za/page-56.html>. (Visited 7 January, 2010.)

Mbembe, Achille. *On the Postcolony.* Berkeley: U of California P, 2001.

Mda, Zakes. *Madonna of Excelsior.* Oxford: Oxford UP, 2002.

Mehta, Brinda. *Diasporic [Dis]Locations: Indo-Caribbean Women Writers Negotiate the Kala Pani.* Kingston, Jamaica: U of West Indies P, 2004.

Meer, Fatima. *Portrait of Indian South Africans.* Durban: Avon House, 1969.

Mishra, Vijay. *The Literature of the Indian Diaspora: Theorising the Diasporic Imaginary.* Oxford and New York: Routledge, 2007.

Mishra, Vijay. "Voices from the Diaspora." In *The Encyclopedia of the Indian Diaspora.* Ed. Brij V. Lal. Singapore, Kuala Lumpur, Paris: Editions Didier Millet, 2006. 120–139.

Moodley, Praba. *The Heart Knows No Colour.* Cape Town: Kwela Books, 2003.

Munsamy, Shireen Sarojini. *From Sunrise to Sunset.* Durban: Afro-Asian Publishing, 1997.

Naidoo, Jay. *Coolie Location.* London: SA Writers, 1990.

Naidoo, Riason. *Indian Ink: The Indian in Drum.* Cape Town: Bell-Roberts Publishing, 2008.

Naipaul, V.S. *A House for Mr Biswas.* Harmondsworth: Penguin, 1961.

Nixon, Rob. "Aftermaths: South African Literature Today." In *Transition: An International Review* 6.4 (72) (Winter, 1997): 64–77.

Nuttall, Sarah and Cheryl-Ann Michael (eds.). *Senses of Culture: South African Cultural Studies.* Cape Town: Oxford UP, 2000.

Nuttall, Sarah and Carli Coetzee (eds.). *Negotiating the Past: The Making of Memory in South Africa.* Oxford: Oxford UP, 2002 [1998].

Okri, Ben. *Infinite Riches.* London: Phoenix House, 1998.

Pillay, Raaz. "Grandmother's Feet," pp. 9–20 in Diesel Alleyn (comp.). *Shakti: Stories of Indian Women in South Africa.* Johannesburg: Witwatersrand UP, 2007.

Poovalingum, Pat. *Anand.* Durban: Madiba Press, 2003.

Rooke, Daphne. *Ratoons.* London: Gollancz and Boston: Houghton Mifflin, 1953.

Sen, Amartya. *The Argumentative Indian: Writings on Indian History, Culture, and Identity.* New York: Farrar, Straus and Giroux, 2005.

Sam, Agnes. "Introduction." In Sam, *Jesus Is Indian, and Other Stories.* Oxford: Heinemann, 1989. 1–13.

Sam, Agnes. "And They Christened It Indenture." In Sam, *Jesus Is Indian, and Other Stories.* Oxford: Heinemann, 1989. 129–131.

Takaki, Ronald. *A Different Mirror: A History of Multicultural America.* Boston: Little Brown & Co., 1993.

Torabully, Khal. *Cale d'etoiles Coolitude.* Reunion: Editions Azalees, 1992.

Walker, Cheryl. "Women and Gender in Southern Africa to 1945: An Overview." In *Women and Gender in Southern Africa to 1945.* Ed. Cheryl Walker. Cape Town: David Philip, 1990. 1–32.

Young, Hershini Bhana. *Haunting Capital: Memory, Text and the Black Diasporic Body.* Hanover: Dartmouth College Press, 2006.

4

Problems of Representation in Raja Rao's *The Great Indian Way: A Life of Mahatma Gandhi*

LETIZIA ALTERNO

Mohandas Gandhi: "the British Gentleman," "the Coolie Barrister" and "the Satyagrahi"

It may come as a surprise, even to those familiar with Raja Rao's work, that he wrote a biography of Mahatma Gandhi: *The Great Indian Way: A Life of Mahatma Gandhi*, first published in New Delhi, India in 1998. However, *The Great Indian Way* cannot be strictly identified as a biography. Rather, as Rao declares in the Preface to his work, it is an ambitious "task" he "dared" to undertake, a biography written "from the inside, desperately, faithfully."[1] Indeed, its author insists that *The Great Indian Way: A Life of Mahatma Gandhi* was not intended in reductive terms as "an extravagant dictionary of dates and facts" (*GIW* 8). This yet "another life of Gandhi" should rather, according to Rao, be true to meaning, not so much to facts (*GIW* 8). What is not surprising to the reader then, even before she or he embarks in the reading of the biography, is that its focus is not the life of Gandhi himself but its "meaning" in the wider historical and political contexts preceding and accompanying the process of Indian independence and the formation of a newly imagined India.

Writing on the "meaning" of Gandhi's life and peculiar politics in this voluminous work, Rao utilizes the example of the Indian leader both as a *metonymy* that shows his contiguousness with the concept of Indian freedom, expressed in Gandhi's conception of *Satyagraha*, and a *synecdoche* for making him – as one Indian individual – represent the entire Indian nation. The issue of representation thus seems to be central to Rao's location of Gandhi within the narrative. I intend to illustrate in this article the limitations of such a centralization together with some complications involved in narrative representation and hope to offer through my analysis a deconstructive reading of *The Great Indian Way*, or a reading "against the grain."

According to Jacques Derrida and Gayatri Spivak, it is the text itself which offers an opportunity for a deconstructive reading, a trace of disorder so to say, which disrupts the balance of textual structure and paves the way to deconstruction. Recalling Derrida, Spivak argues in her introduction to *Selected Subaltern Studies* that "you can only read against the grain if misfits in the text signal the way."[2] In *The Great Indian Way* such misfits are indicated by certain ambivalences inherent in the representation of Gandhi within the narrative. A father to the free Indian nation of today – according to Rao and to many contemporary Indian nationals – Gandhi combined simultaneously two complex and ambivalent positions. On the one hand, he represented an upper-class Indian, British-educated barrister who was relatively free to assert his "freedom" to write in the context of British imperial politics in Africa and India during the end of the nineteenth century. On the other hand, Gandhi represented the position of the *Satyagrahi* and of the colonial subject of the British Empire writing and speaking for the subaltern in his attempt to defend the rights of the coolies who emigrated to Africa during his stay in Natal and their Indian counterparts in his motherland. In this sense, Gandhi may as well be said to represent the modern intellectual, who in Edward Said's terms, "belongs on the same side with the weak and unrepresented."[3]

Mohandas Gandhi: "the British Gentleman"

The following excerpt from Rao's biography illustrates Gandhi's representative position as an upper-class British-educated Indian barrister. The passage reports Gandhi defending himself against the attacks of a train guard in Johannesburg who tries to prevent him from sitting in the first class compartment for which the Indian barrister had lawfully bought a ticket:[4]

In the middle of the journey however, the guard came to examine the tickets. Seeing a coolie in the first class compartment, he became red with anger. "Get out and sit in the van!"

> "*No I will not.* I have a first class ticket."
> "You might have any ticket you like, but a coolie must travel in the van!"
> "I have studied all the rules of the railways. Nowhere do they mention it."
> "I won't argue with you. If you won't listen I will have you pushed out!"
> "No," protested the white passenger. "He is quite harmless. Why do you want to do that to him? He has a first class ticket. He will do no harm to me." The passenger was an Englishman.
> "In that case, please yourself!" shouted the guard, banging the door behind him. (*GIW* 124; emphasis added)

Apart from emphasizing the sense of injustice suffered by Gandhi and his extremely polite, yet categorical refusal to accept this kind of treatment from a representative of authority, the passage also hints at a contradiction commented on by Said in his analysis of the intellectual. According to Said, part of the role of the modern intellectual is to side with an idea of truth which should be respected by a collectivity and collectively so to say, not be exploited by the powerful. In other words, for Said, the intellectual's aim is

> to induce a change in the moral climate whereby aggression is seen as such, the unjust punishment of peoples or individuals is either prevented or given up, the recognition of rights and democratic freedom is established as a norm for everyone, not invidiously for a select few.[5]

Such a contradiction is underlined several times by Gandhi (and by Rao) in the text, for instance when the principles of morality and justice are discussed by the Indian barrister in his "Open Letter" to the members of both the Legislative Council and the Legislative Assembly of Natal, a document that Rao comments "became perhaps the first manifesto of nationalist India" (*GIW* 183). Stirring a comparison between the British, African and Indian political and religious "traditions," Gandhi interrogated the British: "Is their present treatment of the Indian in accordance with the best British traditions, or with the principles of justice and morality, or with the principles of Christianity?" (*GIW* 183).

Interestingly, while Rao quotes a passage from Gandhi's letter that recalls the words of liberal intellectual John Stuart Mill praising the British reputable sense and application of morals and justice, Said recalls the same name in relation to the French intellectual Alexis de Tocqueville, connecting it with the contradiction illustrated by Gandhi above. Indeed, Said comments that, regrettably, Mill's "commendable ideas about democratic freedoms in England [...] did not apply to India."[6] In his "Open Letter," Gandhi expressed a similar concern when in reply to the Natal government, he wrote:

> To bring a man here on starvation wages, to hold him under bondage, and when he shows the least sign of liberty, or in a position to live less miserably, to wish to send him back home where he would become comparatively a stranger and perhaps unable to earn a living is hardly a mark of fair play or justice characteristic of the British nation. (quoted in *GIW* 189)

Trying to confront the British *from within* their preached politics, it is important to note how Gandhi utilizes the same language of legality to "construct" a "truth," expressed by his philosophy of *Satyagraha*, which counterpointed the colonialist's "truth." Examining the intellectual's strategic use of language, Said comments that "[k]nowing how to use language well and knowing when to intervene in language are two essential features of intellectual action."[7]

In his role as an Indian barrister, Gandhi aptly chose his words, making them "speak" the discourse of British justice, which he used to defend the very idea of liberty professed by British liberals such as John Stuart Mill:

> This, then, is the appropriate region of human liberty. It comprises, first, the inward domain of consciousness; demanding liberty of conscience, in the most comprehensive sense; liberty of thought and feeling; absolute freedom of opinion and sentiment on all subjects, practical or speculative, scientific, moral, or theological.[8]

Contrary to Mill's paradoxical statement, which did not historically apply to "all subjects" of Great Britain, the idea of freedom, to recall Said, "cannot be sought invidiously in one territory, and ignored in another."[9] The problem is illustrated by Rao when, following a summary of the advent and establishment of British rule in India, he writes ironically that after the British Crown had taken over absolute rule of India in 1858 from the East India Company, "all Indians became automatically British subjects, and true justice and humanity would now rule the whole land" (*GIW* 149). Rao's irony undermines here the authority of constructed "truths" such as the sense of British justice and humanity, or more appropriately, the discursive practices in which they participate. In questioning the British principles of "true justice and humanity" as applied to the Indian subject, that is constructed as subject by this very system of thoughts and ideas about justice, Rao participates in the critique of discourse initiated by theorists like Michel Foucault,

> underlining how [in Said's words], in a secular world, human beings construct their truths, and that for example, the so-called objective truth of the white man's superiority built and maintained by the classical European colonial empires also rested on a violent subjugation of African and Asian peoples, who, it is equally true, fought that particular imposed 'truth' in order to provide an independent order of their own.[10]

As Said amply elaborated in his analysis of Orientalism, the British imperialistic policies were not as transparent as their ideology would make them appear. The discrepancy between discourse and its application informs Rao's ironic statement about British justice. The writer purposely accompanies this statement with a quotation from Queen Victoria's proclamation reiterating the British principles of liberty and justice:

> We hold ourselves bound to the natives of our Indian territories *by the same obligations of duty which bind us to all our other subjects,*

> and those obligations, by the blessings of the Almighty God, we shall faithfully and conscientiously fulfil. It is our further will that, so far as may be, our subjects, *of whatever race and creed*, be freely and impartially admitted to offices in our service, the duties of which they may be *qualified by their education, ability, and integrity*, duly to discharge. (quoted in *GIW* 149; emphasis added)[11]

The illusion of equal rights for all British subjects is, however, abruptly broken a few pages later by the narrator's comment that "one could say this might be true and right elsewhere but not so in Natal" (*GIW* 163). Rao's comment here illustrates the paradox of unanimous equality disputed by Gandhi. For Rao, Gandhi was "a different type of Indian," one who when he entered his first South African court appeared more like an English gentleman than a stereotypical Indian coolie:

> [Gandhi] spoke faultless Gujarati (after all, a son of a former Prime Minister of Porbandar, the grandson of the famous Ota Gandhi himself) – even so the young Gandhi was also very much a *sahib*. He not only dressed in *impeccable British manner*, he also *ate with fork and spoon*. The only difference, however, was that Barrister Gandhi never touched meat or fish. Nor for that matter did he touch spices. He ate plain, boiled vegetables and *English porridge*, sometimes even fruit and raw vegetables, but never anything very complicated. The only Indian thing about him was his turban. It made him look what he truly was, that is, *a coolie Barrister*. (*GIW* 113; emphasis added)

How was it possible, then, that such an educated and impeccably mannered Indian did endure public humiliation and racial discrimination by the Boers and the British in Africa? In order to illustrate how contemporary Rao's strategic accusation may be here, one may draw a parallel with today's society, or at least with certain societies, and ask for example, how is it *still* possible in "modern" and "civilized" Italy that a vast number of African, Indian, Bangladeshi, Philippine, as well as Romanian or Slovak immigrants – often with a university education – have extremely serious difficulties in finding respectable jobs other than menial occupations such as home or car cleaning for Italian families?

While I do not have the space to develop this point here, I would like to draw attention to the perceived discrepancy between education and representation which appears to embrace Gandhi's paradox in Rao's text. In other words, I would like to ask how Gandhi's paradoxical position is handled – and maybe unwittingly problematized – by the author in *The Great Indian Way*.

Initially, reflecting upon Gandhi's educated position Rao seems to answer this paradox with another paradox, claiming that in fact Gandhi *was not a coolie*: "Mohandas Gandhi was the first Hindu who came to Africa that was not a coolie. He was a British Indian gentleman. And this set more problems than politics or goodwill could resolve" (*GIW* 114).

A few lines later Raja Rao compares Gandhi who "was not a coolie" with a more generic representation of an Indian coolie in Africa under the British and Boer administrations. This depiction touches upon one of the most investigated ideas of current postcolonial theory: the representation of the "other." As Rao claims:

> *A coolie was not* an Arab or a Persian or a Chinaman, a coolie was always a Hindu. For the Indian merchant here [in South Africa], being rich and being Muslim, could claim Arabic descent. The Parsi, though having settled in India, could claim Persian descent. Yet the poor peasant from some obscure South Indian village, he *with his deep Dravidic traditions and layer after layer of religious sensibilities* – his people having died of famine or of poverty, *had hired himself as a legal slave* for five or ten years to his Boer or British masters – *he could not be anything recognisable.* He could not be called a slave (*the British Empire would tolerate no slaves on their territories*) – so he became a coolie. (*GIW* 115; emphasis added)

Apart from emphasizing the idea of a coolie by defining its *différence* in Saussurean style (the signified "Hindu coolie" *differs* for instance in nationality from an Arab or a Persian, or in religious status from a Muslim or Parsi), Rao posits here a Derridian *différance* which *defers* the signified "coolie" from the signified "Indian" to the signified "hired slave." At the same time, Rao polemically emphasizes a zero political visibility of the coolie in the context of British and Boers dominion in Africa, attributing him a class consciousness that makes him consciously choose to be a slave to the Empire *because* of his being devoid of a recognizable political status. To recall Gayatri Spivak's use of the term catachresis, I would like to suggest that Rao's representation of the coolie similarly functions here as an impossible referent (hence not *recognizable*) or "a metaphor that has no literal referent."[12] Rao's irony, strategically attributing a sense of legality to the condition of slavery (the coolie as "*a legal slave*") could not be more explicitly indicated in his comment between parentheses highlighting the paradox of British liberty that I have illustrated above.

Mohandas Gandhi: "the Coolie Barrister"

Yet, in *The Great Indian Way* Gandhi's position as an Indian subaltern to the British is further problematized by an additional position of authority that he appears to represent. Indeed, if Gandhi did not seem to entirely fulfil the position of a coolie-subaltern as defined "according to the lines laid down by the official institutional structures of representation,"[13] how then did he manage to put himself in the position of representing the coolie community through his legal authoritative defence in the eyes of the British and the Boers in Africa?

At this point in the narrative Rao provides the reader with an indication of Gandhi's paradoxical position hinting at a turning point in the life of the Indian barrister during the years 1893 and 1894, when Mohandas Gandhi, with a degree in Law from London, initiated his legal activity in Pretoria, South Africa. Rao illustrates this explicitly in his narrative, writing that "no sooner Mohandas Gandhi landed in South Africa than he discovered himself not only an Indian, but a subject of the British Empire. This was at once his pride and his tragedy. For South Africa was not British. It was British and Boerland and Zululand" (*GIW* 112).

This moment of transition from thinking of himself – though one may wonder if Gandhi's situation was not only Gandhi's but also Rao's – as an "almost the same, but not quite"[14] British, to recall Homi Bhabha's idea of mimicry, to the realization of being a colonized subject constitutes the most interesting turning point in Rao's biography of Gandhi. This moment of transition addresses both the ambivalence of colonial discourse and the dislocation of colonial authority in relation to a subaltern identity. The entire work can indeed be viewed as the author's attempt to resolve this conflict, perceived at the same time as a matter of "pride" but also as "tragedy" in relation to the sorrowful events that this paradox will implicate historically, a matter – stressed in the passage above – that "set more problems than politics or goodwill could resolve" (*GIW* 112).

Hence, in the second passage that I have selected here to illustrate an "other" representation of Gandhi, such a realization becomes central in the way colonial-subject-Gandhi now respond to the British government which, paradoxically, had also empowered him with the very right to respond. The following is an account of Gandhi's engagement with the franchise rights of the coolies in Natal, whom he legally represented, as a coolie barrister. More specifically, Gandhi engaged in arguing against the Asiatic Law Ordinance (22 August 1906) according to which "Indians above the age of eight had to register themselves, giving their finger and thumb impressions, and carry a pass on them which could be asked for by any policeman" (*GIW* 273). His advocacy of the principles of liberty and freedom explicitly pointed out the paradoxical and conflicting ideology sustaining British legislation:

> I would pass the whole of my lifetime in gaol, and I say that in the House of God, in the House of Prayer, and I repeat I would far rather pass the whole of my lifetime in jail and be perfectly happy, than see *my fellow-countrymen subjected to indignity* and I should come out of the gaol.
>
> [...] I should claim that *this country is just as much as mine as any other Colonist's*, and it is in that sense that I put forward that claim *on behalf of my countrymen.* [...] Unfranchised though *we* are, unrepresented though *we* are in the Transvaal, it is open to clothe ourselves with an undying franchise, and this consists in recognising *our* humanity, in recognising that *we* are part and parcel of the great universal whole, [...] and if my countrymen recognise that position I say no matter what legislation is passed over *our* heads, if that legislation is in conflict with *our* ideas of right and wrong, if it is in conflict with our conscience, if it is in conflict with our religion, then we shall not submit to that legislation. (*GIW* 292–293; emphasis added)

Gandhi can almost be heard speaking through Rao's narrative, and the realism of this scene – if we view realism in Terry Eagleton's terms as a form of representation "which seeks to merge itself so thoroughly with the world that its status as art is suppressed,"[15] – offers an imaginative picture of an oxymoronic "reverent revolution" defined by Gandhi's *Satyagraha*, and described by Rao as "the politest, the most courteous revolution history had ever seen" (*GIW* 285).

In addressing his "fellow-countrymen" as one of them, in his use of "we" and "us," Gandhi was *speaking for* the silenced subalterns who according to Spivak are excluded by dominant historiography from the possibility of having a voice. Defining the "meek Indian" in the colonial context of Africa as a third element coexisting with the British and the Boer, Rao also draws attention to the entirely overlooked African indigenous subaltern, remarking that "the native, however, the most populous of the land and who ought have most to say had, of course, *no voice whatsoever* (*GIW* 163). Implicitly similar were the circumstances of the native coolie within the Indian context.

Mohandas Gandhi: "the Satyagrahi"

One further complication emphasized by the Subaltern Studies Group, and particularly by Spivak, is through the "troublesomeness" of *the mechanism of representing* on one side, and *the risk of objectifying* the subaltern on the other, making it participate in the discourse of knowledge as power. In other words, within a narrative context the subaltern can only be seen as a "pointer" to a subaltern consciousness not as "the" consciousness itself, as "in the semioses of the social text, elaborations of insurgency stand in the place of 'the utterance.'"[16] It is in this sense that Gandhi can be said to only imperfectly "represent" the "unrepresented," as he himself called them. In so doing, the Indian leader can be said to perform the role of the intellectual, one which, according to Said,

> cannot be played without a sense of being someone whose place it is publically to raise embarrassing questions, to confront orthodoxy and dogma (rather than to produce them), be someone who cannot easily be co-opted by governments or corporations, and whose *raison d'être* is to represent all those people and issues that are routinely forgotten or swept under the rug.[17]

Hints of Gandhi's position as representing an intellectual who somehow always composedly defied governmental authority in the text are to be found in some of the "sympathetic receptions" to

Gandhi's attempts by newspaper columnists of that time. As Rao writes:

> Thus was Gandhiji defended by the press again and again. In due course the press got involved each time there was a conflict between the Indian community and the whites. [...] Scrupulous with his facts, and always erring on the side of kindness rather than that of accusation, he received the sympathy of both the press and the public. For example, in a legal matter – a matter involving insolvency – Mr Tatham was the adversary. Mr Tatham lost the case and he laughed and made all the court laugh with the remark: "Gandhi is supreme ... The triumph of black over white again!" (*GIW* 183)

As an omniscient narrator, Rao's "voice" here makes one reflect upon the fact that Gandhi is also a fictional character, hence a "construction" of Rao's "truth" of Gandhi's life. What I find particularly significant in *The Great Indian Way* is that through the biographer's representation of Gandhi we enter an extra-diegetic narrative that informs us of yet another reading of Gandhi in a never-ending play of signification that Jacques Derrida called "dissemination." For Rao, Gandhi indicated "the Great Indian Way" of *Satyagraha* – Skt. "firmness of truth." Interestingly, the term was not coined by Gandhi himself but by another Gandhi, whose first name was Maganlal and who responded with the proposition of "Sadagraha" to Gandhi's appeal in *Indian Opinion* to help him find a new word to designate "the Indian struggle."[18]

Another possible reading of the figure of Gandhi which is not examined by Rao comes from the Subaltern Studies Group, particularly from Shahid Amin, who examines several popular perceptions of Gandhi with the aim of showing that "the location of the Mahatma image within existing patterns of popular beliefs and the way it informed direct action, [was] often at variance with the standard interpretations of the Congress creed [...]."[19] Amin concludes that "there is thus no single authorized version of the Mahatma to which the peasants of eastern UP and north Bihar may be said to have subscribed in 1921."[20] Similarly, as I hope to have suggested through my analysis of at least three "representations" of Gandhi in Rao's biography, it is possible to read Rao's attempt to illustrate a meaning of Gandhi's life as the very impossibility of this effort, which translates itself in a dissemination of plural Gandhis as the figures of Gandhi the British gentleman, Gandhi the coolie barrister, and Gandhi the Satyagrahi show.

From an advantaged expatriate condition as Said reminds us (it is indeed not accidental that Rao compares Gandhi to the exiled king of Ayodhya, Sri Rama), it is possible to critically distance one's self and look at the world from the different perspective of being an "outsider" to a specific socio-political reality. For Gandhi this reality was the experience of Indian colonization,[21] as he acknowledged in his *Experiments With Truth*: "Thus service of the Indians in South Africa ever revealed to me new implications of truth at every stage."[22] Similarly, in *The Great Indian Way*, Rao indicates the African experience as "the experiment of South Africa," giving it pre-eminence in Gandhi's life as the account amounts to nearly three quarters of the entire volume. Gandhi's experiment in another country is valued by the biographer as an invaluable and enriching experience informing Gandhi's involvement with India: "It was time therefore to start a satyagraha in India. The experiment in South Africa should prove even better here, this 'the holy land where all acts work for good,' as the Puranas say" (*GIW* 440).

To conclude, I would like to argue that *The Great Indian Way* can be read as Rao's attempt to represent (and complicate) the figure of Gandhi from the perspective of the exiled, which is simultaneously Gandhi's and Rao's. In Rao's narrative, Gandhi's privileged "exilic" condition in Africa emerges as a rare opportunity. In Said's terms, the "exilic" condition is an opportunity "to imagine and investigate in spite of barriers, and always move away from the centralizing authorities towards the margins, where you see things that are usually lost on minds that have never travelled beyond the conventional and the comfortable."[23] I would like to suggest that the figure of Gandhi is represented by Rao as Said's "exilic intellectual" who to some extent "does not respond to the logic of the conventional but to the audacity of daring and to representing change, to moving on, not standing still."[24] Gandhi's courage of daring and representing change through his "Great Indian Way" is shared by his biographer Rao, not least through his privileged condition as an émigré for most of his life.

Notes

1. Raja Rao, *The Great Indian Way: A Life of Mahatma Gandhi*, (New Delhi: Vision Books, 1998), 8. Further references to this work will be given parenthetically in the text, preceded by *GIW*.
2. Gayatri Chakravorty Spivak, "Subaltern Studies: Deconstructing Historiography," in *Selected Subaltern Studies*, ed. Guha and Spivak (New York: Oxford UP, 1988), 21.
3. Edward W. Said, *Representations of the Intellectual: The 1993 Reith Lectures* (London: Vintage, 1994), 17.
4. Before presenting himself at the station to collect his ticket, Gandhi had sent a letter to the station master explaining: "*I am an Indian Barrister* [...]. *I always travel First Class.* I hope you have a ticket for me" (*GIW* 124).
5. Said, 74.
6. Said, 68.
7. Said, 15.
8. John Stuart Mill, *On Liberty* (London: John W. Parker and Son, West Strand, 1859), 26.
9. Said, 66.
10. Said, 67.
11. Also in *The Annual Register or a View of History and Politics of the Year 1859* (London: Longman & Co., 1860), 204.
12. Gayatri Chakravorty Spivak, *A Critique of Postcolonial Reason: Toward a History of the Vanishing Present* (Harvard: Harvard UP 1999), 331.
13. Donna Landry and Gerald MacLean (eds.), *Selected Works of Gayatri Chakravorty Spivak* (New York: Routledge, 1996), 306.
14. Homi K. Bhabha, *The Location of Culture* (London: Routledge, 1994), 127. In other words, Gandhi's realization is that he is not a free British subject, i.e., not "the same" as a "British" as Queen Victoria had proclaimed but simultaneously "its other."
15. Terry Eagleton, *The English Novel: An Introduction* (Oxford: Blackwell, 2005), 10.
16. Gayatri Chakravorty Spivak, "Can the Subaltern Speak?," in *The Post-Colonial Studies Reader*, eds. Ashcroft et al. (London: Routledge, 1995), 28.
17. Said, 9.
18. M.K. Gandhi, *An Autobiography, or The Story of My Experiments With Truth* (Ahmedabad: Navajivan, 2002), 293.
19. Shahid Amin, "Gandhi as Mahatma: Gorakhpur District, Eastern UP, 1921–2," in *Selected Subaltern Studies*, ed. Guha and Spivak (New York: Oxford UP, 1988), 289.

20. Amin, 342.
21. See Said, 47.
22. Gandhi, 201.
23. Said, 47.
24. Said, 47.

Works Cited

Amin, Shahid. "Gandhi as Mahatma: Gorakhpur District, Eastern UP, 1921–2." In *Selected Subaltern Studies*. Ed. Ranjit Guha and Gayatri Chakravorty Spivak. New York: Oxford UP, 1988. 288–348. [Orig. 1985.]

The Annual Register or a View of History and Politics of the Year 1859. London: Longman & Co., 1860.

Bhabha, Homi K. *The Location of Culture*. London: Routledge, 1994.

Eagleton, Terry. *The English Novel: An Introduction*. Oxford: Blackwell, 2005.

Gandhi, M.K. *An Autobiography, or The Story of My Experiments With Truth*. Ahmedabad: Navajivan, 2002. [Orig. 1927.]

Landry, Donna and Gerald MacLean, eds. *Selected Works of Gayatri Chakravorty Spivak*. New York: Routledge, 1996.

Mill, John Stuart. *On Liberty*. London: John W. Parker & Son, West Strand, 1859.

Rao, Raja. *The Great Indian Way: A Life of Mahatma Gandhi*. New Delhi: Vision Books, 1998.

Said, Edward W. *Representations of the Intellectual: The 1993 Reith Lectures*. London: Vintage, 1994.

Spivak, Gayatri Chakravorty. "Introduction – Subaltern Studies: Deconstructing Historiography." In *Selected Subaltern Studies*. Ed. Ranjit Guha and Gayatri Chakravorty Spivak. New York: Oxford UP, 1988. 3–32. [Orig. 1985.]

Spivak, Gayatri Chakravorty. "Can the Subaltern Speak?" In *The Post-Colonial Studies Reader*. Ed. Bill Ashcroft, Gareth Griffiths and Helen Tiffin. London: Routledge, 1995. 24–28.

Spivak, Gayatri Chakravorty. *A Critique of Postcolonial Reason: Toward a History of the Vanishing Present*. Harvard: Harvard UP, 1999.

5

Memory and the Transformation of Identity in Meena Alexander's *Fault Lines*

NISHI PULUGURTHA

'How Shall I Start to Write Myself'

Diaspora involves displacement and uprooting, ensuing in a refashioning of one's identity. This refashioning, then, takes place in the important categories of race, ethnic origin, nation, gender, language and religion – everything that would be needed to define an individual's identity. The very word 'diaspora' means dispersion and hence the notions of temporality and spatiality play an important role in the formation of diasporic identity.

It is a common observation that there is a great longing for home among first generation immigrants. For example, Chandra Talpade Mohanty, in her essay "Genealogies of Community, Home, and Nation," speaks of this idea in the following words:

> What is home? The place I was born? Where I grew up? Where I live and work as an adult? Where I locate my community, my people? Who are "my people"? Is home a geographical space, a historical space, an emotional sensory space? Home is always so

> crucial to immigrants and migrants … . I am convinced that this question-how one understands and defines home-is a profoundly political one. […] Political solidarity and a sense of family could be melded together imaginatively to create a strategic space I could call "home."[1]

Meena Alexander's writing disturbs and reconfigures the representations of nation. This Alexander does by locating her novels and personal narratives on the idea of displacement. This article proposes to study Alexander's memoir *Fault Lines* as a text that raises important questions on the notion of identity formations. Diaspora brings into focus important questions about home, belonging, origin, location, about real and imagined worlds that people in the diaspora inhabit.

'Fault lines' is the term used by geologists to describe cracks in the plates under the earth – Alexander, for her part, uses it to explain the uprooting she has faced all her life. The title suggests a questioning of boundaries. Multiple dislocations have been part of Alexander's growing up, and *Fault Lines* traverses a journey not just across nations but continents as she traces the movement from Kerala to North India, then Sudan and England and finally Manhattan. History functions importantly in the memoir as it is history that brings together the lives of her family members and other people whom she has met and who have in some way or the other influenced her. These various movements and dislocations have worked to shape her present. As Alexander writes in *Fault Lines*, she finds it difficult to locate her identity. When asked about it, innumerable questions crop up in her mind – "Who are you? Where are you from? What do you do?"[2] It is exactly such problematic, problematized identity that Alexander describes in her memoir. Questions of identity are of paramount importance for the diasporic subject. In her memoir, Alexander refers to one such incident involving her four year old son, Adam who is asked questions about his identity. Adam chooses to identify himself as neither American nor Indian, but, rather, a Jedi knight. Alexander asks: "What did my first-born wish for himself? Some nothingness, some transitory zone where dreams roamed, a border country without passport or language?" (*FL* 172).

Fault Lines deals with the theme of establishing one's self and forming an identity independent of one's surroundings. Alexander says, "I am, a woman cracked by multiple migrations. Uprooted so many times she can connect nothing with nothing" (*FL* 3). She distinguishes her self by illustrating the confinement of the many fragments of her identity that do not seem to fit together, creating a dissatisfied and despondent tone. There are many questions that torment her: "Where did I come from? How did I become what I am? How shall I start to write myself, configure my 'I' as Other, image this life I lead, here, now, in America?" (*FL* 2). These questions haunt her being and as she tries to find answers for them, she looks back at her past in an attempt to locate herself and understand her true self. The memoir concerns the answers to many of these questions that help locate her in time and space and fashion her present. There are movements into her distant childhood in Kerala, the various differences that she notices as she begins to move with her family, initially within India and then away from India.

Posing Questions

Early in her youth, Alexander's mother tells her that she must devote herself to raising her children. Alexander's choices, however, take her in a different direction. The process of self-creation for Alexander, therefore, has numerous aspects: creating an identity despite many dislocations and fighting against traditions within society: "My two worlds, present and past, were torn apart, and I was the fault line, the crack that marked the dislocation" (*FL* 15). What Alexander tries to delineate in her memoir is to reveal the various layers that constitute the identity of an immigrant. In her case, the movement away from home and rootlessness has been even more marked since she has moved not to one place but many interim places. Alexander speaks of this rootlessness, of being torn apart with great poetic feeling in *Fault Lines.*

> Sometimes I am torn apart by two sorts of memories, two opposing ways of being towards the past. The first makes whorls of skin and flesh, coruscating shells, glittering in moonlight. A life embedded in a life … . Rooms within rooms, each filled with its

> own scent: rosehips, neem leaves, dried hibiscus leaves that hold a cure, cow dung, human excrement, dried gobs of blood … . Another memory invades me: flat, filled with the burning present, cut by existential choices. Composed of bits and pieces of the present, it renders the past suspect, cowardly, baseless. Place names litter: Allahabad, Tiruvella, Kozencheri, Pune, Khartoum, Cairo, Beirut, Jerusalem, Dubai, London, New York, Minneapolis, Saint Paul, New Delhi, Trivandrum. Sometimes I think I could lift these scraps of space and much as an indigent dress-maker, cut them into shape. Stitch my days into a patchwork garment fit to wear. (*FL* 29–30)

There is a sense of violence in the use of the word "torn" which reveals the pain of an immigrant wonderfully. Alexander's prose vividly brings this idea of pain in the way she describes her sense of existing between two polarities – the past which draws her back and the present so very removed, spatially, temporally and culturally, from the past.

What Stuart Hall says about cultural identity is of importance here. Hall distinguishes two different ways of thinking about "cultural identity." The first defines cultural identity "in terms of one, shared culture, a sort of collective 'one true self,' hiding inside the many other, more superficial or artificially imposed 'selves,' which people with a shared history, and ancestry hold in common."[3] This oneness can be described as national identity and is a very powerful and significant creative force. In the case of immigrants, this oneness is difficult to achieve. This is so because identity formation for the immigrant is more often a position which recognizes that, "as well as the many points of similarity, there are also critical points of deep and significant difference which constitute 'what we really are'; or rather – since history has intervened – 'what we have become'."[4] For Alexander, home is not fixed, and her identity is always hyphenated. In response to certain questions that often crop up, she answers:

> I am a poet writing in America. But American poet? What sort? … An Asian-American poet then? … Poet *tout court*? … Everything that comes to me is hyphenated. A woman poet, a woman poet of color, a South Indian woman poet who makes up lines in English … . A Third World woman poet … . (*FL* 193)

What Hall says about cultural identity can be related to the way Alexander speaks of her identity in her memoir. Since it is an identity that is fractured and fragmented, there is hence no oneness or unity in it. Her cultural identity, because of her multiple dislocations, is characterized precisely by a multiplicity. One instance where this multiplicity is revealed is in her attitude towards the English language.

> Sometimes I think of the English language as a pale skin that has covered up my flesh, the broken parts of my world. In order to free my face, in order to appear, I have had to use my teeth and nails, I have had to tear that fine skin, to speak out my discrepant otherness. (*FL* 73)

English was a familiar language to Alexander which she learnt while in India and one that she had used with great ease in India together with the other Indian languages that she was used to speaking: "Syllables, phrases, sentences of English flowed along as part of the river of my experience" (*FL* 111). However, once away from India, English no longer remained *one* of her many languages, it became the *only* one she could use to communicate with others. As she moves from one place to another cultural nuances begin to surface.

Avtar Brah in *Cartographies of Diaspora: Contesting Identities* argues that "the identity of the diasporic imagined community is far from fixed or pre-given. It is constituted within the crucible of the materiality of everyday life; in the everyday stories we tell ourselves individually or collectively".[5] *Fault Lines*, in the way it presents incidents and people from the past who have now become important to the shaping of its author's psyche, does precisely that. Akhil Gupta and James Ferguson point out that Benedict Anderson's idea of "imagined communities" assume a new meaning in the context of immigrants:

> [It] becomes most visible how imagined communities ... come to be attached to imagined places, as displaced people cluster around remembered or imagined homelands, places, or communities in a world that seems increasingly to deny such firm territorialized anchors in their actuality. ... Remembered places have often served as symbolic anchors of community for

> dispersed people. This has long been true of immigrants, who … use memory of place to construct imaginatively their new lived world.[6]

This remembering about places left behind, about people from the past, forms an important aspect of Alexander's memoir. It is here that nostalgia plays an important role. It is this desire to be rooted and anchored in spite of the various dislocations that work within her consciousness.

> Often I did not recognize myself. I felt I had lost my soul: that it was sucked into the vortex of an Otherness I had no words for; that all I was had contracted into being a wife, being a woman who had crossed a border to give birth in another country. (*FL* 164)

Alexander's feelings of alienation are compounded by her numerous movements and dislocations.

Fault Lines, fragmentary in nature, reveals Alexander's desire for discovering her self in spite of the many displacements that she has had over the years. Alexander tries to recollect her childhood spent in Kerala, her growing up in Allahabad, then in Africa. The displacement that she has been through is figured in terms of a diasporic feminist vision that allows for a questioning of patriarchal n ırratives of nation and identity. In doing so, her memoir rewrites the normative identity category of nation, race, gender and the postcolonial. In *Fault Lines*, she describes her work as "Writing in search of a homeland" (*FL* 3). Her life, she says, changed since the age of five, because that is the time when she began to move along with her family. The movement across countries and continents still haunts her: "In my dreams, I am haunted by thoughts of a homeland I will never find" (*FL* 27). Alexander describes the various houses that she has lived in, right from the house at Tiruvella, "where amma's house stands" (*FL* 7), of the familiar sights and sounds that she associated with that house: "I think of the Tiruvella house, the courtyard, the clear blue of the pre-monsoon sky, as it filled with the spirit of my grandfather. It is where I trace my beginning" (*FL* 8). She then goes on to describe her house in Allahabad, the house that she lived in just after her birth:

> Though I was born there, Allahabad is not my home. It is far from Tiruvella, about a thousand miles due north. *Nadu* is the Malayalam word for home, for homeland. Tiruvella, where my mother's home, Kuruchiethu House stands, where appa's home, Kannadical House, stands, together compose my *nadu*, the dark soil of self. (*FL* 22–23)

Each of the lived-in houses in India have been "real, solid places," "various, multiple," yet bound by the fact that they were all in India (*FL* 53). In the United States, the memories of all these lived-in places and the various memories associated with them haunt her: "There are so many strands all running together in a bright snarl of life. I cannot unpick it, take it apart, strand by strand. That would lose the quick of things. My job is to evoke all, altogether" (*FL* 198). The memoir is composed of all such recollections. This evocation of actual houses that have been lived in seems to be a sort of substitute for the lack of belonging to places that haunt her now. They become emblematic of the displacements that Alexander has undergone.

For Homi Bhabha, the diaspora which flourishes in the intervening spaces of a dominant culture is an empowered space which produces counter-narratives of nations that challenge and displace fixed geo-political boundaries.[7] This is also where Alexander finds her site for neo-colonial resistance by posing questions on identity formations, conflicts between classes, nationalism and its influence on local politics. In *Fault Lines*, Alexander speaks of the reasons why she chose to write:

> I think it is the pain of no one knowing my name that drives me to write. That, and the sense that I am living in a place where I have no history. Where all I am is surface and what is not reducible to a crude postcard dangled round the neck, a torn card with name and address pinned to the blouse, cannot exist, has no place.
>
> In Manhattan, I am a fissured thing, a body crossed by fault lines. Where is my past? What is my past to me, here, now at the edge of Broadway? Is America a place without memory? (*FL* 183)

Struggle for Meanings

Autobiographies and memoirs are often used by immigrant writers as they are great tools to recount events and people from the past which works as a foundation of their identity and literary career. Such writing helps writers create and weave a relationship with the others in their lives. In Alexander, these others include her ancestors, especially the older women in her family, her mother and grandmother. Memoir writing is also a vehicle to situate herself in place, to root herself in geography: "It's as if in all these years as a poet I had carried a simple shining geography around with me: a house with a courtyard where I grew up in Tiruvella" (*FL* 197). In an interview, Alexander notes that this attempt to define one's identity "is a very American project,":

> ... is a very American thing. ... to try to define one's self and to think that in the defining there would be a germ of some kind of essential meaning. This is not the Indian way, if there is an Indian way. ... I think this focus on the self is very peculiar to the culture of North America, and generally, so is the desire to create "autobiography." A constant attempt to vivify what one thinks of as identity by redefining one's self is a very American project.[8]

Writing about herself and her literary life could, therefore, be seen as a means of asserting an identity. Alexander explains,

> I write on paper to reclaim ground. Even in Manhattan, where so little ground is visible. Marginality compels me to it, a territorial thing. And I ponder [...] how Manhattan, with its crowded streets and subways, frames the landscapes of my Indian imagination.[9]

Leigh Gilmore says that "autobiography demonstrates that we can never recover the past, only represent it; yet, it encodes the possibility of recovery as desire".[10] The act of remembering and recording memories satisfy the autobiographer's desire to restore her past.

Unlike autobiographies which use a linear narrative structure, Alexander's memoir is fragmentary in structure and is more in the nature of recollections. Elaine Showalter says that "women's writing should be rule breaking" and "anarchic."[11] One way this could be achieved is by merging *genres*. Alexander's writing not only merges *genres*, but even cultures and languages. Showalter, of course, does refer to the fact that women should write in their mother tongue, this is where Alexander differs and is like most Indian writers writing in English and thereby choosing to write in a language other than their mother tongue. Alexander's response to the immigrant experience is more muted than that of, for example, Bharati Mukherjee's early novels *Wife* and *Jasmine* which present the immigrant experience as exhilarating. Alexander's description of immigrants as patchwork creatures, where each piece of fabric represents an experience picked up from every dislocation, recalls Salman Rushdie's description of himself and others not as "gods but wounded creatures, cracked lenses, capable only of fractured perceptions."[12]

Although Edward Said conjectures that it is a misconception to assume that being exiled is to be totally cut off and isolated from one's place of origin, most often this is precisely the case even though there is nothing barring the immigrant from returning home. Yet, like the exile, an immigrant is constantly reminded of the home left behind and the culture that is no longer as tangible as it once was. It is this uncertainty that makes many immigrants live in a median state, neither completely one with the new place they now live in nor entirely cut off from the old, hence in a state that is characterized both by nostalgia and by a feeling of being an outcast.[13] Alexander's position is comparatively ambiguous. On the one hand, she is aware much like Rushdie that "exiles or emigrants or expatriates, are haunted by some sense of loss, some urge to reclaim, to look back [...] we will not be capable to reclaiming precisely the thing that was lost,"[14] and on the other hand she is also aware that she will always have a bond with her home.

Alexander's memoir has multiple stories being told and it is flexible in its use of time and space. There is a circular pattern in the use of stories within stories, and in the digressions that are reminiscent of the Indian tradition of storytelling. As I have argued, *Fault Lines*, an unusual transnational memoir as it deals with emotions, ideas, poetry and landscapes, rather than with facts and dates and contributes to our understanding of the postcolonial, transnational condition. Diasporic movement characterizes postcolonial people connected by language to the metropolis and by cultural memory to the homeland. Alexander's text reflects her struggle to reclaim the meanings of her own body and subjectivity in the face of multiple migrations.

Notes

1. Chandra Talpade Mohanty, *Feminism Without Borders: Decolonizing Theory, Practicing Solidarity* (New Delhi: Zubaan, 2003), 126, 128.
2. Meena Alexander, *Fault Lines: A Memoir* (New York: The Feminist Press at the City U of New York, 1993; revised edn. 2003), 193. Further references to the book will be given parenthetically, preceded by *FL*.
3. Stuart Hall, "Cultural Identity and Diaspora," in *Colonial Discourse and Post-Colonial Theory: A Reader*, ed. Patrick Williams and Laura Chrisman (New York: Columbia UP, 1994), 393.
4. Hall, 394.
5. Avtar Brah, *Cartographies of Diaspora: Contesting Identities* (London: Routledge, 1996), 183.
6. Akhil Gupta and James Ferguson, "Beyond Culture: Space, Identity and the Politics of Difference," in *Cultural Anthropology* 7.1 (1992): 10–11.
7. Homi K. Bhabha, *The Location of Culture* (New York: Routledge, 1994).
8. Deepika Bahri and Mary Vasudeva, "Observing Ourselves Among Others: Interview with Meena Alexander," in *Between the Lines: South Asians and Postcoloniality*, ed. Deepika Bahri and Mary Vasudeva (Philadelphia: Temple UP, 1996), 36.
9. Meena Alexander, *The Shock of Arrival* (Boston: South End Press, 1996), 16.
10. Leigh Gilmore, *Autobiographics: A Feminist Theory of Self Representation* (Ithaca: Cornell UP, 1993), 86.
11. Elaine Showalter, "American Gynocriticism," *American Literary History* 5.1 (1993): 115.
12. Salman Rushdie, *Imaginary Homelands: Essays and Criticism 1981–1991* (London: Granta, 1992), 12.
13. Edward W. Said, *Reflections on Exile and Other Essays* (Cambridge: Harvard UP, 2002).
14. Rushdie, 10.

Works Cited

Alexander, Meena. *Fault Lines: A Memoir.* New York: The Feminist Press at the City U of New York, 1993; rev. ed. 2003.

Alexander, Meena. *The Shock of Arrival.* Boston: South End Press, 1996.

Bahri, Deepika and Mary Vasudeva. "Observing Ourselves among Others: Interview with Meena Alexander." In *Between the Lines: South Asians and Postcoloniality.* Ed. Deepika Bahri and Mary Vasudeva. Philadelphia: Temple UP, 1996. 35–53.

Bhabha, Homi K. *The Location of Culture.* New York: Routledge, 1994.

Brah, Avtar. *Cartographies of Diaspora: Contesting Identities.* London: Routledge, 1996.

Gilmore, Leigh. *Autobiographics: A Feminist Theory of Self Representation.* Ithaca: Cornell UP, 1993.

Gupta, Akhil and James Ferguson. "Beyond Culture: Space, Identity and the Politics of Difference." *In Cultural Anthropology* 7.1 (1992): 6–23.

Hall, Stuart. "Cultural Identity and Diaspora." In *Colonial Discourse and Post-Colonial Theory: A Reader.* Ed. Patrick Williams and Laura Chrisman. New York: Columbia UP, 1994. 392–403.

Mohanty, Chandra Talpade. *Feminism Without Borders: Decolonizing Theory, Practicing Solidarity.* New Delhi: Zubaan, 2003.

Rushdie, Salman. *Imaginary Homelands: Essays and Criticism 1981–1991.* London: Granta, 1992.

Said, Edward W. *Reflections on Exile and Other Essays.* Cambridge: Harvard UP, 2002.

Showalter, Elaine. "American Gynocriticism." *In American Literary History* 5.1 (1993): 111–128.

6

Nation as the Persistent Centre of Meaning

Dambudzo Marechera and the Zimbabwe Crisis

ANNA-LEENA TOIVANEN

Moving Beyond the Nation

"We need to think ourselves beyond the nation," urges Arjun Appadurai.[1] It is arguable to claim that in the field of postcolonial studies, this call has been heard and answered: the success of concepts such as transnational and even postnational[2] suggest that the boundaries of the nation are loosened and that nationhood is no more seen as the legitimized site of engagement due to "[i]ts failure to provide systems of meaning."[3] The "pastness" of nationhood is declared through the use of notions such as exile, diaspora, and migrancy which, besides expressing the history of displaced communities in the postcolonial era, have become important tropes in cultural criticism.[4] The tropes of displacement and dislocation have been celebrated not least for their capacity to question discourses of fixed origins and pre-given identities that often inform nationalisms.[5]

If the concept of nation is considered out of date in current cultural criticism, then it is no surprise that, by the same token, nationalism is deemed a dubious ideology. Laura Chrisman states that the emergence of postcolonial studies in the 1980s is connected to the decline of anticolonial nationalist movements in the Third World and the rise of violent ethnic communalism. According to Chrisman, these political developments have contributed to the fact that in the field of postcolonial studies, nationalism has come to represent a somewhat detrimental discourse with "[i]nherently dominatory, absolutist, essentialist, and destructive" dimensions.[6] While it must be acknowledged that nationalism as such is not inherently or inevitably detrimental and that it can be used to suit both reactionary and progressive ends,[7] it nevertheless seems that the repudiation of nationalism and, consequently, questioning whether the nation can still stand for a relevant frame of reference are rather necessary undertakings. Indeed, one basic reason for the need to move beyond the nation, according to Partha Chatterjee, is "moral-political": the failed promises of nationalist discourses and the often problematic lived experiences of nationhood that have led the nation into crisis.[8] Francis Ngaboh-Smart exemplifies this aspect by stating that the primary reason for the mistrust in nationhood and nationalism in the African context is that many African nation-states have failed to rid themselves of the violent and undemocratic governing models inherited from the colonial state. Ngaboh-Smart goes on to argue that "[a]fter independence, many nations failed to evolve, let alone reinvent, a discourse that would reconceptualise or redirect nationalist fervor towards a more equitable society." Naturally, dictatorships and genocides have made out that the empowering meanings attached to nationhood have given way to disillusioned understandings.[9] Besides this ethico-political level motivating the need to go beyond the nation, there are empirical reasons, too: past decades have witnessed several social phenomena, such as migrancy, that can not be properly understood in the framework of the nation-state.[10] Andrew Smith emphasizes that the ethico-political and empirical aspects have emerged hand in hand: "There is a link between the loss of hope in anticolonial nationalism and migration."[11]

Naturally, these developments have rendered post/transnational approaches in postcolonial literatures and postcolonial theory rather tempting. While efforts have been made to think beyond the nation, it nevertheless seems sometimes that, as Imre Szeman has put it, "[t]he postcolonial problematic continues to be haunted by the specter of the nation."[12] In a similar vein, Simon

Gikandi argues in a thought-provoking article that despite all the emphasis put on global images and narratives, the postcolonial has not really managed to rid itself of the hauntingly present logic of Enlightenment that it was supposed to deconstruct: the crises within the actual postcolonies[13] disturb the understanding of living a globalized era in which concepts such as the nation are entirely out of date.[14] Discussing the unevenness of globalization, a phenomenon supposed to contribute to transgressing the boundaries of the nation-state, Gikandi states that,

> [w]hile we live in a world defined by cultural and economic flows across formally entrenched national boundaries, the world continues to be divided, in stark terms, between its 'developed' and 'underdeveloped' sectors. It is precisely because of the starkness of this division that the discourse of globalisation seems to be perpetually caught between two competing narratives, one of celebration, the other of crisis.[15]

According to Gikandi, "Postcolonial theorists may have sought to forget the nation in order to become global, but the nation has not forgotten them."[16] Gikandi claims that, busy with celebrating transnationalism, sometimes postcolonial theorists too quickly brush aside meanings that are tied to the logic of the national, and urges researchers to rethink some of the central tropes of postcolonial theory (hybridity, diaspora) from the viewpoint of those living the crisis-ridden realities of the postcolonies. Gikandi emphasizes that despite the deconstruction to which nationhood has been subjected in the realm of postcolonial cultural and literary studies, there is not much evidence of these deconstructive operations working in politics or in people's everyday realities.[17] In Francis Ngaboh-Smart's words, "[w]hether we like it or not, the achievement of nationalism, the nation, is still with us."[18]

And it is not just the nation that is still with us: nationalism is pretty much with us, too, as the observations about the Zimbabwe crisis attest later. Abject conditions of poverty, suffering, and death in the geopolitical space of the postcolony do not always fit to the transnational vocabulary so central in postcolonial studies. Indeed, the abject postcolonial conditions seem to drive merely celebratory rhetoric of dislocation into crisis, rendering it *misplaced*, incongruous. What adds to the problematic of cheering transnationalism, as Meyda Yegenoglu has argued, is that postcolonial discourses with a strong transnational emphasis tend to ignore the disenfranchised groups of the global South:

> The exclusive focus on migrancy, diaspora, hybridity, cosmopolitanism (the buzzwords of Anglo-American cultural studies) is characterised by [...] turning our backs on, never seeing, by remaining deaf to what I will call the 'wasteland' of transnational operations of neocolonial globalization.[19]

The main reason for this is that the migrants in the First World metropolises are taken as representatives of postcolonial subjects in general.[20] Deepika Bahri has also critiqued this kind of vocabulary for the same reason, arguing that concepts such as transnationalism do not have much relevancy for subjects "[i]n the Third World who are facing, with material consequences, the persistence of nationalist ideology that is informed both by colonial and atavistic notions of identity."[21]

While Yegenoglu's and Bahri's observations are important in criticizing the hegemony of transnational imagery in postcolonial studies, the focus in this article is not, as such, on analysing the mechanisms that ultimately silence "the wastelands of transnational operations of neocolonial globalization", but on the question of how crisis in the geopolitical space of the postcolony draws attention to the fact that the currently unfashionable notion of nation *does*, after all, remain relevant. Hence, although the article starts from the assumption that the current era is undeniably marked by diverse manifestations of the transnational, it also wants to question the hurry to go beyond the nation while in some postcolonial crises nationhood remains an important site of struggle. The article discusses this issue through the case of the celebrated Zimbabwean author Dambudzo Marechera (1952–1987), whose relevance in current discussions is legitimized by intertwining his legacy closely with the state of the Zimbabwean nation.[22] This is interesting in the sense that Marechera's authorial vision is at least partly informed by transnational impulses; *at least partly* here implies that while the author declared his dislike of nation-based labels and while some of his non-realist texts, above all *Black Sunlight* and *The Black Insider*, seek to articulate alternative ways of conceiving identity, his last fictional work, *The Mindblast or the Definitive Buddy*, signals a very nation-based approach indeed.[23] Hence, Marechera's own approach to nationhood is rather contradictory. While, on one hand, he seems to be interested in repudiating the concept of nation and envisaging alternative ways of identity construction, on the other his work also offers insights into the problematic of lived nationhood from the viewpoint of subaltern subjects. With this interesting discrepancy in mind, this article starts by contextualizing Marechera's authorship in relation to the questions of dislocation and transnationalism, then moving to a short discussion on some central aspects of the Zimbabwe crisis. Subsequently, the article scrutinizes illustrative extracts of Marechera's current reception in which nationhood proves to play an important role in authorizing the writer's legacy. Finally, the article discusses the ethical necessity of not ignoring instances that contradict the movement beyond the nation. It should be emphasized that while the article approaches some aspects of transnationalism from a critical viewpoint, it by no means wishes to convey that the national/transnational should be conceived as a mutually exclusive binary hierarchy. The global and the local are unavoidably and constantly intertwining with each other: indeed, Marechera's authorial position offers the perfect proof of this. In this sense, there is no denying the value and necessity of the deconstructive operations to which the binary setting of global/local has been subjected in the field of postcolonial studies. What this article sets out to do, however, is to pay attention to the fact that outside the sphere of academic discourses, especially in the material realities in the postcolony, there can be moments that do not so obviously bespeak the pastness of the nation. Ultimately, this problematic can be conceived in terms of the discrepancy between the location of theory and what could be named as the material reality.

Marechera's Negotiations of Nationhood

Marechera's career as a writer was launched in a context in which anti-colonial freedom struggle and nation-building were topical issues: the armed struggle against the colonial settler rule reached its culmination in the late 1970s and Zimbabwe gained its independence in 1980. Marechera's literary debut, the novella *The House of Hunger*, was published in 1978 while the author was still living in the UK. Marechera had left Zimbabwe in 1974, when, like several other students of the then University of Rhodesia, he got expelled as a consequence of student demonstrations. Marechera started his undergraduate studies in English at the New College in Oxford, from where also he got expelled because of his irregular behaviour. After his expulsion from the College, Marechera led a life of a "[w]riter with no fixed employment or abode" in Oxford, Wales, and London.[24] Marechera returned to Zimbabwe in 1982, where his second literary work, *Black Sunlight*, written during the years in exile, had just been banned. In an interview Marechera sheds light on the aspects of the novel that caused the banning: "Their reasons were firstly that it would offend Christians, then that it was obscene and thirdly that its language was so difficult that Zimbabweans would not understand it and fourthly they said that Marechera is trying to be like a modern European writer."[25] Although these arguments were used to justify the banning of one specific work, they capture well the essence of the criticism of Marechera's output in general. Non-realist narrative modes, allusions to European modernism, and provocative language were considered to signal the writer's disregard for "communal issues", which, in the context of anti-colonial struggle and nation-building, were supposed to be the primary site of artistic engagement.

In Marechera's case, the movement beyond the nation can be located as much in his work as in his authorial position. Arguably, the writer's life in exile had its effects on the literary work. However, to classify a writer as migrant on the basis of mere location and circumstance is problematic, as Girma Negash has argued. The physical location of an author is not, by any means, alone sufficient to label authors with classifications (local/national or migrant/transnational) that easily imply complex issues related to style, audience, and commitment.[26] While keeping this caution in mind, it can nevertheless be argued that metonymically, the condition of dislocation constitutes an important part of Marechera's authorial image.

As an author, Marechera was not keen on being labelled as a representative of a certain nation or ethnicity. In his widely-cited comment, he stated that "[I] would question anyone calling me an African writer. Either you are a writer or you are not. If you are a writer for a specific nation or a specific race, then fuck you. In other words, the direct international experience of every living entity is, for me, the inspiration to write."[27] For Marechera, writing transgresses national boundaries, identities, and loyalties. Given the historical context of decolonization and nation-building, these kinds of boundary-crossing affinities were considered dubious. Marechera himself was well aware of the demands that the postcolonial nation-state made on its writers:

> Here we have a deliberate campaign to promote Zimbabwean culture: everyone is talking about it, building it, developing it. When politicians talk about culture, one has better pack one's rucksack and run, because it means the beginning of unofficial censorship. [...] When culture is emphasised in such a nationalistic way, that can lead to fascism.[28]

When looking into Marechera's literary production, it becomes clear that while the author was interested in criticizing the pitfalls of nationalist thinking, he also engaged in examining realities in which such loyalties were of no importance. It is noteworthy, for instance, that in some of his works, namely, in *Black Sunlight* and *The Black Insider*, the settings in which the scenes take place are often left unspecified: they could be as much in Zimbabwe as anywhere else. What is more, often in these novels the ethnic background of the characters is left unarticulated. Marechera's anti-realism refuses to create "African realities" by making links to specific geopolitical contexts through naming places and "races". This open-endedness, as Steward Crehan has argued, is characteristic of Marechera's subversiveness: "If the totalizing closures of realism are nationalist, Marechera's anti-realism (its dislocations and disjunctures, its sudden, unexpected transitions, its movie-like dissolves and cross-generic mixing, its unresolved ambiguities of viewpoint and focalization) is inherently subversive of nationhood."[29] The basis for communal identity in his work does not lie in shared national or ethnic background; more often communal identities are grounded on mutual understanding of suffering and alienation, which is the case of the communities in *Black Sunlight* and *The Black Insider*.[30] This approach deprives the great narrative of nationhood the centrality in identity construction.

Among Marechera's characters there are also those who express exilic sensibilities and lack of territorialized identities.[31] In *Black Sunlight*, for instance, the protagonist's identity is distinctively hybrid: "Europe was in my head, crammed together with Africa, Asia and America."[32] His search for "his true/authentic people" on the basis of shared ethnicity or nationality proves to be a merely futile undertaking. The protagonist's existence is marked by movement, by running "[f]rom one bit of earth to another,"[33] which has made him questioning territorialized loyalties and belongings: "What did it mean that this was my hometown, my country, my continent, my planet, my universe? It could mean anything. It could mean nothing."[34] In *The Black Insider* (written in exile and published posthumously) one of the figures states that, "We are a continent of refugees; one day here, another day there; so much fodder for the boundary makers. There is no sense of home any more, no feeling of being at one with any specific portion of the earth."[35] The existence of a national community is also questioned. At one point, the narrator starts contemplating on how the postcolonial nation is, ultimately, a creation of colonialism:

> The sense of having lost our nation was indivisible from the feeling of the nation having lost us; the smack of some incompetent fate made our eyes sting. Indeed, had there ever been a nation at all? The white pioneers and adventurers who had carved out for themselves farms and estates and had for a time exercised the pirate's right to booty were the sort of origins we had as one nation.[36]

While *The Black Insider* clearly articulates transnational and postnational impulses, it is also concerned with the material conditions of violence and suffering that nationalist discourses, with their fixed conceptions of identity, can cause. Marechera calls this nationalist notion of identity "the African image":

> [W]e raise the African image to fly in the face of the wind and cannot see the actually living blacks having their heads smashed open with hammers in Kampala. We have done such a good advertising and public relations stunt with our African image that all horrors committed under its lips merely reinforce our admiration for the new clothes we acquired at the independence. And, of course, the horrors are themselves one more reason to tighten the screw of our peculiar brand of fascism. For a people seeking freedom we are much practised in intolerance among ourselves.[37]

With respect to the question of dislocation, it is interesting that the last volume of fiction that Marechera got published during his lifetime, *Mindblast or the Definitive Buddy* (1984), is a text compilation that embodies the author's disillusionment with the postcolonial government. Compared to the writer's earlier works written in exile, *Mindblast* marks a shift of focus in Marechera's production. Gerald Gaylard has observed this, and, as his words suggest, the shift in approach might have to do with the change in the author's location:

> "*[T]he House of Hunger* was written in England before Marechera returned to Zimbabwe and is a response to his experience there as well as a re-valuation of his past, with little specific concern for African politics at that time. On his return to Zimbabwe in 1982 after nine years of exile he engaged more directly in African affairs in his subsequent poetry and novel, *Mindblast*.[38]

As several (auto)biographical accounts – such as certain sections of *Mindblast* – attest, after his return from exile, Marechera led a life of an outsider in "his" nation. Could it be that his experiences of living on the fringes of the postcolonial nation contributed to the change in his approach to engage more directly with the conditions of the independent postcolony? To suggest this is not an attempt to resurrect some intentional author figure, but rather, to argue, following Said's conception of worldliness, that texts are conditioned by their material origins, including the conditions that define the writer's situation.[39] In this sense, authorship can be defined as contextually conditioned and partly negotiated positionality. Arguably, material conditions of a migrant writer in the West[40] are not the same than that of a writer positioned in the newly independent postcolony where nation-building discourses make their demands on the writers to be "properly" politically committed. In Marechera's case it seems that the location of authorship does have a bearing on the writer's politics: the author's lived experiences of authoritarian postcolonial nationhood can be interpreted to form the context of engaging the movement towards a multi-voiced re-imagining of the nation, instead of simple repudiation.

Compared to *Black Sunlight* and *The Black Insider*, in *Mindblast* Marechera's strategy is not as much to embrace alternative realities which escape the narrative of the nation, but rather to expose the fringes of nationhood that are disturbing the official "African image". On these fringes, one finds subaltern subjects who do not conform to the national community; "dissident" artists, mentally ill, and homeless alcoholics. These subjects question the relevance of a communal, national narrative and mark the limits of officially defined collective belonging. Whereas *Black Sunlight* and *The Black Insider* are mainly motivated by the need to think beyond the nation in terms of identity and location, *Mindblast* does not really articulate tendencies that might be qualified as transnational. The work is, undoubtedly, very critical of nationalism and expresses a profound distrust in postcolonial nation-state, but instead of engaging in a postnational attempt to envisage realities in which the nation does not have any relevance, it adheres to the nation as an everyday reality that has violent impacts on the lives of those constituting its margins. In *Mindblast*, locations are no more unspecified; stories and plays are explicitly set in Zimbabwe. Comparing *Mindblast* to Marechera's texts that reflect explicitly transnational concerns, David Buuck has argued that "If *The Black Insider* stands as Marechera's singular evocation of the exile experience, *Mindblast* is his documentation of the 'inner exile' that he encountered upon his return to Zimbabwe in 1982 [...]."[41] One of the leading motives of *Mindblast* is the way in which the postcolony makes demands on the production of creative artists and rejects those artists who do not conform to the expectations. This problematic finds its culmination in a text entitled "Prologue. Grimknife Jr and Rix the Giant Cat," in which a writer has been detained for not being "a useful citizen", which is to refer to "Someone who does what he is told. Someone who says exactly what others say. Someone who is the spitting image of Duty, Responsibility, and Patriotism." The writer, who is interpreted as not contributing to the "Progressive Effort", is defined a "dissident" and threatened with execution unless he changes his ways.[42]

Reading Marechera in the Context of Crisis

Concerns circulating around the thematic of the national were, understandingly, topical in a context in which the Rhodesian minority rule gave place to the postcolonial Zimbabwe. However, three decades later nationalist discourses have anything but moved over: the question of nationhood occupies a pivotal position in the current crisis-situation.[43] The crisis of the country has touched all the sectors from politics and economics to human rights. The reasons of the crisis are embodied in the authoritarian regime of Robert Mugabe and his Zanu-PF party, whose ruling methods prove that the violent structures inherited from the colonial settler rule have been anything but replaced. In this sense, Mbembe's notion of *commandement* is applicable to the unconditional use of power at which the Mugabe regime aims.[44]

Although the reasons behind the crisis date farther in the history, the situation started to degenerate in the early 2000s. What happened then was that Mugabe's government started to appropriate and further distribute privately owned farmlands. The project was disguised as an anti-colonial act, linking up with the earlier anti-colonial history of native insurgencies at the time of the colonial invasion in the 1890s and the armed struggle in the 1960s and 1970s, respectively called the First and the Second *Chimurenga* (struggle). The land occupations – officially given the name of "the Third Chimurenga" – were a part of the Mugabe government's strategies of diverting attention away from the actual problem, that is, the misrule of the country. Through this strategy, the real problems were rendered irrelevant, for the primary concern was represented to be the struggle against the imperialist enemy threatening the nation.[45] The land occupations contributed importantly to the deepening crisis by causing hunger and violence. The Third Chimurenga discourse draws from the anti-colonialist imagery and is quick to designate quarters with dissenting opinions as enemies of the nation.[46] Interestingly, then, through the recourse to anti-colonialist and nationalist imagery, "[Z]imbabwe can [...] be said to be entering the future by re-enacting the past [...]."[47]

Thus, during the crisis, the past has been evoked by resorting to anti-colonialist, nationalist discourse that insists on the centrality of the nation and on the ever-continuing relevance of the freedom struggle against the colonial power. In a situation in which the entire narrative of the nation has been so violently appropriated by the ruling government, an urgency to resist this official appropriation rises. Different Zimbabwean cultural texts have been playing an important role in challenging the official national narrative and addressing questions that relate to Zimbabwean history and politics.[48] It must be emphasized that while these cultural texts occupy a counter-discursive position in relation to the official national narrative which is such an elementary part of the current crisis, it is hardly arguable to claim that these counter-discourses would share the logic of the fashionable move beyond the nation. Rather, it would seem that the primary engagement of these counter-discursive voices in this crisis-situation is to envisage new ways of imagining the nation and to reclaim it. Hence, the nation is the centre of debate both in the hegemonic discourses of the government as well as in the counter-discourses that are striving for not letting the official patriotic history have the last word.

After these contextualizing observations, it is time to turn back to Marechera. As to the earlier arguments on how cultural texts have been commenting on and challenging the official national narrative, it must be acknowledged that since Marechera passed away in 1987, his work can not be seen to address directly the current state of the nation, that is, the crisis. In any case, the phrasing of the question here is not as much concerned with the issue of how Marechera's texts might be read as commentaries on the Zimbabwean crisis, but rather, how, in his current reception, the state of the nation stands for the legitimizing context of his literary legacy. This is interestingly incongruous with the general tendency in postcolonial studies of "thinking beyond the nation", and indeed, with the assumption that Marechera himself wanted to distance his authorship from national affiliations which he found restrictive.

Khombe M. Mangwanda, in an essay analysing Marechera's representations of nationhood, observes that critics have "[t]ended to neglect Marechera's representation of the Zimbabwean nation" and that despite this negligence, "[h]is corpus is *of great value* for the way it represents Rhodesia/Zimbabwe."[49] Mangwanda bases his analysis on the idea that nation-state constitutes the inevitable context of all fiction. In a compact analysis of *The House of Hunger*, *Scrapiron Blues*, and *The Black Insider*, Mangwanda points out how Marechera's representations of the nation are marked by violence, marginalization, and corruption and that from the author's view, Zimbabwean nation functions on the division of dominant and subaltern classes. Mangwanda concludes that "[M]arechera is wary of identifying with a nation like this one."[50] In Mangwanda's reading, then, Marechera's repudiation of nationhood and his ways of criticizing nationalist discourses add to the value of his literary legacy. Although Mangwanda mentions that Marechera did not want to be associated with any specific nation, this aspect is not given much consideration in his reading. Marechera's aspirations to go beyond the nation seem to be of less relevance than his concerns with discussing the problems within that very frame of reference.

Another example of highlighting the importance of nationhood in Marechera's output comes from Maurice Vambe. In an article discussing *The House of Hunger* and *Black Sunlight* in terms of national allegories, Vambe makes some interesting remarks as to the problematic of nationhood. While Vambe notes that in *Black Sunlight*, there is no recognisable geopolitical setting[51] – which, as mentioned, can be interpreted as an authorial attempt to evade nation-oriented approaches to the work – he also reads the work as a commentary on African nationalisms, and, even more precisely, as an allegory in the Zimbabwean post-independence context: "As a cautionary tale, the contradictory allegory captured in *Black Sunlight* can only be repeated at the expense of any opposition that poses itself as providing serious resistance to ZANU PF hegemony in post-independence Zimbabwe."[52] Indeed, Vambe sees that through *Black Sunlight*, Marechera, in a rather peculiarly reverse manner, engages the logic of nation-building:

> Marechera's mode of contributing to nation-building in *Black Sunlight* is not to flatter it, so that it becomes complacent and oblivious of the many internal contradictions that define, in the words of Timothy Brennan, its processes of "longing for national form" [...]. *Marechera's own sense of patriotism* implies a paradoxical relation, not only to the discourses of resistance that compete in constructing the ideas of nation-ness, but to the nation itself: the ability to work for one's nation by working against it.[53]

Interestingly enough, in Vambe's reading, Marechera becomes "a real insider" to the nation-building through his subversion of nationalist discourses. The following quote culminates the idea that Marechera's relevance lies, paradoxically enough, in his engagements to the nation: "The self-reflexivity in Marechera's criticism of nationalist discourses of resistance and the notions of 'nation-ness' they authorize is just the kind of internal self-knowledge that a nation such as Zimbabwe needs."[54] In another essay Vambe reads *Black Sunlight* once more as a commentary on recent political developments in Zimbabwe

> Transposed to the post-independence scenario, those political oppositional parties such as the Movement for Democratic Change (MDC) presently led by Morgan Tsvangirai may experience 'fatal' internal problems if they allow individual leaders to impose their views on what is perceived to be mass organization.[55]

Vambe concludes his analysis by stating that Marechera's criticism is indeed "[a] mark of patriotism" and that "It is an expression of the love of one's country to be able to stand up and show where the country is going wrong."[56] Vambe is not alone with this argument. Annie Gagiano, in an article on Marechera's relation to the freedom struggle, foregrounds her analysis with the well-known criticisms of anti-Africanness to which Marechera got subjected, and then goes on to prove the criticism wrong. Gagiano states:

> [M]arechera's engagement with the liberation war [...] is the sign of a writer intensely concerned with the well-being of his own society. It is this loyalty, necessarily critical of the forms of failure and oppression that he saw in Zimbabwe, which emanates undeniably from [...] his work.[57]

In May 2009, an interdisciplinary Marechera symposium was organized at the Trinity College in Oxford. One panel discussion during this celebrative event was entitled "Marechera and the Zimbabwe crisis". In an unpublished conference paper originally presented in this section, Tinashe Mushakavanhu addresses generally the question of the writer's role in the Zimbabwean crisis relating to society and links Marechera's legacy tightly to this context. In his article, Mushakavanhu represents Marechera as the "[t]our guide to understand the complexity of the Zimbabwean problem [...]", who offers an important view on Zimbabwe's developments from colonial to postcolonial era. While Mushakavanhu acknowledges Marechera's dislike of nation-based engagements and belonging, he nevertheless wants to emphasize that Marechera was a Zimbabwean and that "[Z]imbabwe was the centre around which his creativity revolved." Mushakavanhu sees Marechera's importance in the ways he renders visible a multitude of different voices: "While Mugabe attempted from day one to create a whole generation that thinks the ZANU PF way, it is in this context that Marechera helped to keep alive alternative and pluralistic concepts of political and individual morality, social justice and national identity." In this context, Marechera's critical viewpoint is to represent "[h]is great love for his people."[58]

Marechera's legacy has not been forgotten outside the academic world either. Soon after his death, the author became an idolised cult figure who has been an inspiration for several Zimbabwean authors. The contemporary crisis has brought the phenomenon around Marechera to a new level: he is currently represented as a misunderstood prophet who "saw" the crisis coming three decades ago.[59] By definition, in this context, Marechera's meaning is tied to the Zimbabwean nation, not to transnational impulses his work partly embodies. For just one illustrative example, Brian Chikwava, a writer himself, argues: "Not surprisingly, one can still find in Marechera's poetry sentiments that resonate with ordinary Zimbabweans today. That dry cynicism, poetic activism and desire to reach out, which decades ago sounded like causeless mental banditry, fits perfectly into Zimbabweans' circumstances."[60]

Urgent Re-imaginings Within

Whether one takes the empirical or the ethico-political reasons that urge one to take the claims of transnationalism seriously, it must be acknowledged that the nation's empowering potentials still remain alluring.[61] In a crisis situation in which authoritarian *commandment* rule strives for appropriating the nation and charging it with the meanings to suit its own ends, thinking and feeling beyond the nation becomes somewhat impossible. The violence, suffering, and death that the appropriation of the nation by the authoritarian rule generates lend themselves uneasily to an analysis motivated by transnationalism. Governmental violence committed in the name of national unity and safety materializes itself in mutilated bodies whose pain stands in the way of any quick and easy movement *beyond*. In a postcolonial crisis context like that of Zimbabwe, what seems to be more vital than engaging with transnational politics and aesthetics is to resist the seizure of the nation by the authoritarian rule. This resistance is generated by criticizing the official narratives of the nation and by giving voice to alternative, multi-vocal re-imaginings. To challenge the official narration of nationhood does not imply that the concept of nation would be repudiated and done away with altogether: it does not represent a movement beyond the nation, but rather, a revisionist movement *within* it.

Kizito Z. Muchemwa summarizes the current appropriation of the nation's narrative as follows:

> The connection between narrative and nation has many implications in the post-2001 political and cultural scene that has experienced a massive growth in reconstructed versions of the nationalist narrative dominated by a single father figure and single story-teller who will not tolerate rivals.[62]

This appropriation creates the context for urgent revisions of the nation. The urgency of not moving merely beyond the nation but engaging a revisionist movement within it constitutes a motive that marks Dambudzo Marechera's current reception. It is emphasized that while Marechera admittedly criticized the concept of nation, he, nevertheless, did it because of the love for his nation. Marechera's multi-vocal and critical approach to nationhood has been deemed relevant in the context of the Zimbabwean crisis. As to Marechera's own authorial position, his relation to nationhood is somewhat paradoxical: on the one hand, transnational affiliations mark his work and his position of an exiled writer; it is arguable that the texts written in exile embrace transnational poetics and politics. On the other hand, however, it seems that his return to Zimbabwe changed his approach from negotiating the movement to a view in which nation remains a relevant frame of reference that is in urgent need of re-imagining and reclaiming.

To conclude: the need to go beyond the nation can be explained with empirical and ethico-political reasons. However, it is important to acknowledge that in some contexts, claims of the transnational are somewhat incongruous and irrelevant. A postcolonial crisis context, like that of Zimbabwe, which is marked by authoritarian appropriations of nationhood through hegemonic narrations of the nation, calls for an understanding of nationhood as a continuously relevant site of engagement and revision. Authoritarian appropriations of the nation must be resisted and alternative ways of re-imagining the nation envisaged. For those who are living the very material effects of a hegemonic nationalist discourse, the nation is not something to be transgressed, but rather, urgently re-imagined and re-constructed. Dambudzo Marechera's work and his current reception illustrate this urgency: the nation cannot be done away with yet.

Notes

1. Arjun Appadurai, *Modernity at Large: Cultural Dimensions of Globalization* (Minneapolis: U of Minnesota P, 1996), 158.
2. One dimension of the definition of "postnational", according to Arjun Appadurai, is that it "[s]uggests that we are in the process of moving to global order in which the nation-state has become obsolete and other formations for allegiance and identity have taken its place." In his definition the idea of transgressing the territorial space of the nation-state is central. See Appadurai 169.
3. Jean Franco, "The Nation as Imagined Community," in *Dangerous Liaisons. Gender, Nation, and Postcolonial Perspectives*, ed. Anne McClintock, Aamir Mufti and Ella Shohat (Minneapolis: U of Minnesota P, 1997), 133.
4. Aamir Mufti and Ella Shohat, Introduction, in *Dangerous Liaisons: Gender, Nation, and Postcolonial Perspectives*, ed. Anne McClintock, Aamir Mufti and Ella Shohat (Minneapolis: U of Minnesota P, 1997), 2.
5. Avtar Brah, *Cartographies of Diaspora: Contesting Identities* (London: Routledge, 1996), 180.
6. Laura Chrisman, "Nationalism and Postcolonial Studies," in *The Cambridge Companion to Postcolonial Literary Studies*, ed. Neil Lazarus (Cambridge: Cambridge UP, 2004), 183.
7. Elleke Boehmer, *Stories of Women: Gender and Narrative in the Postcolonial Nation* (Manchester: Manchester UP, 2005), 4.
8. Partha Chatterjee, "Beyond the Nation? Or within?" *Social Text* 56 (1998): 57.
9. Francis Ngaboh-Smart, *Beyond Empire and Nation: Postnational Arguments in the Fiction of Nuruddin Farah and B. Kojo Laing* (Amsterdam: Rodopi, 2004), 148.
10. Chatterjee, 57.

11. Andrew Smith, "Migrancy, Hybridity, and Postcolonial Literary Studies," in *The Cambridge Companion to Postcolonial Literary Studies*, ed. Neil Lazarus (Cambridge: Cambridge UP, 2004) 247.
12. Imre Szeman, *Zones of Instability: Literature, Postcolonialism, and the Nation* (Baltimore: Johns Hopkins UP, 2004), 18.
13. The concept of *postcolony* in Achille Mbembe's thinking is illustrative in this context, as it embodies the idea of the violent inheritance of colonialism: "['p]ostcolony' identifies specifically a given historical trajectory – that of societies recently emerging from the experience of colonization and the violence which the colonial relationship involves," Mbembe, *On the Postcolony* (Berkeley: U of California P, 2001), 102.
14. Simon Gikandi, "Globalization and the Claims of Postcoloniality," in *Postcolonialisms: An Anthology of Cultural Theory and Criticism*, ed. Gaurav Desai and Supriya Nair (Oxford: Berg, 2005), 610.
15. Gikandi, "Globalization," 609. See also Revathi Krishnaswamy, "The Criticism of Culture and the Culture of Criticism: At the Intersection of Postcolonialism and Globalization Theory," *Diacritics* 32.2 (2002): 123.
16. Gikandi, "Globalization," 618.
17. Gikandi "Globalization", 618–619. See also Gikandi in interview with David Jefferess, "Postcolonialism's Ethical (Re)Turn," *Postcolonial Text* 2.1 (2006): n.pag, and Gikandi, "Theory, Literature and Moral Considerations," *Research in African Literatures* 32.4 (2001): 15–17.
18. Ngaboh-Smart, 154.
19. Meyda Yegenoglu, "Cosmopolitanism and Nationalism in a Globalized World," *Ethnic and Racial Studies* 28.1 (2005): 104.
20. Yegenoglu 104. Of course, it must be highlighted that not all migrant postcolonial subjects are in a privileged position: the modes of postcolonial dislocation cover also such less privileged conditions as that of the refugees, illegal immigrants, or low-paid migrant labour. See Revathi Krishnaswamy, "Mythologies of Migrancy: Postcolonialism, Postmodernism and the Politics of (Dis)location," *ARIEL* 26.1 (1995): 129–130; also Brah 178–183.
21. Deepika Bahri, "Once More with Feeling; What is Postcolonialism?" *ARIEL* 26.1 (1995): 58.
22. The formulation "the state of the Zimbabwean nation" has been inspired by the title of a recently published collection of Zimbabwean poetry, *State of the Nation: Contemporary Zimbabwean Poetry*, ed. Tinashe Mushakavanhu and David Nettleingham (Kent: Conversational Paperpress, 2009).

23. See Flora Veit-Wild, *Dambudzo Marechera. A Source Book* on to *Mindblast*, the posthumously published text collection Scrapiron Blues, that Marechera wrote after his return to Zimbabwe, adopts a more nation-based stance.
24. See Flora Veit-Wild, *Dambudzo Marechera. A Source Book on His Life and Work* (Trenton: Africa World, 2004), xvi.
25. Dambudzo Marechera, interview with Kirsten Holst Petersen, in Marechera, *An Articulate Anger: Dambudzo Marechera, 1952–87* (Sydney: Dangaroo, 1988), 23.
26. Girma Negash, "Migrant Literature and Political Commitment: Puzzles and Parables in the Novels of Biyi Bandele-Thomas," *Journal of African Cultural Studies* 12.1 (1999): 78.
27. In Flora Veit-Wild and Ernest Schade, *Dambudzo Marechera: 4 June 1952–18 August 1987*. Pictures, Poems, Prose, Tributes (Harare: Baobab, 1988), 3.
28. In Veit-Wild 39.
29. Stewart Crehan, "Down and Out in London and Harare: Marechera's Subversion of 'African Literature'," in *Emerging Perspectives on Dambudzo Marechera*, ed. Flora Veit-Wild and Anthony Chennels (Trenton: Africa World, 1999), 269.
30. Daniela Volk, "'In Search of My True People': Universal Humanism in Marechera's Writing," in *Emerging Perspectives on Dambudzo Marechera*, ed. Flora Veit-Wild and Anthony Chennels (Trenton: Africa World, 1999), 304–307.
31. In her analysis, Annie Gagiano identifies seven different ways of "[e]xperiencing and imagining" exile in Marechera's work: there are the ontological and autobiographical dimensions; cultural alienation caused by colonialism; Africans' experiences in the UK; alienation in the postcolony; exile as theme; and finally, psychological effects of exile. As Gagiano aptly states, these different concepts do not emerge distinctively, but are intertwined and related to each other; see Gagiano, "Concepts of Exile in Dambudzo Marechera's Early Work," *African Literature Today* 22 (2000): 4–9.
32. Dambudzo Marechera, *Black Sunlight* (London: Heinemann, 1982), 3–4.
33. Marechera, *Black Sunlight*, 9.
34. Marechera, *Black Sunlight*, 21.
35. Dambudzo Marechera, *The Black Insider* (London: Lawrence & Wishart, 1992), 108.
36. Marechera, *The Black Insider*, 141–142.

37. Marechera, *The Black Insider,* 114.
38. Gerald Gaylard, "Dambudzo Marechera and Nationalist Criticism," *English in Africa* 20.2 (1993): 91. Very similar suggestion, although in a less explicit manner, has been made by Elleke Boehmer who defines *The House of Hunger* and *Black Sunlight* as books that were published during Marechera's stay in England and that "[r]eflect largely on the internal conflicts [Marechera] experienced from early childhood, the dilemmas of 'colonised consciousness', and his alienated situation as a black 'colonial' artist claiming international precursors." *Mindblast,* on the other hand, is represented as "[t]he book he published after his return to home" in which "[M]arechera [...] engage[s] directly at certain points with the condition of newly-independent Zimbabwe." See Boehmer 150.
39. Edward W. Said, *The World, the Text and the Critic* (London: Vintage, 2003), 31–53. See also Gikandi, who argues that "The texts we call postcolonial are texts which reflect in their thematic and linguistic interests the materiality of the conditions in which they emerge." Gikandi, "Postcolonialism's Ethical (Re)Turn: An Interview with Simon Gikandi," by David Jefferess, *Postcolonial Text* 2.1 (2006): online; available at: <http://journals.sfu.ca/pocol/index.php/pct/article/view Article/464/845> (visited 18 December 2009).
40. It must be noted that Marechera's conception of exile and the exile that he lived, partly without fixed domicile, are not really glorious.
41. David Buuck, "African Dobbelganger: Hybridity and Identity in the work of Dambudzo Marechera," *Research in African Literatures* 28.2 (1997): 127.
42. Dambudzo Marechera, *Mindblast or the Definitive Buddy* (Harare: College Press, 1994), 45–46.
43. Terence Ranger, "Rule by Histography: The Struggle over the Past in Contemporary Zimbabwe," in *Versions of Zimbabwe. New Approaches to Literature and Culture,* ed Robert Muponde and Ranka Primorac (Harare: Weaver, 2005), 217.
44. Mbembe, 24–65.
45. Christine Sylvester, "Remembering and Forgetting 'Zimbabwe': Towards a Third Transition," in Political Transition: Politics and Cultures, ed. Paul Gready (London: Pluto, 2003), 44–46.
46. See, for instance, Amanda Hammar and Brian Raftopoulos, "Zimbabwe's Unfinished Business: Rethinking Land, State and Nation," in *Zimbabwe's Unfinished Business: Rethinking Land, State and Nation in the Context of Crisis,* ed. Amanda Hammar, Brian Raftopoulos and Stig Jensen (Harare: Weaver, 2003), 27–28.

47. Ranka Primorac and Robert Muponde, Introduction, "Writing against Blindness," in *Versions of Zimbabwe. New Approaches to Literature and Culture*, ed. Robert Muponde and Ranka Primorac (Harare: Weaver, 2005), xiv.
48. Primorac and Muponde xiv–xv.
49. Khombe M. Mangwanda, "Dambudzo Marechera's Zimbabwe: A Nation of Captives," *Commonwealth Essays and Studies* 26.2 (2001): 37 (emphasis added).
50. Mangwanda, 45.
51. Maurice Taonezvi Vambe, "The Instabilities of National Allegory: The Case of Dambudzo Marechera's *The House of Hunger* and *Black Sunlight*," *Current Writing* 13.1 (2001): 72.
52. Vambe, "Instabilities," 80.
53. Vambe, "Instabilities," 81 (emphasis added).
54. Vambe, "Instabilities," 81–82.
55. Maurice Taonezvi Vambe, "Orality in the Black Zimbabwean Novel in English," *Journal of Southern African Studies* 30.2 (2004): 247.
56. Vambe, "Orality," 248.
57. Annie Gagiano, "Marechera's Wordhorde and the Scrapiron of War," in *Versions of Zimbabwe. New Approaches to Literature and Culture*, ed. Robert Muponde and Ranka Primorac (Harare: Weaver, 2005), 45.
58. Tinashe Mushakavanhu, "Dambudzo Marechera and the Zimbabwe Crisis," Conference paper at "Dambudzo Marechera: A Celebration," Trinity College, Oxford University, Oxford, 15 May 2009.
59. See Anna-Leena Toivanen, "'Hänen henkensä elää': Dambudzo Marecheran nerous," *Kulttuurintutkimus* 26.2–3 (2009): 31–46.
60. Brian Chikwava, "Blasting the Poet," *Guardian* 31 March (2005), available at: <http://www.guardian.co.uk/books/2005/mar/31/zimbabwe.society> (visited 29 January 2008).
61. Boehmer, 4.
62. Kizito Z. Muchemwa, "'Why Don't You Tell the Children a Story?': Father Figures in Three Zimbabwean Short Stories," in *Manning the Nation: Father Figures in Zimbabwean Literature and Society*, ed. Kizito Z. Muchemwa and Robert Muponde (Harare: Weaver, 2007), 14.

Works Cited

Appadurai, Arjun. *Modernity at Large: Cultural Dimensions of Globalization.* Minnesota: U of Minnesota P, 1996.

Bahri, Deepika. "Once More with a Feeling: What is Postcolonialism?" *ARIEL* 26.1 (1995): 51–81.

Boehmer, Elleke. *Stories of Women: Gender and Narrative in the Postcolonial Nation.* Manchester: Manchester UP, 2005.

Brah, Avtar. *Cartographies of Diaspora: Contesting Identities.* London: Routledge, 1996.

Buuck, David. "African Dobbelgänger: Hybridity and Identity in the Work of Dambudzo Marechera." *Research in African Literatures* 28.2 (1997): 118–131.

Chatterjee, Partha. "Beyond the Nation? Or within?" *Social Text* 56 (1998): 57–69.

Chikwava, Brian."Blasting the Poet." *Guardian* 31 March (2005). Available at: <http://www.guardian.co.uk/books/2005/mar/31/zimbabwe.society>. (Visited 29 January 2008.)

Chrisman, Laura. "Nationalism and Postcolonial Studies." In *The Cambridge Companion to Postcolonial Literary Studies.* Ed. Neil Lazarus. Cambridge: Cambridge UP, 2004.183–198.

Crehan, Stewart. "Down and Out in London and Harare: Marechera's Subversion of 'African Literature'." In *Emerging Perspectives on Dambudzo Marechera.* Ed. Flora Veit-Wild and Anthony Chennels. Trenton: Africa World, 1999. 265–281.

Franco, Jean. "The Nation as Imagined Community." In *Dangerous Liaisons: Gender, Nation, and Postcolonial Perspectives.* Ed. Anne McClintock, Aamir Mufti and Ella Shohat. Minneapolis: U of Minnesota P, 1997.130–137.

Gagiano, Anne. "Concepts of Exile in Dambudzo Marechera's Early Works." *African Literature Today* 22 (2000): 1–12.

Gagiano, Anne. "Marechera's Wordhorde and the Scrapiron of War." In *Versions of Zimbabwe: New Approaches to Literature and Culture.* Ed. Robert Muponde and Ranka Primorac. Harare: Weaver, 2005. 41–54.

Gaylard, Gerald. "Dambudzo Marechera and Nationalist Criticism." *English in Africa* 20.2 (1993): 89–105.

Gikandi, Simon. "Globalization and the Claims of Postcoloniality." *South Atlantic Quarterly* 100.3 (2001): 627–658. Rpt. in *Postcolonialisms: An Anthology of Cultural Theory and Criticism.* Ed. Gaurav Desai and Supriya Nair. Oxford: Berg, 2005. 608–634.

Gikandi, Simon. "Theory, Literature, and Moral Considerations." *Research in African Literatures* 32.4 (2001): 1–18.

Gikandi, Simon. "Postcolonialism's Ethical (Re)Turn."Interview with David Jefferess. *Postcolonial Text* 2.1 (2006): online. Available at:

<http://journals.sfu.ca/pocol/index.php/pct/article/viewArticle/464/845>. (Visited 18 December 2009.)

Hammar, Amanda and Brian Raftopoulos. "Zimbabwe's Unfinished Business: Rethinking Land, State and Nation." In *Zimbabwe's Unfinished Business: Rethinking Land, State and Nation in the Context of Crisis.* Ed. Amanda Hammar, Brian Raftopoulos and Stig Jensen. Harare: Weaver, 2003. 1–41.

Krishnaswamy, Revathi. "The Criticism of Culture and the Culture of Criticism: At the Intersection of Postcolonialism and Globalization Theory." *Diacritics* 32.1 (2002): 106–126.

Krishnaswamy, Revathi. "Mythologies of Migrancy: Postcolonialism, Postmodernism and the Politics of (Dis)location." *ARIEL* 26.1 (1995): 125–145.

Mangwanda, Khombe M. "Dambudzo Marechera's Zimbabwe: A Nation of Captives." *Commonwealth Essays and Studies* 26.2 (2004): 37–45.

Marechera, Dambudzo. *An Articulate Anger: Dambudzo Marechera, 1952–87.* Interview with Kirsten Holst Petersen. Sydney: Dangaroo, 1988.

Marechera, Dambudzo. *The Black Insider.* London: Lawrence and Wishart, 1992.

Marechera, Dambudzo. *Black Sunlight.* London: Heinemann, 1982.

Marechera, Dambudzo. *Mindblast or the Definitive Buddy.* Harare: College Press, 1994.

Mbembe, Achille. *On the Postcolony.* Berkeley: U of California P, 2001.

Muchemwa, Kizito Z. "'Why Don't You Tell the Children a Story?': Father Figures in Three Zimbabwean Short Stories." In *Manning the Nation: Father Figures in Zimbabwean Literature and Society.* Ed. Kizito Z. Muchemwa and Robert Muponde. Harare: Weaver, 2007. 1–16.

Mufti, Aamir and Ella Shohat. Introduction. In *Dangerous Liaisons. Gender, Nation, and Postcolonial Perspectives.* Ed. Anne McClintock, Aamir Mufti and Ella Shohat. Minneapolis: U of Minnesota P, 1997. 1–12.

Muponde, Robert and Ranka Primorac, eds. *Versions of Zimbabwe: New Approaches to Literature and Culture.* Harare: Weaver, 2005.

Mushakavanhu, Tinashe. "Dambudzo Marechera and the Zimbabwean Crisis." Conference paper at "Dambudzo Marechera: A Celebration." Trinity College, Oxford University, Oxford. 15 May 2009.

Mushakavanhu, Tinashe and David Nettleingham, eds. *State of the Nation.* Kent: Conversational Paperpress, 2009.

Negash, Girma. "Migrant Literature and Political Commitment: Puzzles and Parables in the Novels of Biyi Bandele-Thomas." *Journal of African Cultural Studies* 12.1 (1999): 77–92.

Ngaboh-Smart, Francis. *Beyond Empire and Nation: Postnational Arguments in the Fiction of Nuruddin Farah and B. Kojo Laing.* Amsterdam: Rodopi, 2004.

Primorac, Ranka and Robert Muponde. Introduction, "Writing against Blindness." In *Versions of Zimbabwe: New Approaches to Literature and Culture.* Ed. Robert Muponde and Ranka Primorac. Harare: Weaver, 2005. xiii–xxii.

Ranger, Terence. "Rule by Histography: The Struggle over the Past in Contemporary Zimbabwe." In *Versions of Zimbabwe: New Approaches to Literature and Culture.* Ed. Robert Muponde and Ranka Primorac. Harare: Weaver, 2005. 217–243.

Said, Edward W. *The World, the Text, and the Critic.* London: Verso, 1991.

Smith, Andrew. "Migrancy, Hybridity, and Postcolonial Literary Studies." In *The Cambridge Companion to Postcolonial Literary Studies.* Ed. Neil Lazarus. Cambridge: Cambridge UP, 2004. 241–261.

Sylvester, Christine. "Remembering and Forgetting 'Zimbabwe': Towards a Third Transition." In *Political Transition: Politics and Cultures.* Ed. Paul Gready. London: Pluto, 2003. 29–52.

Szeman, Imre. *Zones of Instability: Literature, Postcolonialism, and the Nation.* Baltimore: Johns Hopkins UP, 2004.

Toivanen, Anna-Leena. "'Hänen henkensä elää': Dambudzo Marecheran nerous." *Kulttuurintutkimus* 26.2–3 (2009): 31–46.

Vambe, Maurice Taonezvi. "Orality in the Black Zimbabwean Novel in English." *Journal of Southern African Studies* 30.2 (2004): 235–249.

Vambe, Maurice Taonezvi. "The Instabilities of National Allegory: The Case of Dambudzo Marechera's *The House of Hunger* and *Black Sunlight.*" *Current Writing* 13.1 (2001): 70–86.

Veit-Wild, Flora. *Dambudzo Marechera: A Source Book on His Life and Work.* Trenton: Africa World, 2004.

Veit-Wild, Flora and Ernest Schade. *Dambudzo Marechera: 4 June 1952–18 August 1987. Pictures, Poems, Prose, Tributes.* Harare: Baobab, 1988.

Volk, Daniela. "'In Search of my True People': Universal Humanism in Marechera's Writing." In *Emerging Perspectives on Dambudzo Marechera.* Ed. Flora Veit-Wild and Anthony Chennels. Trenton: Africa World, 1999. 299–312.

Yegenoglu, Meyda. "Cosmopolitanism and Nationalism in a Globalized World." *Ethnic and Racial Studies* 28.1 (2005): 103–131.

7

The Ethics of Representation in *The Glass Palace* by Amitav Ghosh

TUOMAS HUTTUNEN

Unvoiced Histories through Dialogues

Among the main aims of Amitav Ghosh's writing are revealing areas of the past that have not been taken up by orthodox history books (or represented in fiction) and creating links where they have not been perceived traditionally. Although *The Glass Palace* (2000)[1] on the surface seems to adopt the form of the family saga, at the same time it relates the histories of the teak and rubber trade, the Burmese royal family, the British Indian Army, the Indian National Army and the general history of India, Burma (Myanmar) and Malaysia from 1880s to 1990s. One of the main aims of the novel seems to be to provide a kind of intermediate viewpoint to the history of India, Burma (Myanmar) and Malaysia, bringing to the fore the many interconnected elements of these areas and giving voice to those who have largely been left in silence by mainstream fiction or historiography. World War II, for instance, has rarely been narrated from the point of view of the soldiers in the British Indian army or the Indian National Army. In a similar manner, Burma (Myanmar) and Malaysia have not been among the most famous scenes of war in European historiography or fiction. This intermediate viewpoint is created through the coming together of Western-originated ideologies and technologies on the one hand and the heterogeneous and mixed histories of the areas of India, Burma (Myanmar) and Malaysia on the other.

These histories are conveyed by characters stemming from various social classes and backgrounds. Ghosh's stock of characters includes, among others, the rapacious and opportunistic businessman Rajkumar, the idealist activist Uma, the Western-trained middle-class bureaucrat the Collector, the inward-turned humanist photographer Dinu and the initially happy-go-lucky soldier Arjun. The physical characteristics of the characters more or less conform to the ideologies they represent. The actual plot proceeds mainly through discussions in which differing ideologies are pitted against each other in a manner that vindicates none of them. Such juxtaposition brings into view more clearly the pros and cons of each way of seeing the world. Between the discussions the reader finds meticulous descriptions of the practical procedures of teak and rubber trade that read like a guide or a manual and descriptions of the private lives of the various characters. While the novel has a separate narrator, large sections are focalised through its many characters. At the level of narrative technique, the novel draws on the *genres* of the classic realist historical novel, romantic fiction, oral stories and the style of textbooks or manuals.

Two differing viewpoints, or ideologies, are usually introduced in the discussions. None of the views that emerge are given priority, no one "wins" the argument. Instead, the many standpoints are placed in a dialogical relationship with each other. This kind of technique, while obviously professing a link with Rabindranath Tagore's *Gora*[2] and "the novel of Ideas," is also reminiscent of the idea of an ethical relationship to another person. Ethics has been steadily gaining ground within the field of literary studies during the last twenty years. The contemporary ethical criticism is closely linked with discussions of otherness. It examines among other things the questions of how to represent otherness in a text, how to respond to the other and bring the concept of otherness to bear on the experience of reading. This article will concentrate on the first two of these questions. I aim to examine from the point of view of ethics Ghosh's choices of what to represent and how to represent it in the novel. In what follows I will first examine the strategies for presenting the other in the narrative, both through discussions and as a way of delineating the characters. I will then move on to look at how image and language are juxtaposed as representational models in the narration, before examining the strategy used for creating connections between different discourses within the narrative. I will finish by placing the outcome of these considerations within the framework of ethical theory by trying to outline how the representative ethics of the novel works.

Ethical Representation of the Other

The basic idea in ethically aware representation is to secure the distinctive features of the target/s of representation. Ethics is about searching for connection with the other, be that a person or a discourse. What usually happens when we meet someone on a personal level is that we appropriate this other into our own knowledge of the world, our views on it and experiences of it. But the encounter with the other should not constitute mere knowing and describing of the other from our point of view and through our discourse, because this effaces the other almost completely and leaves it without a voice or agency of its own. The idea behind all this is that we cannot know without language/discourse. Consequently, to know something is to project a certain discourse on it, a discourse that we have produced and that makes the target of knowledge understandable to us. But this does not reveal the real other as it stands on its own. It has been changed through our knowing it. Emmanuel Levinas, among others, maintains that the other cannot be properly reached by the self. However, we should aim at forming a relationship with it by letting the other show itself to us on its own, as it were, without us projecting our own value systems on it. Both the self and the other should remain as independent and self-sufficient, but still in relationship with one another. Here self-sufficiency and independence imply difference and the existence of a relationship refers to connections and wholeness. When forming an ethically aware representation of the other we should let it stand on its own to the extent it is possible. I shall next examine how *The Glass Palace* represents the differing viewpoints of its characters through dialogue and then take a look at how it represents these characters themselves.

The narrative does not offer overt commentary on the many discussions it features. Nor does it take sides: the narrator in a way stays in the background and lets each point of view in the dialogue stand on its own. The opposing views do not melt into any peaceful union, nor does any of them gain any advantage. But despite this, the reader is given a glimpse of the larger whole through this juxtaposing of viewpoints. The idea is not that the characters in the novel are necessarily open to each other's views in an ethically aware manner, but that the narrative represents their views as equals in such a manner, not giving discursive priority to any of the standpoints it brings forth. Although the opposing views are presented as equals on the level of dialogue, the narration as a whole is not as impartial as its method of juxtaposing different views might imply. By choosing what to narrate and how to narrate it, the narrator, when emerging, manipulates and directs the reader. Consequently, although the various viewpoints in the dialogues are given a chance to get heard on their own without manipulation, it is usually quite clear where the narrator wants the allegiances of the reader to lie.

The discussions Arjun Roy has with other characters on the position of Indians in the British Indian Army and whether or not they should separate themselves into a national army (*GP* 405–407, 416–417, 437–439) form one of the most resonant of all the ethical problems in the novel.[3] As the first person in his family to join the army, Arjun is at first overwhelmed by its glamour and is proud of his supposed freedom, ostensibly gained by access to British officers as well as British language and food:

> "Look at us!" Arjun would say, after a whisky or two, "we're the first modern Indians; the first Indians to be truly free. We eat what we like, we drink what we like, we're the first Indians who're not weighed down by the past."
>
> To Dinu this was profoundly offensive. "It's not what you eat and drink that make you modern: it's a way of looking at things ..." He'd fetch reproductions that he'd cut out of magazines, of photographs by Stieglitz, Cunningham and Weston.
>
> Arjun would shrug these off with a laughing retort: "To you the modern world is just something you read about. What you know

> of it you get from books and newspapers. We're the ones who actually live with Westerners ..." (*GP* 279)

There seems to be tension between theory (Dinu) and experience (Arjun) as well as duty (Arjun) and emotion (Dinu), which get into each other's way and complicate the situation of both those who act in practice and those who stay aside and reflect on things from afar. As the result both characters gradually change in the opposite direction in the course of the novel. Dinu becomes more active (the meetings he arranges in his photo-studio) and Arjun becomes more aware of himself and the world, as we shall see later. The views and ideologies that Arjun and Dinu represent are here juxtaposed as self-sufficient and independent. The dialogue fades away with neither view 'winning' the argument. The reader is provided with the pros and cons of each view without narratorial manipulation.

But Hardayal (or Hardy), who was born into a family which had served the army for generations, is the one who has doubts to begin with. At the Military Academy in Dehra Dun, they were told that the safety, honour and welfare of their country must always come first. But where and what exactly was this country they were supposed to defend? The moral dilemma of the Indians in the British army comes to the surface in a hiding place in Burma where the company lie injured after a Japanese attack. Hardy can no longer go on with his divided life and says to Arjun:

> "In the trenches [...] I had an eerie feeling. It was strange to be sitting on one side of a battle line, knowing that you had to fight and knowing at the same time that it wasn't really your fight – knowing that whether you won or lost, neither the blame nor the credit would be yours. Knowing that you risked everything to defend a way of life that pushes you to the sideline. It's almost as if you're fighting against yourself."
>
> "I can't say I felt the same way, Hardy." (*GP* 406)

Arjun's code of honour will not allow him to think the way Hardy does. In his view the idea of joining the Japanese for the liberation of India would only mean exchanging one set of rulers for another. But in Hardy's view, the important thing is that they would for once be making their own decision instead of just taking orders. The conflict is further complicated by Arjun's relationship with his loyal batman Kishan Singh who wants to know what the English word 'mercenary' means – and his close relationship to his British commanding officer (*GP* 416–417). These relationships, again, are presented in the form of dialogues in the narrative.

Hans-Georg Gadamer has approached the issue of ethical representation from the viewpoint of hermeneutics. As Peter Haney observes, Gadamer equates the relationship between the text and its interpreter with the relationship between the participants in a discussion.[4] Ethical relationships demand self-deliberation in "the immediacy of a given situation,"[5] rather than the placing of the other participant into a premeditated conceptual or representational system. In other words, "a person or a text is present [...] to the degree that the person or text maintains its otherness"[6] and is not appropriated into the already existing thought model or worldview of the interpreter or interlocutor. In this way, the participants are in a sense subordinated to the discussion, the "truth" of which transcends their original truths, or viewpoints. In the words of Gadamer, the participants have to "transpose" themselves for this to happen:

> Transposing ourselves consists neither in the empathy of one individual for another nor in subordinating another person to our own standards; rather, it always involves rising to a higher universality that overcomes not only our own particularity but also that of the other. [...] To acquire a horizon means that one learns to look beyond what is close at hand – not in order to look away from it but to see it better, within a larger whole and in truer proportion.[7]

This way of representing interhuman relationships is ethically aware. In a sense, no idea exists independently, but only in a dialogical relationship with something else (meaning the other). The "truth" emanating from the communication with the other is intermediate in the sense that it has elements from both the views that are brought into dialogical relationship with one another. But this truth resulting from their meeting is not merely the sum of the views in question, but a truth of a higher level, as it were, revealing the larger context of the particular meeting.

The narrative in *The Glass Palace* never brings out an opinion or a viewpoint without providing an antithesis to it. Further, these viewpoints are never formulated as abstract generalizations or cultural comments by the narrator, but everything is placed in the mouths of the characters "in the immediacy of a given situation", to borrow Gadamer's phrase.[8] But although these discussions are narrated in a manner that honours the demands of ethically aware representations of interpersonal relationships, the topics under discussion are very much a part of the sociopolitical, or the public. For instance, Arjun's ethical dilemma is contextualized precisely within the moral code of the army, in other words, within rules set by the "society" to which he belongs. I have stated elsewhere that the writing of Ghosh arrives at universal issues through the examination of particularity.[9] In a parallel way, he arrives at the questions of moral conduct by way of the ethical, and to the representation of sociopolitical schemes through the examination of the interhuman in particular circumstances and situations.

In the novel, the abode of the Burmese Royal family, *The Glass Palace*, can be seen as symbolizing the self-other problem caused by the artificial divisions of cultures into separate nations. The walls of the central dome of the palace are made of glass, and the ceiling of mirrors. Consequently, inside the dome one can look out but also see oneself. *The Glass Palace* is also the name of Dinu's photo-studio set up in Myanmar in the 1990s. The notion of *The Glass Palace* containing the idea of both window and mirror can also be seen as symbolizing the seclusion of the Royal family of Burma in their castle and later in Outram house in Ratnagiri, as well as the seclusion of the modern state of Myanmar caused by the repressive military regime. Seclusion is also characteristic of Dolly, who ends up in a nunnery a few years before her death.

But there is also the implicit reference to the Empire (even the whole world) as a glass palace: many of the characters in the novel are very much the mirrored images of the stereotypical American/European types. The opportunistic Rajkumar resembles the capitalist individualist businessman who is only interested in his own benefit, even trading his fellow Burmese to make money. The young Rajkumar is characterized in the novel as "a feral creature, unaware that in certain places there exist invisible bonds linking people. [...] Beyond the ties of blood, friendship and immediate reciprocity, Rajkumar recognised no loyalties, no obligations and no limits on the compass of his right to provide for himself." (*GP* 47) This kind of ideology seems very close to the stereotypical myth of the self-made American.

Similarly, the other characters represent types not alien to European-American cultures. While her marriage lasts, Uma is reminiscent of the typical colonial administrator's wife during the days of the Raj: she misses home and has nothing to do apart from official commitments. The pedantic Cambridge-trained Collector is evidently the mirror image of the mentioned European colonial administrator; his position not different from that of Arjun's who is an officer in the British Indian army. At the end of her marriage Uma becomes an idealistic political activist not unfamiliar to the Western reader.

The characters also come from hybrid backgrounds. One of the most striking examples is Saya John (or John Martins), who has two names, wears European clothes, looks Chinese, speaks Hindustani, was born in Malaysia and has received a Catholic education (*GP* 9). But although the ethnic features/differences of the characters are brought clearly into view and although their physical features develop almost into caricatures of the various ideologies they represent, these differences are not emphasized for their own sake. Rather, they are related with the purpose of assuring each character their distinctive features, by this means avoiding their appropriation into any one homogenizing discourse. The setting and target of representation in the novel as a whole maintains its heterogeneity, while aspiring to create connections. Consequently, as Ranjita Basu has remarked in a discussion of Ghosh's first novel, *The Circle of Reason* (1986), in the end the characters' "emotions and passions are related to their universal humanity rather than to their racial identity."[10] The ethnic or other identities in Ghosh's narration are secondary to a "broader, more human context that transcends the boundaries"[11] between races and ethnicities in search of ethically established connections. And this context is achieved through an ethically aware representation of interpersonal relationships, which in the case of *The Glass Palace* happens largely through discussions.

Image and Language/s

In Ghosh's writing, one recurrent theme related to the ethical representation of the other is the depiction of realities through both images and language. Ghosh seems to present the creation of pictures and texts as alternative modes of representation. In *The Glass*

Palace this problematic is present mainly in two occasions – those of Dinu and Arjun. The thematic of image is most obviously present in the character of Dinu. Dinu is quiet by nature and when he speaks it is mostly in fragments. His way of looking at the world is through the viewfinder of a camera. In other words, in a sense he prefers images to words. This causes some bewilderment in Alison:

> "I'm not just a thing, for your camera to focus on. Sometimes it's as if you have no other interest in me but this." [...] "I see more of you in this way that I would in any other," he said. "If I were to talk to you for hours I wouldn't know you better. I don't say this is better than talking ... it's just my way – my way of understanding ..." (*GP* 357)

For Dinu looking through the viewfinder is "'the most intimate way that I can know anyone ... or anything" (*GP* 358). Ghosh's writing does not take part in the discussion of what comes first, the word or the image. In his texts the two appear as alternatives for realizing the world. Language appears as the more dangerous of the two, due to its reality-constructing and power-inflicting nature. The theme of photography is also hinted at on the level of narrative technique. As Ira Pande observes in a review of the novel, Ghosh's prose "mimics photography" in its construction of "word pictures,"[12] for instance in the passage describing the long march from Burma to India (see *GP* 466–474).

Later *The Glass Palace* becomes the name of Dinu's photo-studio in Myanmar. People come to the politically dubious meetings held at the studio to seek connections and to find themselves through discussions on topics and pictures forbidden by the regime. They also get a view of the world outside the closed state through foreign magazines and photos that Dinu has managed to find despite the all-invading censorship. The novel also approaches the self-other problematic through Dinu's photography. He comments on the miracle of the photograph:

> When you print by contact ... when you lay the negative on the paper and watch them come to life ... the darkness of the one becomes a light of the other. The first time I saw it happen I thought, what must it be like to touch like this? ... with such utter absorption? ... For one thing to become irradiated with the shadows of another? (*GP* 404)

While this of course refers to what happens to the negative in the development process, the same reciprocal relationship exists between the photographer and the target observed through the viewfinder. The viewfinder is not merely a window, through which the photographer can project his/her own world-view onto the world by choosing the target and then manipulating it by deciding what kind of picture to take; nor is it merely a mirror, which denies access to the outside world by reflecting this world-view back on to the photographer. The idea of a window also implies that someone may look in. Similarly, the target of observation looks back at the photographer through the viewfinder.

Consequently, the taking of a photograph constitutes a two-directional act of looking, a moment of contact between two active participants. In a sense, then, the observers "become irradiated with the shadows of another" (*GP* 404). Ghosh seems to present the self-other problematic as two-directional on both the personal and the communal level. One cannot simply observe the world by either trying to know it, or by trying to know oneself by looking at it: the world, or the other, also looks back. Consequently, the other is not merely an inert object that can be appropriated to one's own discourse claiming to "know" it or used for purposes of self-definition: the other is active and looks back at the observer.

In the case of Arjun, image takes the place of language, which seems to be inadequate as a tool for creating his personality anew. Arjun has to recreate his identity, because he has lost the basis on which he has been built by the British military discourse. When he lies wounded, hiding from the Japanese with Kishan Singh, he starts to ponder on the reasons that make him do what he does. He gradually comes to the conclusion that he has no will of his own, but that he has been moulded by the influences of the British. He realises that he does not even have the words and the language to talk about things other than military. He wants to ask Kishan Singh about his marriage and his relationship with his wife, but finds himself unable to do that:

> He tried to form the sentences in his head and found that he did not know the right words in Hindustani; did not even now the tone of voice in which such questions could be asked. These were things he did not know how to say. There was so much he did not

> know how to say, in any language. [...] How was that possible? Was it because no one had taught them the words? The right language? Perhaps because it might be too dangerous? (*GP* 428)

He has no tools of self-consciousness, no language, through which to know that he possesses a within. The imperialist discourse in its military form, affecting him through the English language, has moulded him into a weapon in the hands of the British and without a will of his own. In the words of Hardy, he has no way of "connecting his hand and his heart," because his inner self has been suppressed. And this has happened without his noticing it. He has a hallucinatory vision, where he and Kishan Singh appear as lumps of clay whirling on potters' wheels. He is immediately formed and shaped by his unseen potter: "he had come a thing unto itself – no longer aware of the pressure of the potter's hand, unconscious even that it had come his way" (*GP* 430–431), while Kishan Singh remains unformed by the touch of his potter. The implication is that Kishan Singh is capable of resisting outside influence because he is conscious of his motives and his past that directs these motives. Arjun has been educated under the influence of the imperial discourse, which has more or less robbed him of words of his own and made him a puppet directed by others. He is unable to act on his own and has turned into "a crafted mimicry," of a British soldier.

Language and agency are intertwined, and the losing of one means the losing of the other as well. In a sense, Arjun no longer has either. But after the revelation he experiences while lying wounded in his hide-out, he gains agency and a will of his own. The problem is, where to place his loyalties now that the grip of the Empire has loosened:

> But who would claim his loyalty now? The old loyalties of India, the ancient ones – they'd been destroyed long ago; the British had built their Empire by effacing them. But the Empire was dead now – he knew this because he had felt it die within himself, where it had held its strongest dominion – and with whom was he now to keep faith? [...] How would one begin the work of re-creating the tissues that bound people to each other? (*GP* 441)

Arjun decides to place his loyalties not with the Japanese like his friend Hardy, but with India, and joins the Indian National Army.

Despite references to photographs/images as an alternative mode of representation in the novel, language is obviously still the primary tool for the creation of connections here. In this role, one language is even allowed to appropriate other languages into its discourse. This is commented on in the novel, when Dinu and Ma Thin Thin Aye discuss the writing of the latter. Dinu asks why all the characters in her stories speak Burmese, although they come from different linguistic and ethnic groups. This does not startle her: "'Where I live,' she said softly, 'every house on the street speaks a different language. I have no choice but to trust my reader to imagine the sound of each house. Or else I would not be able to write at all about my street – and to trust your reader is not a bad thing'" (*GP* 533). When Dinu contemplates how wonderful it would be if the readers could actually hear the mingling of several languages when reading the stories, Ma Thin Thin Aye answers: "'Why do you think they don't? A word on a page is like a string on an instrument. My readers sound the music in their heads, and for each it sounds different'" (*GP* 533).

Representing a multilingual group through one language makes the different languages and the socio-cultural discourses carried by them understandable as a whole to those fluent in the language in question, which in Ghosh's quest for connections is an end in itself. As a result, someone fluent in Burmese may gain access to the diverse lives of the people living in the street. If everyone were represented in the language they speak, no one would be able to grasp the whole and these particularities would remain incommunicable and separate. And it is just such separations and partitions that Ghosh tries to transcend by creating connections. The set of characters in the novel itself is very heterogeneous consisting of people coming from various linguistic groups. The language of the novel is English, with foreign words used only when there is no equivalent in English. But in the text there is always indication of which language or dialect is actually being spoken. The implied languages and dialects of the novel include Burmese, Hindustani, Bengali as Chittagong dialect and as a mainstream version from Calcutta, Tamil, Konkani and English. Dinu's conversation with Ma Thin Thin Aye described above can therefore be seen as a comment on the linguistic strategy of the novel as a whole.

Creating Connections

The tendency of Ghosh's writing to move somewhere between a kind of universal humanism and the poststructuralist realm emphasizing difference and "discourse as power" has been noted before.[13] Parallel with the search for interhuman relationships and the universal features of mankind there is an awareness of the world as a narrative and discursive social construction where knowledge is produced discursively by those versed in the hegemonic language/discourse. *The Glass Palace* comments on the all-pervasiveness of politics, which as a form of discourse easily invades all areas of the human society. When Dinu and Jaya are listening to Aung San Suu Kyi give a speech, the former says that Suu Kyi is the only leader he has ever been able to believe in, because:

> She's the only one who seems to understand what the place of politics is ... what it ought to be ... that while misrule and tyranny must be resisted, so too must politics itself ... that it cannot be allowed to cannibalise all of life, all of existence. To me this is the most terrible indignity of our condition – not just in Burma, but in many other places too... that politics has invaded everything, spared nothing... religion, art, family... it has taken over everything... there is no escape from it ... (*GP* 542)

By refusing to allow herself be swallowed by the discourse of politics (or the idea of discourse *as* politics), Suu Kyi has in Dinu's view already defeated the regime which is only capable of seeing reality as politics. In Dinu's words, she has "robbed them of words, of discourse." (*GP* 542)

In addition to the awareness of discourse as power and knowledge, Ghosh's narration attempts to construct instances of communication which transcend the claim to knowledge requiring a specific language or discourse. In *The Glass Palace*, this comes through in the scene from Dinu's photo studio in the Myanmar of the 1990s. People of various social and ethnic backgrounds come to the studio to talk of things forbidden by the regime. When Jaya expresses her worry about the spies sent to the meetings, Dinu answers:

> They would never be able to understand the attraction that brings people here [...] And when we talk of politics it is in such ways

> that they cannot follow ... we don't say things they can pin down ... in Myanmar nothing that is worth saying can be spoken in ordinary language ... everyone learns other means of communication, secret languages. (*GP* 509)

The people in the meetings communicate outside the discursive world of the regime and therefore the spies sent to the meetings cannot understand what is going on. It seems that subaltern agency exists, and can only exist, outside the discursive reality of the hegemonic group.

The regime represents a totalitarian discourse where there is no possibility of transcending the political, which has invaded all levels of society. The passage from ethics to politics has been of interest to Simon Critchley, who has constructed a model based on deconstruction and Levinasian ethics to explain the idea of a just society: "Justice must be informed by proximity; that is to say, the equality and symmetry of the relations between citizens must be interrupted by the inequality and asymmetry of the ethical relation."[14] The society has a double structure. People are equal and have the same rights as citizens but, at the same time, everyone is in an unequal relationship to the other. If this balance is broken, injustice follows: "Injustice – not to mention racism, nationalism, and imperialism – begins when one loses sight of the transcendence of the other and forgets that the State, with its institutions, is informed by the proximity of my relation to the Other."[15] The state should allow itself to be criticized and interrupted by the principle of the ethical relationship and the irreducibility of difference that it implies: "political discourse must be both a language of justice and a language of critique, legitimizing the *polis* while simultaneously letting the *polis* be interrupted by that which transcends it: a politics of ethical difference."[16] In the Myanmar depicted in *The Glass Palace* this does not happen. The group gathering at Dinu's photo studio clearly represents the ethical, or the transcending of the political totality of the regime, but it has to communicate in secret ways. As I implied above, the discussion group at the studio is very heterogeneous:

> It consisted of a motley mix of people, old and young, girls and boys, men and women. They were all Burmese but some looked to be of Indian origin, some Chinese. Some were smartly dressed

> while others were wearing cast-offs. There was a student in a black cap that said *Giorgio Armani*, and in one corner there sat a group of three monks in saffron robes. (*GP* 506–507)

This, then, is a group where difference is not reduced and everyone gets to speak: Dinu says that he only starts them off – then it is everyone else's turn. But the totalitarian discourse of the regime does not allow the group to interrupt its ontology and the imbalance between the ethical and the political remains in *status quo*. The ideal of a politics of ethical difference has not been reached, because the state does not allow its politics to be interrupted or criticized by the irreducible difference that Dinu's group stands for, both on the level of discourses they use and on the level of the heterogeneous whole they form.

In *The Glass Palace*, the main connector that does away with power politics and international schemes is love. The novel features several love relationships, beginning with the surprising love of King Thebaw and Queen Supayalat, which is described as a "startling new development, something that threw everybody's calculations off kilter" and occurs "in defiance of the protocols of palace intrigue" (*GP* 38). There are also the relationships between Dolly and Sawant, Dolly and Rajkumar, Manju and Neel, Alison and Dinu and, in the end, even Rajkumar and Uma, who in the beginning represent totally opposite ideologies and worldviews. Love, then, be it one-sided or mutual, seems to be a major connecting force, often functioning against, and in spite of, the world of power politics and wars, creating connections across geographical as well as social and ideological distances.

In his article on anthropology, cultural representation and privileged discourse, R.S. Khare sketches an alternative direction in representation of the other to what he calls "postmodernist temper" that "raises only issues of power, domination, and control in different guises."[17] This would be to view the relationship to the other in terms of "love". His argument is that love, besides power politics, is also a "pervasive and potent human sentiment" carrying "a *universal* human content and purpose."[18] The fact that the relationships between characters in the novel are directed by love at least as much as by things belonging to the realm of politics and power, can perhaps be seen as representing an ethical attitude to the description of the self and the other.

The strategy for representing love in *The Glass Palace* is somewhat surprising. Many of the 'love scenes' contain overtly soapy passages reminiscent of romantic fiction. Most of the novel reads like a classic realist historical novel, although the subject material is not typical of this *genre*. But especially the scenes describing the relationship of Dinu and Allison, while stressing the power of love, contain passages that are sentimental to the extreme, even banal:

> He pulled her closer. He did not care what had happened between her and Arjun; nothing mattered but this – that she loved him and he loved her. Nothing else was of any account, not the planes, not the bombs, nothing but this. This was what happiness was – he'd never known it before; this melting away, this exaltation, your guts spilling into your head, filling your eyes – your mind transformed into your body, your body indistinct with the joy in your mind; this sensation of reality having met its end. (*GP* 401)

And here is Manju arriving in Rangoon shortly after her marriage to Neel:

> It was only now, circling above the city that was to be her home, that she acknowledged how completely she was in love. He was her present, her future, the entirety of her existence. Time and being held no meaning without him. She slipped her hand into his and looked down again on the great muddy river and the spire of gold. 'Yes,' she said. 'I'm home.' (*GP* 301)

Again we are presented with a new discourse: that of romantic fiction. There is also love at first sight when Rajkumar sees Dolly in the palace (*GP* 34–35), parting and reunion after several years in Ratnagiri, and even a romantic last minute change of mind when Dolly rushes to the harbour just in time to stop Rajkumar (*GP* 166–169). This constitutes a typical example of Ghosh's tendency to mix genres and use their representative techniques for new purposes.

The same thing happens with the passages on the teak or rubber business, which read like a school book or a manual. Ghosh's technique in almost all his writing is to use both the creative imagination and archival research as the sources of revisions of traditional historiography, or uncovering events or sections of the past eclipsed by the same historiography. When not chosen as the subject of one of the discussions, the larger historical and sociopolitical schemes in the novel mostly appear implicitly. In a sense, they form the background for the lives of the characters. But the sections on the theory and praxis of teak (*GP* 68–71) and rubber trade, or the description of anthrax (*GP* 92) and the history of the discovery of petroleum in Burma (*GP* 122) are related in a mode of narration containing traits of the styles of manuals or textbooks, even philological research:

> Teak is a relative of mint, *tectona grandis*, born of the same genus of flowering plant, but of a distaff branch, presided over by that most soothing of herbs, verbena. It counts among its close kin many other fragrant and familiar herbs – sage, savoury, thyme, lavender, rosemary and most remarkably holy basil, with its many descendants, green and purple, smooth-leaved and coarse, pungent and fragrant bitter and sweet. (*GP* 70)

These passages are not set apart from the main narrative typographically as passages written in another discourse (for example, excerpts from a newspaper) as they are in some postmodern novels, but they appear to be woven into it, not quite separate but not quite a part of the main line of the text either. This tendency to mould passages written in a style associated with textbooks (or romances) into the main flow of the narrative can be seen as a strategy for not appropriating all the sectors of life into one mode of discourse, or one knowledge production strategy.

On the level of narrative technique, or choice of discourse, there seem to be traits of an ethics of interdiscursive connections matching the ethics of interhuman relationships apparent in the content of the novel. There also seems to be an acute awareness of how to balance imaginative knowledge with the knowledge gained from factual research. For instance, in addition to the matter of fact, scientific explications of anthrax and the running of a teak camp, there is the mysterious ghost tale of an elephant avenging the death of its keeper on a teak camp told orally by Saya John (*GP* 96–103). In this way, several levels of reality, or several discursive realizations of the teak business, become narrated.

In addition to the circulation of people and ideologies, the narrative also contains numerous references to technological development in the form of meticulous descriptions of car and camera models etc. One of the functions of this emphasis on the circulation of cultural objects is to describe the spreading of the products and ideology of Western originated capitalism. But, as with the passages on the teak and rubber trade, which are also offsprings of the developments in Western industries, the description is again meticulous to the extreme, enough to distract someone not familiar with the terminology:

> Mrs Khambatta's camera was an instrument of superb craftsmanship: a 1901 Graflex single-lens reflex, with a cube-like body, a bellows extension and a foursided hood. It was fitted with a Globe wide-angle lens which proved perfect for the panorama deployed before the shutter. (*GP* 170)

> This was a Duisenberg Model J Tourster, Matthew explained. It had a hydraulic braking system and a 6.9 litre, straight-8 engine. It had chain-driven overhead camshafts and could go up to 90 m.p.h. in second gear. In top gear it could cruise at 116. (*GP* 218)

Again, these kinds of descriptions (of which there are many more in the novel) based on careful research can be seen as balancing the imaginary contents of the narrative with factual descriptions. And they can be taken as results of a social anthropological interest in the circulation and spreading of technological advancement. Either way, they serve to create a fuller picture of the background of the characters in the novel, while providing the reader with yet another discourse through which to access the reality of the narrative as a whole.

The Ethics of Connections

As I have tried to show above, the ethical project of Ghosh seems to be firmly based on the creation of connections both between people and between various discursive and epistemological models. He aims at the provincialization of various colonial and national discourses, which are very much dependent on the construction of differences through the setting of geographical, ethnic, religious, linguistic etc. borders, and attempts to reveal realities eclipsed by these discourses. Ghosh is also careful not to provide just one truth on any matter at hand. On the content level, he always brings in two or more differing views on the same subject, as was seen in the frequent discussions/arguments in the novel. On the level of narrative technique, he usually represents the same target through an amalgamation of different discourses, as was seen in the case of the teak business, which is described through straightforward realist narration, the style of manuals or schoolbooks and through the mysterious oral tale told by Saya John. Otherwise, the realist narrative weaves together anthropological details on technical advancements and overtly soapy scenes in the style of romantic fiction.

These different styles, or strategies, of narration create connections on the level of discourse and consequently on the levels of different discursive realities. The subject material of the narrative is not typical of the stereotypical realist historical novel, although large parts of the narrative are represented in this form. The South Asian scene would be rather strange for a novel of this type, especially when the narration is limited to this area. Also, the large social scale of the characters, not to mention their heterogeneous backgrounds, is uncharacteristic of the mentioned genre, as is the lack of a neat narrative pattern that would lead from the beginning to the end. This narrative has several beginnings and ends that actually hint at a cyclical model of history. In a sense, then, the novel uses the narrative mode of the realist historical novel to dismantle the ideology and thought models that originally gave birth to this *genre.*

Current ethical criticism has its foundation in the examination of interpersonal relationships. Zygmunt Bauman has made a distinction between "modern" and "postmodern" ethics. In his view, modern ethics emphasized the similarity between the self and the other. The idea was that there was a common essence in all humans that was attainable through the removal of particularities. The function of the encounters with others was to help the ego on the way to this common essence, which was its real self.[19] Conversely, postmodern ethics emphasizes difference. The main representative here is probably Emmanuel Levinas, who subordinates the self to the other and denies the possibility of any kind of fusion or unification between the two, characterizing the relationship between them as alterity. In Levinas' view, the other exists outside the ontology of traditional Western philosophy, which conceives of all being as a projection of the self. Consequently, the other, as well as that which is ethical, cannot strictly speaking be described in discourse, but are transcendental. Levinas tried to develop a philosophy and language that would preserve the self and the other as independent and self-sufficient but still in relationship with one another.[20]

In relation to the problematics of modern and postmodern ethics introduced by Bauman, it seems that Ghosh occupies, once again, a position somewhere in the middle of the two. In Bauman's view, the idea of modern ethics was to remove all particularities from man so that "what is common to all men as such, can emerge in him as his essence."[21] Consequently, the relationships with other people are conceived as stops along the road through which the ego reaches its self. The characters in the novel do develop: their opinions and value-preferences change through discussions with others. The most obvious example would probably be Arjun, who, through his dialogues with Kishan Singh and Hardy, finally manages to gain agency and a will of his own.

But the problematic part is the implied similarity of all men beneath the disposable particularities, the "common essence" of all men, which is revealed as an independent, self-sufficient and asocial way of being.[22] In Ghosh's narration, the unity of people and the universal features of human existence are characterized primarily by connections across various social barriers, not so much through the idea of common essence, let alone an essence indicating an independent and separate mode of being. Due to their heterogeneous backgrounds, the characters in the novel are very difficult to pin down to any essence, or essentialist origin or characteristic. The only thing in common to be found in the characters is the ability to love and feel compassion, and even this is realised in different ways in different cases. Furthermore, as already stated above, love is described as a connecting force, not as a characteristic in the manner of for instance shyness or boldness.

In the representative ethics of the novel, the obstacles to be removed are the various kinds of geographical, discursive, class-related and linguistic borders, instead of particularities or differences. And the thing to emerge after this removal is (re-)established connections. And here also lies the dissimilarity of the narrative's ethics to the Levinasian postmodern version. According to Levinas, there is no possibility of a fusion, but the relationship of the self to the other is characterized as an opposition, an encounter between irreconcilable differences. What is more, in Levinas' view, the self is subordinated to the other. The narration of Ghosh does not try to do away with difference, but neither does it highlight difference in any obvious way. Difference appears as an integral part of the narrative, as a normal characteristic of everyday life. But the opposition between self and other is something that the narrative does try to alleviate through connections and dialogue. Consequently, there is no subordination of the self to the other on the narrative level, but the characters' views are presented as equals in the dialogues.

In general, the self/other problematic in Ghosh's narration is somewhat different from that of, for example, the Western modernist novel, because his narrative on the whole does not back up the notion of the individual subject as the centre of consciousness from which the world is constructed. In *The Glass Palace*, the world comes to being through various different views and ideologies represented by several characters. These worldviews enter into dialogue through the discussions in the narrative thereby forming a representation of the whole.

It seems to me that Ghosh is primarily attempting to create narrative representations that create connections across all kinds of culturally constructed borders, be they those of language, ethnicity, religion, social class, or those between different epistemological models (for instance image *vs.* language) and representative techniques/discourses (oral tales, the style of manuals, the narrative modes of the classic realist novel, romantic fiction or the "novel of ideas"). This transcending of borders inevitably requires a certain emphasis on difference, as well as an awareness of realities as discursive constructions. In a sense, Ghosh has to play the (language)games of textuality and "discourse as power" to be able to avoid discursive appropriation and abstract homogenizing of heterogeneous groups to be able to secure the distinctive features of all the represented varieties.

By transcending culturally constructed borders through interhuman relationships and connections that are ethically aware in the ways demonstrated in this text, he tries to set the standard for the description of larger social and political issues, which are always present in the background of his writings. Inevitably this also presupposes the idea of some kind of common denominator, even if that were only the capacity for imaginative empathy needed for the establishment of interpersonal relationships. In Ghosh's writing there is no gap between the level of interhuman connections (ethics, personal) and the functioning of the society (politics, public), but the latter comes into existence as the natural offspring of the former.

Ghosh has embarked on a project that is ethical, but also politically valid. We all know what happens when a political model (such as, for example, nationalism) is brought in from the outside to define the relationships between people. The novels by Ghosh offer us a glimpse of how it might be if things were conducted the other way around and societies were built on the scene of interpersonality and interhumanity.

Notes

1. Amitav Ghosh, *The Glass Palace* (London: HarperCollins, 2000); references are to this edition, and they are given parenthetically, preceded by *GP*.
2. See Rabindranath Tagore, *Gora* (London: Macmillan, 1961). [Orig. 1909.]
3. Among similar kinds of discussions are for instance the one on Gandhi and the Ghadar party by Uma and Dolly (*GP* 222–224), the argument Uma and Rajkumar have on theoretical ideals *versus* practical action (*GP* 247–248), the discussion Dinu and Arjun have on Indians in the British army (*GP* 276–285), the argument Dinu and Uma have on Congress *versus* anti-facist viewpoints on World War II (*GP* 292–295).
4. David P. Haney, "Aesthetics and Ethics in Gadamer, Levinas, and Romanticism: Problems of Phronesis and Techne," special Issue on "Ethics and Literary Study," *PMLA* 114 (1999): 39.
5. Hans-Georg Gadamer, *Truth and Method*, 2nd ed., trans. Joel Weinsheimer and Donald Marshall (New York: Continuum, 2000) [orig. 1960), 322.

6. Haney 39.
7. Gadamer, 305.
8. Gadamer, 322.
9. For discussion of universalism and particularism in the works of Amitav Ghosh, see Tuomas Huttunen, "Narration and Silence in the Works of Amitav Ghosh," *World Literature Written in English* 38.2 (2000): 28–43.
10. Ranjita Basu, "Amitav Ghosh's Fiction: Turning the Full Circle," in *Indian-English Fiction 1980–90: An Assessment*, eds. Nilufer E. Bharucha and Vilas Sarang (Delhi: B.R. Publishing Corporation, 1994), 152.
11. Basu, 153.
12. Ira Pande, Review of *The Glass Palace* by Amitav Ghosh (2000), available at: <http://www.amitavghosh.com.html> (visited 28 December 2009).
13. See, e.g., Robert Dixon, "'Travelling in the West': The Writing of Amitav Ghosh," *The Journal of Commonwealth Literature* 31.1 (1996): 3–24, or Anshuman A. Mondal, "Allegories of Identity: "Postmodern" Anxiety and "Postcolonial" Ambivalence in Amitav Ghosh's *In An Antique Land* and *The Shadow Lines*," *The Journal of Commonwealth Literature* 38.3 (2003): 19–36, for detailed discussions on this issue.
14. Simon Critchley, *The Ethics of Deconstruction: Derrida and Levinas*, 2nd ed. West Lafayette: Purdue UP, 1999), 233.
15. Critchley 233.
16. Critchley 236.
17. R.S. Khare, "The Other's Double: The Anthropologist's Bracketed Self: Notes on Cultural Representation and Privileged Discourse," *New Literary History* 23 (1992): 15.
18. R.S. Khare 15.
19. Zygmunt Bauman, *Postmodern Ethics* (Cambridge: Blackwell, 1993), 82.
20. Emmanuel Levinas, *Totality and Infinity. An Essay on Exteriority*, trans. Alphonso Lingis (Pittsburgh: Duquesne UP, 1969).
21. Bauman, 82.
22. Bauman, 82.

Works Cited

Basu, Ranjita. "Amitav Ghosh's Fiction: Turning the Full Circle." In *Indian-English Fiction 1980–90: An Assessment.* Ed. Nilufer E. Bharucha and Vilas Sarang. Delhi: B.R. Publishing Corporation, 1994. 151–160.

Bauman, Zygmunt. *Postmodern Ethics.* Cambridge: Blackwell, 1993.

Critchley, Simon. *The Ethics of Deconstruction: Derrida and Levinas.* 2nd ed. West Lafayette: Purdue UP, 1999.

Dixon, Robert. "'Travelling in the West': The Writing of Amitav Ghosh." *The Journal of Commonwealth Literature* 31.1 (1996): 3–24.

Gadamer, Hans-Georg. *Truth and Method.* 2nd ed. Trans. Joel Weinsheimer and Donald Marshall. New York: Continuum, 2000. [Orig. 1960.]

Ghosh, Amitav. *The Circle of Reason.* London: Granta, 1998. [Orig. 1986.]

—. *The Glass Palace.* London: HarperCollins, 2000.

Haney, David P. "Aesthetics and Ethics in Gadamer, Levinas, and Romanticism: Problems of Phronesis and Techne." Special Issue on "Ethics and Literary Study." *PMLA* 114 (1999): 32–45.

Huttunen, Tuomas. "Connections beyond Partitions: Amitav Ghosh's *In An Antique Land.*" *The Atlantic Literary Review* 4.3 (2003): 87–107.

—. "Narration and Silence in the Works of Amitav Ghosh." *World Literature Written in English* 38.2 (2000): 28–43.

Khare, R.S. "The Other's Double – The Anthropologist's Bracketed Self: Notes on Cultural Representation and Privileged Discourse." *New Literary History* 23 (1992): 1–23.

Levinas, Emmanuel. *Totality and Infinity. An Essay on Exteriority.* Trans. Alphonso Lingis. Pittsburgh: Duquesne UP, 1969.

Mondal, Anshuman A. "Allegories of Identity: 'Postmodern' Anxiety and 'Postcolonial' Ambivalence in Amitav Ghosh's *In An Antique Land* and *The Shadow Lines.*" *The Journal of Commonwealth Literature* 38.3 (2003): 19–36.

Pande, Ira. Review of *The Glass Palace* by Amitav Ghosh (2000). Available at: <http://www.amitavghosh.com.html>. (Visited 28 December 2009).

Tagore, Rabindranath. *Gora.* London: Macmillan, 1961. [Orig. 1909.]

8

Transnational/Transcultural Subjectivities and Chronotopes in Diasporic Literature

MADINA TLOSTANOVA

"The writer's art is his real passport and not his nationality."

– Vladimir Nabokov

"It is OK to be a homeless ... but only if you are a homeless in Armenia."

– Agassi Ayvazyan (an Armenian writer)

Problematizing Diaspora, Diasporic Self and Diasporic Literature in the Post-national World

There are many definitions of diaspora and a number of leading cultural theorists have contributed to the interpretation of this concept in the last decades – from Edward W. Said's secular criticism with its non-ethnic-nationalist stance[1] to Homi K. Bhabha's unhomeliness,[2] from James Clifford's travelling cultures[3] to Paul Gilroy's rethinking of double consciousness in the Black Atlantic.[4] In the last few years diaspora has been theorized more and more in a subjunctive mood as well as in the context of the nation, and associated with a metaphoric and imaginary nature. William Safran called diaspora a "metaphoric designation" taking it out of the racial, ethnic or religious constraints.[5] Robin Cohen attempted to rework the definitions offered by Clifford and Gilroy, when he defined diasporas as positioned somewhere between "nations-states" and "travelling cultures" in that they involve dwelling in a nation-state in a physical sense, but travelling in an astral or spiritual sense that falls outside the nation-state's space/time zone.[6] The 1990s brought a further shift in the understanding of diaspora which merged more and more with transnationalism and transnational communities seen through the lens of globalization. This led even more to virtualization and problematization of diaspora. Some theorists even argue in favour of the insufficiency of the term 'diaspora' itself, in the analysis of more and more common *transnational* and *transcultural* aesthetic phenomena. The idea that one nation (in the political sense) equals one culture has always been conditional, even in the case of the most monocultural states. When we turn to post(neo)colonial, plurinational, diasporic phenomena, the relations between culture and nation become even more problematic. If national culture belongs to the imaginary of the nation, then transnational and transcultural are aimed at dismantling of the nation, in a way, overcoming it, each on its conceptual level. In the relations between transcultural and transnational, the clash between political and cultural that the traditional understanding of the nation attempted to alleviate, comes forward.

Diasporic literature is a concept that has existed for a long time, but earlier it was regarded more as a deviation from the national canonical form with its predictable combination of language, literary tradition, ethnic belonging and fixed territoriality that defined the author's identity. Diasporic writing often remained unaddressed in the study of world literature as a constellation of national literatures. However, it is obvious today that the critical mass of diasporic writing overweighs the traditional national canon and in the post-national age it shifts more and more towards the centre of the global literary process.

A simple analysis of the uses of diaspora in literary studies today demonstrates that this concept is often utilized as a synonym of immigrant and postcolonial literature. In the latter case, it replaces postcolonial as a less politically engaged term. It remains obvious however that colonialism and coloniality[7] as a residue of the long-term power structures created within colonialism and still defining culture, labour, inter-subjective relations and knowledge production, constitute the main frame for the diasporic literature and imagination today, as diasporas are historically linked with forced migrations, collective traumas and exile. It is true that in the last two decades at least, this major meaning of diaspora has been gradually changing to less openly violent forms, not marked by slave trade or genocide overtones. I do not mean the unregistered migrants, human trafficking and other grim forms of dispensability of lives today, but the more optimistic commercial and commodified forms of negotiating diasporic identities which, in the long run, can just as easily lead to painful dislocations and disorientations. Today, the previously existing cultural links between ex-colonies and ex-empires are blurred and diasporic writers often find themselves in someone else's metropolis or in the symbolic global cultural metropolis of neo-liberal age – the USA. With the decline of neo-liberal globalization this situation is likely to change in the coming decades. In case of many authors we find a complicated imperial-colonial ligature of attractions and alienations which gives birth to a specific poetics, reflecting their multiple crossing of modern spaces and the ontological dimension of transit.

It would be a mistake to say that diasporic, immigrant and postcolonial literature are simply synonyms. The problem with postcolonial theory and criticism is that it has been formulated for a particular space in particular historical context, using particular ideological and cultural logic. Thus, it cannot become a travelling theory for other imperial-colonial relations and locations. In the same way as postcolonial theory, diaspora cannot be a travelling term as several theorists have pointed out recently. Thus, Ruediger Heinze[8] argues that 'diaspora' has become an umbrella term and tends to look for unification and similarity in cases where intercultural and transcultural difference and tensions play a much more important role in fiction than an imaginary diasporic unity. On a more fundamental level, the problem with the term 'diaspora' as a theoretical tool is, in my opinion, that, identical to postcolonial studies, it fails to question the terms and the content of conversation with modernity, retaining its basic myths and intellectual operations based on subject-object dichotomy. Seemingly deconstructing the nation, diasporic studies paradoxically still keep it as the norm and a point of reference. As any travelling theory, it unavoidably leads to distortions and oversimplifications. Thus, the concepts of diaspora and diasporic literature are highly problematic.

Like the majority of difference and diversity discourses in modernity, diaspora and its cultural products are linked with rethinking of the nation-state, its frontiers, discourses and identities. In Gilroy's opinion, the nation-state is the institutional means to terminate diaspora dispersal: on one side, through assimilation and, on the other side, through return.[9] One can add that the nation-state itself is one of the major manifestations of the colonial matrix of power which even when it is transformed today, cannot quite accommodate diaspora and strives to take it this way or the other to the economy of sameness and thus, to assimilation and control. Even if the new forms of transnational business elite, and transcultural diasporic cosmopolitan elite – easily tamed and commodified as the new form of "colonial goods," the majority of diasporic lives in the world remain dispensable. Historically and spatially situated the relational concept of nation-state and the national itself undergoes a major transformation today, not just a superfluous remodelling as in the case of multiculturalism or identity politics. And it seems that theorizing this shift and the birth of a specific corresponding subjectivity requires concepts other than diaspora.

Steven Vertovec points out the three main meanings of diaspora: "diaspora" *as social form*, "diaspora" *as type of consciousness*, and "diaspora" *as mode of cultural production*. He insists on an identified group characterized by its internal relationship – despite dispersal. In his opinion, diasporic members are still linked by a commonality (ethnic, racial, religious, historical, linguistic, and so on).[10] Thus, the concept of diaspora retains in this case a strong sense of place, an association with a homeland, a necessity of re-territorialization, even if imaginary, while a contemporary subject tends to associate himself/herself more and more with migration and transit. If he/she arrives at some place, it is not likely to be a new home where he/she can and wants to re-territorialize, but an airport, to quote a contemporary Black Diasporic writer Caryl Philips.[11] In other words, there is a pronounced focus on movement, not on locality, on unhomeliness and in-between-ness as a paradigmatic state and on hybridity as a chosen identity. We can speak of the emergence of a post-diasporic self which juggles and shuffles cultures and which does not regard its deterritorialized condition as something that has to be overcome. Place in this case is not just a topographic space, but also a way of life in its material and spiritual manifestations. In the centre of such existential condition there lies the problem of cultural, linguistic, epistemic translation as an interpretation in the course of self-identification, a reconstruction of the past, as a result of which many recollections are erased and only some of them remain relevant – giving birth to the myth of exile and often turning the past into a commodity. The state of exile and in-between-ness is interesting from the point of view of the signifier and the signified and the problematic of referentiality. The in-between-ness of an exiled person, his/her being outside the common system of coordinates almost prescribes a non-stop movement, a dynamics, a change as a result of which the stability of the signifier and the signified and the peculiar logic of the sign and referent interaction are being constantly questioned and disturbed.

These people are border dwellers, not border crossers. And the fiction they write is not centred or arranged around previous hierarchies and binaries of home and exile, motherland and foreignness, immigration and exodus. Here, there is a constant threat of sliding towards a commercialized literature as (post-)colonial goods which is possible to overcome only through self-conscious irony, fluidity, flexible unsettled selves and forever changing masks avoiding any stable definition and playing on previous models of assimilation. This set of features is born out of necessity but can and does become a new and productive aesthetic mode. The majority of most interesting writers who are traditionally regarded as diasporic, have radically questioned and re-conceptualized their links with a particular locale and communal identity, opting instead for a transcultural mode of living and creativity. That is why, in the books written by transcultural writers – Gloria Anzaldúa, Achmat Dangor, Andrey Volos, Salman Rushdie and many others – we encounter vivid metaphors of such de-centred existence and negotiating self from continent to continent. To quote Bharati Mukherjee, they write of the "hurly-burly of an unsettled magma"[12] between two or more cultural worlds. Mukherjee calls herself a four hundred-year-old woman, stressing the duration of her cultural journey from Faridpur to Manhattan. However, it is not New York that is the centre or a new reference point in the unsettled magma of her narratives – there are no concepts of centre and periphery here any more, India flows into America and *vice versa*. While new meanings and selves are constantly generated in these boiling points, whirlpools and spatial-temporal lacunas; the meanings and selves in their turn are to be questioned, deconstructed and arranged into a new and unfinished design by the authors.

William Safran insists on the founding myth and memory of the original homeland as the gist of diasporic disposition, the pessimism about the possibilities of assimilation and finally the dream of return.[13] I would argue that in most cases today some or all of these conditions won't work. The original homeland is questionable, particularly in the case of those writers who were born in immigrant families abroad, who are mixed racially, linguistically and culturally, who have no access to native languages and whose allegiance to a possible nation-state is highly problematic. Their assimilation can and is often quite successful, particularly if they choose a commercialized boutique multiculturalist stance. Most of them came voluntarily to the first world and do not plan to go back to the third world ever, or visit it only as tourists. Group consciousness and solidarity in their case has more to do with critical non-Kantian cosmopolitanism than any diasporic imagination *per se*. Their India, Russia or Africa is on a bookshelf or in a museum rather than in reality. If in Goethe's time with his idea of world literature, a literary text as a reservoir of foreign experience travelled long distances and was translated into different cultures, today it is often the writer himself or herself who travels and becomes a translated individual, forever hybridizing and creolizing his/her initial culture(s) with the new ones in the process of double epistemic translation. There have always been hybrid and creolized cultures such as the Caribbean, but previously there was no language and no conceptual frame to theorize them properly. After a postmodernist re-reading of the impact of modernity and globalization on societies, these tendencies have become increasingly common and in a sense, we can say that the whole world has become diasporic and uprooted today. Transcultural writers are particularly sensitive to the constant chaotic movement of great masses of people – looking for better jobs, better life, protection, basic human rights, survival under of a growing sense of lacking roots, national cultures, traditions, time as past, or belonging to any particular group.

Walter D. Mignolo has suggested that we create a new philology that would study not texts and aesthetics, but systems of literacy, the distribution and functioning of languages, based on border epistemology, taking into account the plurilanguaging, the transcultural and transimperial tendencies, not so closely connected with the discourses of national language and literatures, thus reconsidering the existing idea of comparative studies.[14] Rethinking literature from the viewpoint of imperial-colonial side of modernity is an understanding of literature as a floating signifier, without grounding it in any particular sanctified tradition. And transcultural writings are an example of such floating signifiers *per se.*

Rethinking Hybridity, Transculturation, Transgression and Diaspora

In Gilroy's *The Black Atlantic: Modernity and Double Consciousness*, diaspora is theorized mainly through hybridity.[15] This understanding of diaspora seems more fitting today when the number of fluid diasporas *versus* the crystallized ones is constantly growing,[16] as compared to any insistence on common origins and focus on primordialist locality or going back to something. A winning concept of double consciousness which Gilroy takes from African-American William Dubois, who formulated it a century back, is not only the concept of *Africana*, as it is to be found today practically in all diasporic cultural products. The question remains, however, as to what to do with this double consciousness. How to create a liveable world with its help, a world of multiple options and playful juggling of cultures instead of schizophrenic focusing on rejection and alienation?

Instead of hybridity which is used to describe diasporic mixing of previous elements with the new ones in order to create a certain presumably homogenous unity, I prefer to talk about transculturation, as theorized by a Cuban anthropologist Fernando Ortiz[17] and later rethought in the project of decolonization[18] as the main diasporic mode, because it describes in a better way the mutual double process as a result of which both diasporas and their host societies are changing in spite of the remaining power asymmetry. What is important here is the mutual dialogue, the reciprocal nature of this process and the impossibility of homogenous synthesized worlds and selves.

In the previously dominating Eurocentric linear model, it was generally accepted that the multicultural artistic phenomena can be divided into archaic and assimilationist. The deficiency of such a classification is obvious today when practically all transcultural writers cling to the in-between hybrid model, balancing the asymmetry of assimilation and transculturation which was typical of diasporic writings earlier. Rejecting the linear temporal matrix also means rejecting the idea of going back in time to some tradition or going forward to modernity. Space in this case is rehabilitated and taken out of the generally accepted model of time prevailing over space. But at the same time space is virtualized and problematized and re-rooting takes place based on principles other than language, soil, religion, and so on. Embracing almost all sides of identification, from the national which it largely denies, to the ethnic-racial and ethnic-cultural and gender problematic and regional differences, from the ecological discourse to the efforts to formulate the basis of the post-human existence, the aesthetics of transculturation focuses on the genealogy of colonial and imperial differences, within which the concrete local histories defining the creative worlds of various writers have been shaped.

Understanding diaspora today requires a set of tropes rather than scientific approaches, a non-rationalist metaphoric imagery rather than binary thinking. In the case of Africana diaspora, the Atlantic Ocean acts as a graphic symbol of constant dis(re)location. In the case of other diasporas, there are also visual metaphors of exodus, transit and crossing. Thus, an Adygean diasporic anthropologist Seteney Khalid Shami points out the importance of the imagery of ship as a symbol of dis(re)location for the gendered diasporic imagination of Northern Caucasus people who left their land *en mass* in the mid 19th century, as a result of its annexation by the Russian empire and crossed the Black Sea in unbearable conditions, packed in many ships in the direction of the Ottoman Sultanate. In Shami's formulation, this largely unknown diaspora, like the well-known Black or Indian diasporas, was also a prehistory of globalization and generated a complex negating-continuing attitude to the homeland.[19] Many of these people who later dispersed all over the Middle East and today venture to go back sometimes to their motherland, were forced to change their identities literally on board – from pagan to Islamic, from peasant to warrior, often from free to slave. A modern diasporic self in contrast to these historical instances, feels truly at home only in transit – in the airport, on board a ship, on the road, and in transgression. But the question remains, how diasporic is it? Or is it diasporic at all?

Transgression is a postmodernist term but we can also theorize it within the frame of leaving the logic of modernity and its rhetoric as an act of epistemic delinking, in Mignolo's words.[20] It is crucial that transgression questions the linearity of the process and rejects the previous idea of continuity, offering instead the familiar either/or logic, the possibility of a non-positive assertion, in Michel Foucault's understanding. What is crucial here is crossing the border that used to be uncrossable, going beyond some unsurmountable limit. Within the postmodernist frame this limit remains inside the Western tradition, even if critically assessed. In case of alter-modern paradigms (and many transcultural post-diasporic writers belong precisely there), it is connected with the fact that people do not just cross borders, they become borders themselves, to quote Anzaldúa: "To survive the Borderlands/you must live *sin fronteras*/be a crossroads."[21] What is at work here is the birth of a new subjectivity which leaves not only the commercial paradigm, but also the deeper epistemic and ontological grounds of Western modernity performing a rupture and delinking from the rhetoric of modernity and its hidden logic of coloniality. The aesthetics of transculturation seems to be one of the most fitting places to practise this new subjectivity.

Transculturation is based on the dynamic multiplicity, primarily of the epistemic and not just ethnic-cultural or linguistic nature, presupposing a new understanding of borders, migrations, multilingualism, cultural diversity, transnational languages and traditions. Transculturation as a new episteme is based on the cultural polilogue in which there should not be a complete synthesis, a complete cultural translation, where cultures meet, interact, but do not merge, retaining their right to "opacity." The Caribbean philosopher and poet Edouard Glissant claims that linguistic creolization inevitably leads to epistemic creolization. Hence, his famous metaphor rejecting the usual understanding of pure and simple language, clearly reflecting as in a mirror, the object under cognition. Glissant speaks not only of the right to difference but also the right to opacity, "that is not enclosure within an impenetrable autarchy but subsistence within an irreducible singularity. Opacities can coexist and converge, weaving fabrics. To understand this truly one must focus on the texture of the weave and not on the nature of its component."[22] Mukherjee echoes this stance when she comments that there is never a complete merging of past and present, first and third world, there are always certain parts of the fractured self that are not subject to confluence, that always remain Indian or American in her case, that slide along the surface of the masks of newer selves.[23]

Transcultural subjectivity is a trickster of the era of globalization marked by a ludic identity, which is a non-competitive, non-Gadamer and non-Huizinga kind of game, described by Maria Lugones in her essay on playfulness, world-travelling and loving perception.[24] It has nothing to do with a deadly Western agony. Instead, Lugones' and other transcultural tricksters' playfulness refers to a loving attitude while travelling across other people's "worlds." It is an openness to self-construction and the idea that no rules are sacred: "We do not worry about competence ... We do not abandon ourselves but we are not stuck in any particular world ... We are there creatively."[25] This kind of a playful trickster is devoted to the process of constant metamorphosis and his/her subjectivity is a masquerade, but it necessarily has a contesting dimension. In Chela Sandoval's words, this subjectivity is an

> oppositional agent who accesses differing identity, ideological, aesthetic and political positions. This nomadic morphing is not performed only for survival's sake, as in earlier, modernist times.

> It is a set of *principled conversions* that requires (guided) movement, a directed but also diasporic migration in both consciousness and politics, performed to ensure that ethical commitment to egalitarian social relations to be enacted in the everyday, political sphere of culture.[26]

Metamorphosis is expressed not only in the creative idea of the world as a re-enchanted space, as a non-ending chain of changing, impossible to fix, rationalize and define once and for all, negating the very possibility of naming, but also in the principles of constructing the fictional characters and the negotiating narrative itself. Metamorphosis is often considered in connection with the mythology of opposition, survival, tricksterism, developed practically in every colonized tradition. The Guyanese writer Wilson Harris has analysed the close relationship of bodily metaphors and metamorphosis in Caribbean literature and the folklore origin of trickster motifs, such as the image of Anansi spider and the limbo dance, which recreates the way from Africa to the New World. Harris expresses this in the image of a dismembered but never dying God or a man, approaching the ideal of unstable protean physical nature and non-finite metamorphosis of living and dead, resurrected and changed, which corresponds to the spiritual awakening and is also expressed in the corporeal metamorphosis, when the imagined and the real disappearance and shifting towards the new and different condition help to cope with the unbearable and oppressing world around.[27]

A poetic play on metamorphosis dressed in the garb of peculiar canonical counter discourse is *Kafka's Curse*[28], an ironic novel by Achmat Dangor African writer of Indian and Muslim origin. It is transcultural and transgender palimpsest. We meet a modern trickster Omar Khan passing for Oscar Kahn in order to win a place in the apartheid society and later – the love of his White Anna, and a more radical angry female stance of the psychoanalyst Amina Mandelstam – a young woman with a Muslim name and a Jewish surname, whose role in the story seems to be that of a destroying goddess, punishing all males. Kafka's curse afflicting Oscar (as Majnoen, he turned into a tree) is a punishment for his urge to assimilate, for his breaking the nature to fit the life of the White establishment. Oscar and his wife somehow switch the usual assigned gender roles – she, as a White person, performs the part of the desiring actor. It is not the husband who looks at her with desire but rather she herself gazes at him with a typical Western male gaze, at the same time remaining a chaste female on a pedestal. But we would find practically no description of Oscar's gazing at Anna while he remains apprehensive in a typically colonial way of how others see him, instead of focusing on looking at others. His fantastic association with the tree introduces tactile rather than visual overtones into the text.

There are many variants of tricksters in transcultural fiction – a Hodja Nasreddin and a lumpen, a rogue and a homeless person. Sometimes all these identities merge in the image of a new Ahasuerus, a paradigmatic example of which is Rushdie's Moraes Zogoiby. If earlier there was a firm connection of identity with the concept of home in a wider metaphorical sense, today individuals radically change their sense of belonging together with the collapsing institutes of state, family, economics, education, and so on, that provided the stability and socialization earlier. For many, home is nowhere and it can be their own choice or a forcefully imposed condition. Such people become adventurers without stable and far-reaching motivations. They become the modern rogues or picaros without biographies, with just a chain of loosely connected adventures in each of which they act in a new role and in a sense-create themselves anew.

Countless variants of exile and deterritorialization metaphors are particularly interesting in those cases when the authors attract attention to the ontological and existential aspects of this problem, when the characters undergo not just a physical transplanting, but an involuntary movement from one system of values and discourses into another – in the form of internal migration or a violently imposed immigrant status. The problem of cultural translation and un-translatability acquires then a specific meaning because it is not always connected with a clear juxtaposition of linguistic and even epistemic models. Without such a translation – however inadequate and tentative – an exiled person remains without an identity and hence invisible. In this situation the easiest way out is self-irony and tricksterism, manifested in today's fiction in an infinite number of unruffled ironists with easily hurt souls and a slightly detached attitude to their own translated image.[29]

The Aesthetics of Transculturation and the Imperial/Colonial Chronotope

No matter if transcultural writers today occupy a celebrating or a negating position, focus on nostalgia or melancholy, the basic (post-)diasporic problems in literature will be those of time and space, consequently home and memory, border crossings and border dwellings and a (post-)diasporic persona – who she or he is, what his or her ways of adapting to multiple realities are, how he or she is created as a playful, forever changing trickster. These issues are brilliantly embodied in the works of many transcultural writers – from Achmat Dangor to David Dabydeen, from Salman Rushdie to Bharati Mukherjee.

The in-between space of transculturation gives birth to its own epistemology, to its own discursive practices and aesthetics, based on the optics of stereoscopic vision and creation of the specific fictional reality under an angle to the real one, the stylistic and discursive collages, and certain recurrent leitmotifs, the essentially unfinished and open metamorphosis, the turning of the self *vs.* other dichotomy inside out, the inclination to complex grotesque forms and the fantastic, as well as certain metaphors, such as the metaphor of home and symbolic un-home-li-ness and hybridity, to specific images, such as the image of the ex-empire and ex-colonizer, an interest in the creation of the chronotope of in-between-ness and constant transit, to the negative time-space, giving birth to the migrating, self-rejecting, de-centred narrative forms.

Transcultural aesthetics is a multiple re-conceptualizing of epistemic, cultural, social and economic, as well as physical de-territorialization which is considered from an in-between position avoiding modernity/tradition dichotomy. The aesthetics of transculturation can be defined through the multiplicity and, at the same time, unfinished position and subjectivity of the practising individual, who is between the ironically and critically regarded European aesthetics and epistemology, as he/she clearly sees its contextuality and limitations, and the episteme of the marginalized, of the absolute and non-absolute others.

Living and writing in various locales, growing out of different traditions (national, philosophic, ethnic-cultural, linguistic) many contemporary writers refer to the same or similar problems, themes, images, metaphors – not because there is a "spiritual telepathy" between them or the traditional influences and borrowings, but because they cannot avoid the rhetoric of modernity with its hidden logic of coloniality, against which their art is inevitably oriented. Transcultural sensibility is best expressed in the problematics and metaphors of migrations, in-between-ness, transit, defining the existential situation of the subject of this world – a radically deterritorialized individual. But this radically deterritorialized nature of his/her new existence in the global world cannot erase the sense of specific locale that he/she is attached or used to be attached to, be they real or imagined, national or ethnic, sexual or social.

It seems that the pure diaspora model refers to the 1960–1970s with their ethnic revivals and black-and-white restrictive logic. While transcultural literature of the 1990s and global literature of the 2000s is characterized by a different and open mentality and transforming, not conserving culture, not going back to something. Evolution of diasporic imagination in the 1990s goes in the direction of further problematizing space and weakening of its links with any concrete locale. The graphic realization of this tendency is the emergence of transcultural in-between chronotope in ex-diasporic writings.

Mikhail Bakhtin singled out a specific type of existential psychological chronotope connected with human self-identification and exceeding the frame of static mythic and folklore elements. The scholar named it a border chronotope or a threshold chronotope.[30] Obviously, Bakhtin was not interested in imperial/colonial relations and even less in imperial and colonial differences. That is why, his border chronotopes are silent about imperial and colonial power differential. But what happens if we depart from Bakhtin's "border chronotope" and look at this concept through the lens of "coloniality of being"[31] as it manifests itself in the works of transcultural writers coming from or writing about the cultures that have been marked with imperial/colonial difference. The imperial/colonial chronotope is characterized by in-between-ness, the protean nature, the constant state of transit, nonfinality, parallel deterritorialization and dehistorization (that is, falling out of space and time) – in short, by everything that Rushdie has called "being elsewhere,"[32] thus defining a possible territory of transcultural fiction, which is not limited politically or linguistically, but only in an imaginative sense. Contrary to Rushdie, I think that it is not just the blurred category of imagination that is at work here, but a particular condition of transcultural subjectivity – that of restless non-belonging and a specific double consciousness, which generates complex relations with time and space and works for the creation of transcultural chronotope that in its turn defines the subjectivity of its inhabitants and the ways in which they cope with imperial/colonial differential.

The degree of invented-ness of the colonial/imperial topos, of the imagined nature of space – is different in the works of various transcultural writers, but almost always it negates the conglomerate of locale, ethnic culture and time as the basis of poetological system, typical for authenticity discourses. The way out of the dilemma of permanent transit has been looked for at the juncture of western and non-western epistemologies and aesthetics. If we deal with subaltern Eurasian empires and colonial spaces which are situated between such imperial configurations, the number of traditions, played on, questioned and interrelated in such transcultural works becomes much wider and more complex, leading to additional split nature of identification and particular models of imperial/colonial chronotope.[33]

The "imagined geography" of transculturation is an intentionally invented space, based on playing on various cultural topoi, recreating and rethinking the artistic reality, distorting the angles under which it is placed in relation to the real world. It is built on the tendency to subjectification, to the more and more pronounced isolation from any real locales, to the unimaginable and ephemeral nature of spaces, which gradually leads the authors further and further away from any spatial stability and materiality. For example, Rushdie, marked with a specific imperial-colonial history, who began with the highly politically engaged and rooted in reality Peccavistan in his *Shame*, gradually came to such consciously utopian constructed spaces as Palimpstine and Mooristan in *The Moor's Last Sigh*, that exist entirely inside the character's mind, inside his split "self" and are often based on fictional and mythic rather than any real political overtones.

In the imperial/colonial chronotope, topos largely recreates the old model of utopia or dystopia adding to it the mutopian element as well.[34] The idea of nowhere-ness, lying in the basis of this chronotope, is close to the meaning of the word "utopia" itself. What comes to mind here is not even Thomas Moore's *Utopia* (1516),[35] but rather such transcultural works as Anglo-Australian author Samuel Butler's *Erewhon* (1872)[36] – an anagram of the word "nowhere" and a literal translation into English of the Greek "utopia," where we encounter the theme of naming as the creation of the symbolic and real "home" that lies in the basis of many literary works from various locales, sensitive to the imperial/colonial problematic. A classical example in this case would be the Caribbean aesthetics. Migrations in the mutopic or dystopian space are a metaphoric way to salvation by means of some magical reality which turns into a mirage intrigue, a vicious circle, a wandering in the literal and figurative sense, based on temptations and semblances. Wonderings and deceptions, the mirage glimmering and enchanted space lie in the basis of the characters' misadventures in many fictional works. The enchanted nature of such 'another world' with its highly subjective time and relative space can be defined as the deception of space, where the characters' existential adventures are set in a number of plot elements – each of which has its own mini-topos and often a number of well-known and actively re-conceptualized literary allusions and myths.

Transcultural sensibility is often the sensibility of exile, deterritorialization, which Kateryna O. Longley aptly called "the fifth world", populated with the uprooted and displaced people for whom it becomes almost impossible to find their way through the impenetrable fence of barriers and obstacles.[37] The logic of interaction of cultural influences in the subaltern empires and their colonies is deeply rhizomic and based on the horizontal links and non-systemic differences, while any efforts to impose binarity on these locales from outside, ultimately fail. At the same time the cultural, religious and ethnic incompatibility of the colonizers and the colonized in the space of Russian/Soviet or Ottoman empires has never been clearly asymmetrical in favour of the more modernized colonizer, as it was in the case of Great Britain or France.

Time in the chronotope of in-between-ness changes its usual characteristics, such as linearity, one dimension and irreversibility, becoming multidimensional and moving with different speeds and in different directions, while the point of non-return (irreversibility) becomes highly arbitrary and can easily be negated. The Christian linear evolutionary idea of time, dominant in modernity, as well as the efforts to correlate it with the destiny of humankind, is constantly presented as relative and arguable. This leads, on the one hand, to the revival of various concepts of cyclical time, both connected with traditional cultures and newly created and on the other hand, sometimes, in the works of the same authors, the concept of time correlates with the re-conceptualized but recognizable idea of time and history, coming from natural sciences. That is why a character from transcultural fiction easily combines the cyclical half-forgotten traditions, the logic of a net-game and notions of post-human existence.

The external and seemingly more objective time moves in several directions, so that linearity entangles and clashes with cyclical and backwards time models. Several time models also coincide in the minds of transcultural characters who cannot be easily attributed to the archaic cyclical model of time, because they live in the lacunas and gaps between the linearity of western modernity, the inadequacy of which they realize sharply, and other time structures, which are being created in their minds in various situations and often act together. A relatively subjective time which is born as a result, does not have a duration in the usual understanding of the word, or, in Bakhtin's definition, "falls out of the normal flow of biographical time."[38] Subjectification of external time leads to extreme relativity of personal time, to its arbitrary acceleration or (less often) slowing down, sometimes, thickening, when another acquires the ability to live out several lives – no matter how short or unhappy they are. Such characters live out several lives which seem to be crammed into one physical existence, pressed like a spring – in accordance with the fairytale beginning of Mukherjee's novel *Jasmine*: "My past happened many lifetimes ago."[39]

City Chronotope in Transcultural Fiction

Let us now look at the chronotope of the imperial and colonial city in contemporary transcultural fiction from the point of view of imperial and colonial difference. The imperial city is often a sinister space where the imperial myths take shape and are embodied in the life stories of various people. Here, the colonial subject is defenceless and invisible. The imperial side of the city is viewed in utmost ruthless and phantasmagoric details by the individuals rejected and exiled by this space. They can be both colonial subjects and representatives of empire, carrying its deadening nature in themselves. Such a fearful and sickeningly attractive space is Moscow for the Baktinian character of Afanasy Mamedov,[40] or Istanbul in Orhan Pamuk's *Black Book*,[41] and London in Rushdie's *Satanic Verses*.[42] Transcultural authors often juxtapose the colonial city topos and the space of the imperial capital. Depicting the colonial city as a crisscrossing of various imperial and colonized cultures, they do not necessarily base it on predictable accusations and resentment, but rather mark these portraits of colonial spaces with paradoxical nostalgia for the lost and imperfect, but still a paradise. Hence comes the idealizing of his childhood in *Baku* by Mamedov and of *Khurramabad* (Dushanbe) by Andrey Volos,[43] and hence comes Bombay and Hong Kong nostalgia of Salman Rushdie and Paul Theroux.[44]

Giles Deleuze and Felix Guattari, reflecting on the contrast of the state and the nomadic war machine, divided spaces into smooth and striated, giving an example of Chess and Go – the smooth space of Go in contrast with the striated space of Chess game, nomos against polis.[45] The chaotic postimperial and postcolonial space often reacquires the quality of smoothness and stops to be striated, but it retains the traces of previous times, of crisscrossing of various imperial state machines, and it is important to try to understand the logic of these half-erased lines, which effect the psychological reactions of the people living in these spaces.

The imperial city is the centre of metropolis and its miniature model, a conglomerate of its main discourses, both verbal and non-verbal, connected with human behaviour, with architecture and with the very way of domesticating the space. The colonial city is a playful space of mimicry, of non-identical copy of the metropolis, where not only the recognizable signs of colonization are palpably present in all their forms, but also the stability of the original is effectively shaken, leading to its hybridizing. Both topoi – the imperial and the colonial – undergo various artistic interpretations in the frame of the fantastic, the magic, the metamorphosing, giving birth to imagined hybrid urban spaces, particularly if the time aspect of the urban chronotope corresponds to the moment of disintegration of the empire and its reference system. The global urbanization of the postmodern space in its relation to exodus and re-rooting of deterritorialized people in the imagined gigantic cosmopolis, also brings forward rethinking of the city chronotope, where the modernizing logic with its linear progressivist change from rural to urban is reversed, particularly in the locales of civil wars and political turmoil today.

The most interesting interpretations of imperial/colonial city chronotope emerge in the works of those writers whose cultural, linguistic, ethnic, imperial/colonial and religious positioning is marked with a paradigmatic insuperable in-between-ness. They cannot be classified unanimously within one local history, living on the crossroads of many instead, and not accepting any of the histories completely. Their works cannot be so easily compared with the well-known postcolonial or diasporic fictional models. Very often, there are two or more cities living inside such writers, creating a third one in the author's imagination. Rushdie, who can easily be regarded as a paradigmatic case of such sensibility, called himself and people marked with the insuperable sense of exile and loss – "the world community of displaced authors."[46] This becomes not only the acceptance of their often immigrant status, but also the sign of the deep internal spiritual exile, a metaphysical outside-ness out of which their very art is born.

An Australian living in New York (Peter Carey), a Turkish author (Pamuk), a Muscovite with Bakinian roots (Mamedov), or a Russian from Tadzhikistan (Volos) – all offer different spatial and temporal transcultural models often based on the fairytale, fantastic imagery of utopian or dystopian kind, on the subjective, many-directional time. Within the city chronotopes presented in these writers' works, there are several recurrent minitopoi organizing the space and the time of the imperial and colonial city – the market square, the cemetery, the underground and so on. Their works are also stories of painful modernization, fighting with and conquering the previous local traditions, bringing forward its own myths, meta-narratives and unresolved dilemmas of subjectivity. This happens in Pamuk's case in a semiotic way, takes a nostalgic Proustian form in case of Mamedov, acquires a fantastic postmodernist twist in Carey's fiction,[47] is expressed in the specific double vision, circulating between the oriental fairytale and the cruelty of almost documentary in Volos's narrative, while the empire itself acts for many new modern Ahasueruses as an absent and hostile space, where they do not and indeed cannot feel at home.

Coda: Transnational, Transcultural, Transgressive Authors

To sum up, I must say that I am a little skeptical about diaspora as a viable theoretical concept in the contemporary world. Maybe it has to do with my own critically cosmopolitan and decolonial stance and a refusal to associate myself with a particular locale, even if imaginary, with a particular language, ethnicity or religion. Living in a cultural metropolis of the ex-Soviet empire, I do not find any points of contiguity with Moscow Caucasus or Central Asian diasporas that I am linked with by blood alone, just as I do not feel many points of congruence with ethnic Russians. The diasporic seclusion rejects people like me by definition and refuses to come to terms with any ironic rendering of sacred nation myths by any transcultural post-diasporic writers, as I had a chance to find out recently after I published my own transcultural fictional experiment. In my view, it is precisely the writers who are overcoming diaspora that are most symptomatic for today's cultural dynamic and also throw a bridge into the future. It is more fitting to call them transnational, transcultural and even transgressive authors, although each term has to be reconsidered in order to properly theorize such (post-)diasporic writing and thinking, which acutely reflects our complex and constantly changing world. My article only posed some problems in this area while their proper conceptualization is definitely a task for the future.

Notes

1. Edward W. Said, *The World, the Text and the Critic* (Cambridge: Harvard UP, 1983).
2. Homi K. Bhabha, *The Location of Culture* (London: Routledge, 1994).

3. James Clifford, "Travelling Cultures," in *Cultural Studies*, ed. Lawrence Grossberg, Cary Nelson and Paula Treichler (New York: Routledge, 1992), 96–116.
4. Paul Gilroy, *The Black Atlantic: Modernity and Double Consciousness* (London: Verso, 1993).
5. William Safran, "Comparing Diasporas: A Review Essay," *Diaspora* 8.3 (1999): 255–291.
6. Robin Cohen, *Global Diasporas: An Introduction* (London: University College of London Press, 1997).
7. Anibal Quijano,"Coloniality of Power, Eurocentrism, and Latin America," *Nepantla: Views from South,* 1.3 (2000): 533–580
8. Ruediger Heinze, "A Diasporic Overcoat? Naming and Affection in Jhumpa Lahiri's *The Namesake*," *Journal of Postcolonial Writing* 43.2 (August 2007): 191–202.
9. Paul Gilroy, "Diaspora," *Paragraph* 17.1 (1994): 207–212.
10. Steven Vertovec, "Three Meanings of 'Diaspora', Exemplified among South Asian Religions," *Diaspora* 6.3 (1997): 277–299.
11. Caryl Philips, *A New World Order: Selected Essays* (London: Secker & Warburg, 2001).
12. Bharati Mukherjee, "A Four Hundred-Year-Old Woman," in *Critical Fictions: The Politics of Imaginative Writing*, ed. Philomena Mariani (Seattle: Bay Press, 1991), 27.
13. William Safran, "Diaspora's in Modern Societies: Myths of Homeland and Return," *Diaspora* 1.1 (1991): 83–84.
14. Walter D. Mignolo, *Local Histories/Global Designs. Coloniality, Subaltern Knowledges, and Border Thinking* (Princeton: Princeton UP, 2000), 220–221.
15. See Gilroy, *Black Atlantic.*
16. Alain Médam, "Diaspora/Diasporas: Archétype et typologie," *Revue Européenne des Migrations Internationales* 9.1 (1993): 59–66.
17. Fernando Ortiz, *Cuban Counterpoint: Tobacco and Sugar*, trans. Harriet de Onís (Durham: Duke UP, 1995). [Orig. *Contrapunteo cubano del tabaco y el azúcar*, 1940.]
18. See Mignolo, *Local Histories*; Madina Tlostanova, *Postsovetskaya literatura i estetika transkulturatsii* [Postsoviet Literature and the Aesthetics of Transculturation] (Moscow: Editorial URSS, 2004).
19. Seteney Khalid Shami, "Prehistories of Globalization: Circassian Identity in Motion," *Public Culture* 12.1 (2000): 177–204.
20. Walter D. Mignolo, "Delinking: The Rhetoric of Modernity, the Logic of Coloniality and the Grammar of Decoloniality," *Cultural Studies* 21.2–3 (March–May 2007): 449–514.

21. Gloria Anzaldúa, *Borderlands/La Frontera: The New Mestiza* (San Francisco: Spinsters/Aunt Lute, 1999), 217.
22. Edouard Glissant, *Poetics of Relation*, trans. Betsy Wing (Ann Arbor: U of Michigan P, 1997) [orig. *Poétique de la relation*, 1990].
23. Mukherjee, "Four Hundred-Year-Old," 26.
24. Maria C. Lugones, "Playfulness, 'World'-Travelling, and Loving Perception," in Lugones, *Pilgrimages/Peregrinajes: Theorizing Coalition against Multiple Oppressions* (Lanham: Rowman & Littlefield Publishers, 2003), 77–102.
25. Lugones, 96.
26. Chela Sandoval, *Methodology of the Oppressed* (Minneapolis and London: U of Minnesota P, 2000), 62.
27. Wilson Harris, "The Limbo Gateway," in *The Post-Colonial Studies Reader*, ed. Bill Ashcroft, Gareth Griffiths and Helen Tiffin (London and New York: Routledge, 1995), 378–382.
28. Achmat Dangor, *Kafka's Curse* (New York: Vintage International, 1997).
29. Madina Tlostanova, *The Sublime of Globalization? Sketches on Transcultural Subjectivity and Aesthetics* (Moscow: Editorial URSS, 2005).
30. Mikhail Bakhtin, "Formy Vremeni i Khronotopa v Romane: Ocherki po Istoricheskoy Poetike" [Forms of Time and Chronotope in the Novel: Sketches on Historical Poetics], in Bakhtin, *Voprosy Literaturi i estetiki* [Questions of Literature and Aesthetics] (Moscow: Khudozhestvennaya Literatura, 1975), 234–407.
31. Nelson Maldonado-Torres, "On the Coloniality of Being: Contributions to the Development of a Concept," *Cultural Studies* 21.2–3 (March–May 2007): 240–270.
32. Salman Rushdie, *Imaginary Homelands: Essay and Criticism 1981–1991* (London: Granta Books, 1991), 12.
33. Madina Tlostanova, "The Imperial-colonial Chronotope: Istanbul-Baku-Khurramabad," *Cultural Studies* 21.2–3 (May–March 2007): 406–427.
34. Istvan Csicsery-Ronay, "Notes on Mutopia," *Postmodern Culture*, An Electronic journal of interdisciplinary criticism (http://jefferson.village.virginia.edu/pmc) 8.1 (1997); available at: <http://pmc.iath.virginia.edu/text-only/issue.997/csicsery.997> (visited 9 January 2010).
35. Thomas Moore, *Utopia*, trans. Ralphe Robynson (London: Chatto, 1908) [orig. 1516; trans. 1551].
36. Samuel Butler, *Erewhon* (London: Trübner & Co, 1872).

37. Kateryna O. Longley, "Fifth World," in *Striking Cords: Multicultural Literary Interpretations*, ed. Sneja Gunew and Kateryna P. Longley (Sydney: Allen & Unwin, 1992), 23.
38. Bakhtin, 399.
39. Bharati Mukherjee, *Jasmine* (New York: Fawcett Crest Books, 1991 [1989]), 5.
40. Afanasy Mamedov, *Khazarsky Veter* [Khazar Wind] (Moscow: Text, 2000).
41. Orhan Pamuk, *Chernaja Kniga* [Black Book], trans. V. Feonova (Sankt-Peterburg: Amfora, 2000) [orig. *Kara Kitap*, 1990].
42. Salman Rushdie, *The Satanic Verses* (New York and London: Viking, 1988).
43. Andrey Volos, *Khurramabad* (Moscow: Nezavisimaja Gazeta, 2000).
44. Paul Theroux, *Kowloon Tong* (Boston: Houghton Mifflin, 1997).
45. Giles Deleuze and Felix Guattari, *Nomadology: The War Machine* (New York: Semiotext(e), 1992), 4.
46. Rushdie, *Imaginary*, 15.
47. Peter Carey, "Do You Love Me?" in *Colonial and Postcolonial Fiction: An Anthology*, ed. Robert Ross (New York and London: Garland, 1999), 121–132.

Works Cited

Anzaldúa, Gloria. *Borderlands/La Frontera: The New Mestiza.* San Francisco: Spinsters/Aunt Lute, 1999.

Bakhtin, Mikhail. "Formy Vremeni i Khronotopa v Romane: Ocherki po Istoricheskoy Poetike" [Forms of Time and Chronotope in the Novel: Sketches on Historical Poetics]. In Bakhtin, *Voprosy Literaturi i estetiki* [Questions of Literature and Aesthetics]. Moscow: Khudozhestvennaya Literatura, 1975. 234–407.

Bhabha, Homi K. *The Location of Culture.* London: Routledge, 1994.

Butler, Samuel. *Erewhon.* London: Trübner & Co, 1872.

Carey, Peter. "Do You Love Me?" In *Colonial and Postcolonial Fiction: An Anthology.* Ed. Robert Ross. New York and London: Garland, 1999. 121–132.

Clifford, James. "Travelling Cultures." In *Cultural Studies.* Ed. Lawrence Grossberg, Cary Nelson and Paula Treichler. New York: Routledge, 1992. 96–116.

Cohen, Robin. *Global Diasporas: An Introduction.* London: U College of London P, 1997.

Csicsery-Ronay, Istvan. "Notes on Mutopia." *Postmodern Culture.* An Electronic journal of interdisciplinary criticism (http://jefferson.village.virginia.edu/pmc) 8.1 (1997). Available at: <http://pmc.iath.virginia.edu/text-only/issue.997/csicsery.997>. (Visited 9 January 2010.)

Dangor, Achmat. *Kafka's Curse.* New York: Vintage International, 1997.

Deleuze, Giles and Felix Guattari. *Nomadology: The War Machine.* New York: Semiotext(e), 1992.

Gilroy, Paul. *The Black Atlantic: Modernity and Double Consciousness.* London: Verso, 1993.

Gilroy, Paul. "Diaspora." *Paragraph* 17.1 (1994): 207–212.

Glissant, Edouard. *Poetics of Relation.* Trans. Betsy Wing. Ann Arbor: U of Michigan P, 1997. [Orig. *Poétique de la relation,* 1990.]

Harris, Wilson. "The Limbo Gateway." In *The Post-Colonial Studies Reader.* Ed. Bill Ashcroft, Gareth Griffiths and Helen Tiffin. London and New York: Routledge, 1995. 378–382.

Heinze, Ruediger. "A Diasporic Overcoat? Naming and Affection in Jhumpa Lahiri's *The Namesake.*" *Journal of Postcolonial Writing* 43.2 (August 2007): 191–202.

Longley, Kateryna P. "Fifth World." In *Striking Cords: Multicultural Literary Interpretations.* Ed. Sneja Gunew and Kateryna P. Longley. Sydney: Allen & Unwin, 1992. 19–28.

Lugones, Maria C. "Playfulness, 'World'-Travelling, and Loving Perception." In Lugones, *Pilgrimages/Peregrinajes: Theorizing Coalition against Multiple Oppressions.* Lanham: Rowman & Littlefield Publishers, 2003. 77–102.

Maldonado Torres, Nelson. "On the Coloniality of Being: Contributions to the Development of a Concept." *Cultural Studies* 21.2-3 (March–May 2007): 240–270.

Mamedov, Afanasy. *Khazarsky Veter* [Khazar Wind]. Moscow: Text, 2000.

Médam, Alain. "Diaspora/Diasporas: Archétype et typologie." *Revue Européenne des Migrations Internationales* 9.1 (1993): 59–66.

Mignolo, Walter D. *Local Histories/Global Designs. Coloniality, Subaltern Knowledges, and Border Thinking.* Princeton: Princeton UP, 2000.

Mignolo, Walter D. "Delinking: The Rhetoric of Modernity, the Logic of Coloniality and the Grammar of Decoloniality." *Cultural Studies* 21.2-3 (March–May 2007): 449–514.

Moore, Thomas. *Utopia.* Trans. Ralphe Robynson. London: Chatto, 1908. [Orig. 1516; trans. 1551.]

Mukherjee, Bharati. "A Four Hundred-Year-Old Woman." In *Critical Fictions: The Politics of Imaginative Writing*. Ed. Philomena Mariani. Seattle: Bay Press, 1991. 24–29.

Mukherjee, Bharati. *Jasmine*. New York: Fawcett Crest Books, 1991 [1989].

Ortiz, Fernando. *Cuban Counterpoint: Tobacco and Sugar*. Trans. Harriet de Onís. Durham: Duke UP, 1995. [Orig. *Contrapunteo cubano del tabaco y el azúcar*, 1940.]

Pamuk, Orhan. *Chernaja Kniga* [Black Book]. Trans. V. Feonova. Sankt-Peterburg: Amfora, 2000. [Orig. *Kara Kitap*, 1990.]

Philips, Caryl. *A New World Order: Selected Essays*. London: Secker & Warburg, 2001.

Quijano, Anibal. "Coloniality of Power, Eurocentrism, and Latin America." *Nepantla: Views from South* 1.3 (2000): 533–580.

Rushdie, Salman. *The Satanic Verses*. New York and London: Viking, 1988.

Rushdie, Salman. *Imaginary Homelands: Essay and Criticism 1981–1991*. London: Granta Books, 1991.

Safran, William. "Comparing Diasporas: A Review Essay." *Diaspora* 8.3 (1999): 255–291.

Safran, William. "Diaspora's in Modern Societies: Myths of Homeland and Return." *Diaspora* 1.1 (1991): 83–99.

Said, Edward W. *The World, the Text and the Critic*. Cambridge: Harvard UP, 1983.

Sandoval, Chela. *Methodology of the Oppressed*. Minneapolis and London: U of Minnesota P, 2000.

Shami, Seteney. "Prehistories of Globalization: Circassian Identity in Motion." *Public Culture* 12.1 (2000): 177–204.

Theroux, Paul. *Kowloon Tong*. Boston: Houghton Mifflin, 1997.

Tlostanova, Madina. *Postsovetskaya literatura i estetika transkulturatsii* [Postsoviet Literature and the Aesthetics of Transculturation]. Moscow: Editorial URSS, 2004.

Tlostanova, Madina. *The Sublime of Globalization? Sketches on Transcultural Subjectivity and Aesthetics*. Moscow: Editorial URSS, 2005.

Tlostanova, Madina. "The Imperial-colonial Chronotope: Istanbul-Baku-Khurramabad." *Cultural Studies* 21.2–3 (May–March 2007): 406–427.

Vertovec, Steven. "Three Meanings of 'Diaspora', Exemplified among South Asian Religions." *Diaspora* 6.3 (1997): 277–299.

Volos, Andrey. *Khurramabad*. Moscow: Nezavisimaja Gazeta, 2000.

9

Globalizing European Peripheries

The Transnational and the Translocal in Monica Ali's *Alentejo Blue*

JOPI NYMAN

Introduction: An Alternative View of Globalization

In the context of the expansion of the European Union and the increased mobility of transnational migration, ranging from labourers to ERASMUS students exchange and from tourists to settlers, it has become evident that globalization affects the construction of European identities in ways that go beyond the traditional colonizer/colonized opposition and other similar dualisms. What this means is that the identities of European nation-states are changing because of both global and intra-European flows of migration generating new cultural expressions. While postcolonial literary studies have tended to prioritize the entry and experiences of the formerly colonial migrant in the metropolis over other forms of mobility, the new challenges of cultural contact call for new ways of reading postcolonial narratives to account for the peculiarities of increased cultural contacts.[1]

It is the aim of this article to explore the impact of such everyday contacts and "vernacular cosmopolitanisms" through an analysis of their representation in *Alentejo Blue* (2006), the second novel by the British Asian writer Monica Ali.[2] While Ali is known primarily for *Brick Lane* (2003), a novel narrating Bangladeshi immigrant lives in East London, *Alentejo Blue* addresses different conditions of contemporary migration. In my analysis, I will argue that this underrated novel set in rural Portugal deserves critical attention as it is an attempt to examine, through narratives of travel and stay, the problematics of migration and the transformed meanings of centre and periphery. Through a series of snapshots of European tourists, travellers, and their hosts in the small and remote Portuguese village of Mamarrosa, *Alentejo Blue* shows the presence of globalizing forces and the transnational in the locality, emphasizing that the global and the local are not oppositions but work in a parallel manner. Rather than simply representing globalization as threatening the alleged purity or tradition of a rural village with its premodern lifestyle, Ali's novel, read in a transnational framework, uncovers its silenced histories and links it with the wider world in order to counter dominant views of cultural contact. In doing so it shows how all identities, including those in European peripheries, are mobile and constructed in multiple ways in relation to the global. In other words, what I will argue is that *Alentejo Blue* provides an alternative to views of globalization that emphasize its metropolitan nature and reveals how it extends everywhere by showing how global flows affect the local in various ways.

Contextualizing Globalization

Contemporary cultural narratives of migration are embedded in the transnational processes of globalization which transform the ways in which national and other identities are lived and imagined. As such, the processes of globalization are not entirely new as world system theorists and critics of colonial discourse have shown, but the nature of contemporary globalization is somewhat different from its earlier historical predecessors.[3] While the links and nodes between different civilizations predate the conquests of European civilizations, transforming histories and creating cultural hybridities, the processes of today's globalization, owing to digitalization and the development of rapid communications technology, are experienced simultaneously in different parts of the globe. Unsurprisingly, the social theorist Anthony Giddens describes globalization as an expression of an era characterized by "the intensification of worldwide social relations which link distant localities in such a way that local happenings are shaped by events occurring many miles away and *vice versa*."[4]

In her book *A Sociology of Globalization* (2007), the sociologist Saskia Sassen argues that globalization involves two distinct modes. On the one hand, the term denotes the emergence of global actors and institutions such as the World Trade Organization as well as that of new global processes including financial markets and the transformation of cosmopolitanism.[5] On the other hand, it describes processes that at the current point in time are less evident at the global level but are transforming the naturalized meanings of the national and the local. In Sassen's view, processes such as the emergence of transnational activist networks and the replacement of national institutions and standards with international ones are examples of this:

> Although localized in national – indeed subnational – settings, these processes are part of globalization in that they involve transboundary networks and entities connecting multiple local or "national" processes and actors, or the recurrence of particular issues or dynamics in a growing number of countries or localities.[6]

What is important in Sassen's reading of globalization is that it involves a transformation in the relationship between the global and the local: issues and processes formerly understood as national may in her view be instances of the "localization of the global."[7] In other words, the nation-state is no longer a closed entity but the global is present in its processes, practices, and the daily life of its inhabitants, generating a variety of cross-border and transnational phenomena. It is this transformation in the role of the nation in contemporary globalization that characterizes contemporary globalization, to the extent that many theorists arguing for new modes of analysis describe studies focusing on merely one nation and country as examples of "methodological nationalism."[8] At the same time, however, in addition to nation, globalization changes the nature of the local, stripping it of its assumed isolation and allegedly peripheral status. Owing to increased transnational mobility that is not merely unidirectional, emigration and new forms of communication technology, the nature of the locality also transforms and "is no longer the prime referent of our experiences."[9]

While the transformed locality has been described by using such terms as "glocal" and "hybrid", terms that address its socio-cultural peculiarities, in this article I prefer to address Ali's representation of an apparently peripheral Portuguese village by using the term *translocal* to emphasize the role of locality. As proposed by the influential anthropologist James Clifford, this term is able to describe the contacts between cultures, contacts that in his view "begin with historical contact, with entanglement at intersecting regional, national, and transnational levels."[10] Following Clifford, I will argue that from the perspective of the village and the travels of its inhabitants this term is better able to account for its role in on-going identity construction. While the notions of the transnational and the diasporic would link Mamarrosa with larger cross-border networks and communities and the concept of glocalization would emphasize the adaptation of readymade global models by local people, the idea that the *translocal* conveys is the transformed sense of life in a particular locality – here a village community – in the era of globalization characterized by increased travel and cultural contact. In other words, my argument is that Mamarrosa functions as intercultural space or "a contact zone," as a locale where "the making and remaking of identities [...] takes place, along with the policed and transgressive intercultural frontiers of nations, peoples, locales."[11]

The Translocal Alentejo

For many readers and critics, Monica Ali's second novel was a disappointment. Readers familiar with her acclaimed first novel *Brick Lane* that explored global mobility and life in multicultural London, a cosmopolitan world city inhabited by displaced Asian migrants, may have found the focus and thematics of *Alentejo Blue* unexpected, strange, and alienating.[12] Set in rural Portugal and consisting of individual chapters telling of particular characters, it may also appear too loosely structured and lacking focus. Natasha Walter, reviewing the book for *The Guardian*, wishes that Ali had written about something closer to her heart – or to her status as the chronicler of Bangladeshi immigrants in Tower Hamlets: "you can't help wishing that Monica Ali had chosen to write about somewhere she knew better, or wanted to know better."[13] To quote Walter:

> The further you go in *Alentejo Blue*, the further you seem to get from *Brick Lane*. While her first novel grew cumulatively, with characters who were gradually revealed through different situations, this novel is structurally piecemeal, a collection of vignettes with no forward narrative thrust at all.[14]

Yet, as I will argue, the choice of setting as Portugal, while apparently masking Ali's interest in the effects of mobility and globalization and thus open to comments such as Walter's, is beneficial to the novel as it enables Ali to transcend a more limited British perspective by allowing an examination of the effects of globalization. Admittedly though, the choice is also one emphasizing the exotic and the touristic, as can be seen in some readers' reviews on the Amazon (UK) website.[15] Yet others praise her ability to convey a view of Portugal that is not superficial or merely stereotypical. However, it can be argued that it is through its setting that *Alentejo Blue* writes against a dominant trend that locates globalization in cities or other blatantly hybridized spaces.

Alentejo Blue consists of nine intertwined chapters each of which foregrounds a particular individual or couple. The characters, who are at the same time individuals and types peculiar to globalization, range from traditional labourers to *au pairs* and include omnipresent British tourists as well as a somewhat stereotypical representation of writer in exile through the character of Harry Stanton. It can be argued that the presence of these characters in a remote village is indeed what makes the novel a transcultural and translocal one. As the German critic Sissy Helff has recently argued, the transcultural novel can be characterized through its use of one or more of the following three features:

> [F]irst, if the narrator and/or the narrative challenge(s) the collective identity of a particular community; second, if experiences of border crossing and transnational identities characterize the narrators' lifeworld (*Lebenswelt*); and third, if traditional notions of "home" are disputed.[16]

Ali's novel can be seen to apply these ideas in a variety of ways. While the village appears quiet and traditional, a local community with its peculiar patterns of interaction and social life, it is not without links to the wider world. This becomes evident when the following passage from the second chapter of the novel describing a typical afternoon in Vasco's bar/restaurant is examined closely. While it apparently portrays a pure, untouched local space, in reality the identities of its inhabitants are formed through various border crossings, intercultural encounters and links with the globalized world, links that range from personal migration to the use of the internet (see *AB* 260). In other words, this means that the photographic image contained in the novel is lacking in depth, and to understand it the reader needs to locate its content, the image and the "memories" of the old men, in their proper historical context(s):

> The old men stood at the bar caressing their Macieiras and coughing up memories. In the black felt fedoras and black waistcoats, red handkerchiefs tied at the neck, they appeared to Stanton like postcards from the past, as picturesque as the crooked streets, the whitewashed houses, the doors and windows framed gaily in blue and yellow. (*AB* 26)

In this passage the use of the touristic as a narrative strategy is a mask hiding unspoken histories of cultural contact and dislocation and it shows how all identities are formed transculturally. By framing the traditional in the touristic, the novel contrasts an apparently national and folkloric past (extending to the present) with the allegedly modern values of the outside world – yet the national is always embedded in the transnational. At the same time the passage creates another false juxtaposition by contrasting an allegedly passive and objectified periphery with a supposedly active modernity with its representatives, British tourists and readers, gazing at a relic-like lifestyle. The bar, however, as the site where the men spend their time, tells another story. Rather than a site of a pure national past, it is an intercultural space hiding different narratives of globalization and border crossings as becomes evident in the people crowding it. For instance, its proprietor Vasco is a returned migrant, who has spent twelve years abroad, a time known as his "legendary stint as a barman in Provincetown, Cape Cod, the United States of America" (*AB* 27). In addition to revealing Vasco's past, the scene foregrounds the intercultural thematic as all other characters introduced in detail are similarly part of the global and the local. These include the exiled British writer Stanton, his friend Dieter, a German builder who is part of contemporary seasonal intra-European migration, and Ruby Potts, the promiscuous fifteen-year-old daughter of the expatriate British Potts family living a disorderly and drunken life in the vicinity of the village.

Hence, the function of the characters of the novel is to contribute to its imagining of globalization and to link Mamarrosa with the wider world. In doing so the novel presents characters who reflect on their position and identity in the current situation. To use Sissy Helff's words, they are examples of what she refers to as transcultural narration, "a process in which the narrative and the reader are constantly crossing and shifting boundaries between intercultural and transcultural spaces."[17] While this Portuguese village is apparently peripheral to contemporary globalization, the novel makes its links explicit in two ways, first, by showing how its inhabitants go out into the world, and, second, by showing how the foreigners, *estrangeiros* (*AB* 45), enter the village and thus make it an intercultural space.

The novel's references extending beyond the nation include both those that emphasize Portugal's connection with the wider world and often revolve around the nation's erstwhile glorious Empire and those bringing the world to the village. In the first case it is the restaurant owner Vasco in particular who plays an important role: migration is a part of his personal and family background. In addition to revealing Vasco's tragic experiences in the USA, the novel mentions that several members of his family have left the village before him. While Uncle Humberto opted "for a new life in Mozambique, of metal mines and miscegenation," Uncle Henrique desired "to fight the savages in Angola and save them from themselves and international communism" (*AB* 77) but never returned. The Portuguese empire is, indeed, a thing of the past, and a comparison between Portugal and the United States as a global empire-builder makes the former a laughing matter for Vasco: "'We had a big empire too' – Vasco turned purple and began to wheeze, tears in his eyes. It dawned on Stanton that he was laughing. 'Five hundred years ago'"(*AB* 41). Similarly, in Vasco's view the future belongs to Americans who will spread their ideologies and language all over the world, destroying local values and practices:

> In America now romance is dead. The feminists killed it and the men are scared. If a man opens a door for a woman he will end up in court. Sex discrimination.
>
> "You think it could never happen here?" he said. "These crazy Americans? Let me tell you, in my opinion it is only a matter of time."
>
> It's the way the world is. Even the Alentejo cannot escape. The United States of America is the Superpower and it is not just a question of guns. He said to Bruno, "What language do you think your grandchildren will speak?"
>
> Bruno pushed up his cap and grunted. Bruno is not a great thinker.
>
> "English, my friend," Vasco informed him. "With an American accent." (*AB* 86)

As Arjun Appadurai, a well-known scholar of globalization, has argued, the different global flows are not limited to the mobility of human beings from one nation and culture to another (ethnoscape) but globalization also involves the transmission of ideoscapes (as testified in Vasco's rendering of American sex discrimination in the passage above), financescapes, technoscapes, and mediascapes.[18] Mediascapes in particular flow across borders and construct what Appadurai calls imagined worlds, linking different cultures with each other.[19] Indeed, the inhabitants of the village are portrayed as consumers of globalized popular culture with shared values, watching Brazilian telenovellas (*AB* 190, 210), using Vodafone (*AB* 137), and wearing either Manchester United shirts (*AB* 54) or shirts with "big Chinese letters, or Japanese, down the front" (*AB* 185). Similarly, popular local music is rejected: "'Mariza? You're kidding. That's what we'll play when we break up'" (*AB* 185), as Teresa's boyfriend comments on her choice of music on their last night together. As a result of being linked with the wider world, Mamarrosa is at least partially losing its cultural specificity and entering the homogeneity of global culture. In today's Mamarrosa, then, it is possible to find a barman reading a

Las Vegas hotel brochure, dreaming that the flows of the mediascapes and ideoscapes will be followed with the flow of global capital (financescape) into the village. This shows that the village is fully embedded in the global network:

> "Listen," said Vasco. "Treasures of the ages await at Hotel Luxor's Giza Galleria. Located on the main level of the East Tower, enchanting fountains, beautifully sculpted statues and elegant stone walkways greet visitors when shopping Luxor-style at Giza Galleria." He passed a fat hand over his mouth. "Only in America, yes?"
>
> Stanton conceded this to be so.
>
> "But maybe also in the future in the Alentejo. Nothing is impossible." (*AB* 66)

International Migrations

As a sign of participation in the global economy, the novel juxtaposes more traditional internal migration with international economic migration but reveals that the former is not without its international aspects. While contemporary work-related migration patterns are addressed through such characters as Dieter the German builder, Telma Ervanaria (who has spent 15 years in Paris), and Teresa, a young girl desiring a position as an *au pair* in London, their historical counterpart is addressed in the narrative of the eighty-four-year-old labourer João and his friend and one-time lover Rui. This is not a mere juxtaposition but rather hints at continuity and transformation, emphasizing that the village has never existed in isolation but has always functioned as a node in the networks of modernization and internationalization. In doing so the narrative challenges what Helff has defined as the community's conventional collective identity.[20] Other spaces are indeed represented as providing opportunities for learning and expanding one's world view, as means of escaping the backwardness and oppressive politics of Salazar's Portugal and learning the internationalist ideologies of solidarity:

> He had been in France after the war, with all the other illegals, working the construction sites. He learned to read and write. "*Liberté, égalité, fraternité*," he said. "In France," he said, "a man has rights. He has dignity. He has respect." (*AB* 17)

In other words, what the narrative voices, is a view arguing that cultural contact and migration are part of the formation of European identities. This is confirmed in the dialogue between the novel's group of bowling old men; it reveals that for migrant labourers, European cities are not much different from the Portuguese capital:

"My granddaughter wants to go to Lisbon," said José.

"My son left London and went to Glasgow," said Rui. (*AB* 14)

In this context of migration the figure of the *au pair*, represented in the novel in the character of Teresa, provides a further example. According to the critic Bruce Robbins, who has studied its representations in diasporic writing by Jamaica Kincaid and Bharati Mukherjee, the *au pair* is often used in literary narratives as a marker of global modernity and upward social mobility, relocating a peripheral character in the metropolis and providing her with "universal civilization."[21] Robbins, however, also suggests that the *au pair's* travel to the metropolis does not necessarily mean that "nation and race are merely skins to be shed in the interest of quicker acculturation" but that the *au pair* narrative may also function as an expression of "explosive, even unconscious anger" and resistance.[22] *Alentejo Blue* appears to use the *au pair* narrative to address similar questions of global mobility but also shows seeds of resistance to global hegemony. While it is Teresa's wish to leave the restrictive life in Mamarrosa – where she, "like a social worker" (*AB* 169), is forced to take care of her widowed mother who spends most of her time in front of the television – for a better life in London, her decision is not unproblematic and is rooted in her family's financial problems: ever since being forced to leave the school following the death of her father Teresa has worked as a shop assistant in the daytime and sold life insurance policies in the evenings (*AB* 131, 159). For Teresa, London, or her fantasized version of it, promises social mobility and a glamorous lifestyle. Its modern conveniences are clearly contrasted with the backwardness of the village:

> João had no electricity. When the sun went down he would go to bed. Teresa imagined herself on an aeroplane, a mile high in the sky; she thought of herself in London, coming out of a restaurant or nightclub; she saw herself on an escalator, travelling through a

> department store that reached nearly as high as the plane. [...] In London, though, she would have her own television. Her room would be modern, perhaps with fitted wardrobes. She was to have her own bathroom. (*AB* 145, 154)

Regardless of the pull of London, Teresa remains uneasy about the change and its effects on her own life and relationship with her boyfriend Antonio. This is seen in her inability to tell her family and friends that the letter of acceptance from the office has arrived, revealing an uneasiness partially stemming from her limited knowledge of English. In negotiating her identity, she decides that she will go to London "as a woman" (*AB* 147), lose her virginity to Antonio, a decision aiming to liberate him from waiting for her: "It would be her gift to him. To make him free like that" (*AB* 147). The chapter ends with Teresa and Antonio having sex, but rather than orgastic pyrotechnics it is described in melancholic terms: "She kept her eyes open the whole time, watching the bamboo ceiling and counting the insects that fell" (*AB* 191). What is more significant, however, is what Teresa, now high on a spliff and beer, has understood right before the intercourse. Upon reflecting on her own position as a potential migrant, she deconstructs the pull of the metropolis and realizes that the centre and the periphery are literally *au pair*, equal, as Robbins reminds us,[23] rather than in a hierarchical relationship. The centre is not an object of fantasy and desire that will offer constant gratification. The following passage constructs global relationships as reciprocal, based on mutual exchange and transnational flow of people going in both directions:

> What was the point, though, really? Why was she going there? Those children with their Indian headdresses and their thoughtless expectation of love. Who would she be in London and who would be there to see? She would be there and the writer would be here, and the tourists would come or they wouldn't, Marco Afonso Rodriguez went and was coming back, and Telma Ervanaria was in Paris and Vasco was in Provincetown, and Mãe was lost in Brazil and everyone was going round and round and it didn't make one bit of difference as far as she could understand. They come here and I go there. Round and round. This bed, that bed, new bed, old bed. If the room would just hold still! (*AB* 190)

In short, the *au pair* narrative as used in Ali's novel seeks to resist hegemonic narratives of globalization that promote unidirectional relationships between the centre and its alleged peripheries. Teresa's realization, which takes place significantly on the same day when the first internet café opens in the village (*AB* 161), is that the centre does not provide a fixed identity. Rather, as a migrant her identity is in a flux, constantly negotiated, always between here and there, rather than strictly linked with one particular place. This indeterminacy of identity is also reflected in the words uttered by the young British boy Jay Potts. Displaced in a foreign country with his dysfunctional parents, he wonders: "Am I Portuguese now?" (*AB* 102).

At first sight the character of Marco Afonso, a migrant who returns to Mamarrosa in the final chapter of the novel, also appears to criticize a traditional understanding of the centre-periphery relation and the alleged primacy of economic migration. While all of the inhabitants in the village believe that Marco has made a fortune abroad, either in hotel business, electrical appliances, or dry cleaning (*AB* 264), he returns to the village practically empty-handed in a taxi, wearing a black cape and carrying no more than one bag. In the fantasies of the villagers, Marco Afonso is a messiah who will build either a 400–bed hotel or a centre for rural tourism (*AB* 262–263), depending on whom the question is addressed to. In the view of the cynical writer Stanton, Marco with his aphoristic comments on the mind and "Awareness" is a fake hippie-cum-philosopher: "Stanton knew what Marco was. Some old hippie, fresh from an ashram where they chanted and indulged in free love" (*AB* 273). As Marco turns out to have no plans for developing the village but prefers "to live in the present" (*AB* 287), the promise of his return is emptied out in his privileging of individualism. In the end, if discussed by using the terms introduced by the sociologist Anthony D'Andrea, Marco appears to embody a particular condition generated by globalization and hypermobility, namely neo-nomadism: "neo-nomads migrate through sites of practice and experience in search of excitement and insight into themselves."[24] In Ali's novel such self-centred travel resting on Marco's alternative New Age subjectivity appears problematic and ethically unsound to the entire community and by the end of the novel some villagers decide to ask him to leave. Unsurprisingly, Marco has already left the village in the middle of the night, leaving behind a piece of paper with a short and mundane message: "peace" (*AB* 298).

Regardless of their particularities, all migrants and travellers in the novel, representing the presence of global migration and the significance of cultural contacts in the formation of identity, are examples of the migratory character of contemporary societies. The sociologist Ulrich Beck claims that the movement of migratory masses has transformed the experience of mobility in the West, and he defines this phenomenon as contemporary "cosmopolitanization"[25] or as "cosmopolitanism from below."[26] This is a term referring to the experiences of ordinary, everyday border crossers rather than those of a limited class, as is the case in the traditional use of the term cosmopolitanism. It is also argued that the migrant's experience of travel, work, and stay abroad problematize the claims of nationalism and that the transnational migrant subject may have multiple alliances.[27] As Beck writes:

> Migrants embody all gradations of both/and: they are native foreigners and foreign nationals whose social competences are not only indispensable but also enrich cultural and public life by making it more colourful, contradictory and conflictual. Migrants are what is analytically excluded by the national either/or.[28]

In my discussion of the presence of transnational networks and translocal identities in the novel, I have emphasized the links of the traditional inhabitants of Mamarrosa with the global and shown how identity construction and transculturation take place in this locale. In addition to the transformation of the identities of its original inhabitants, *Alentejo Blue* also shows the presence of foreign nationals in Alentejo as its characters include both tourists and foreign nationals living in the village. The role of traditional tourists in the village, however, appears rather traditional since the foreign space is used for acting out (pre-)marital problems and finding one's self. These processes are triggered by a foreign lifestyle and, in the case of the young British couple Huw and Sophie, the moribund elements of the Roman Catholic religion as seen in their responses to a local tomb, the Chapel of Bones, full of human bones and skulls (*AB* 224–230). Similarly, the elderly tourist Eileen manages to challenge her husband's patronizing and sulking behaviour. The end of the chapter shows her sitting on a bench by the city square and telling him that "[i]t is my holiday [...] And I'd like to sit here and do nothing" (*AB* 129).

The British Abroad

The novel's most significant foreign nationals include the writer Stanton and the Potts family. The representation of the latter is particularly interesting as it reverses the more conventional modes of narrating of British travellers and their intercultural encounters. It is a family consisting of an alcoholic father Michael (a.k.a. China), a "dishcloth" (*AB* 39) mother Chrissie, and their two teenage children, promiscuous Ruby and lonely Jay. Having arrived in Mamarrosa with hopes of settling down and building a house, the family has run out of money and lives in an unfinished house with a swimming pool-cum-mudpool on the outskirts of the village. The dismal living conditions of the family emphasize their decay: while shown sitting "on high-backed leather-padded chairs" (*AB* 50) in their living room, linking them with a more luxurious past, the present includes the corpse of a dead and stinking cow in their yard (*AB* 48–49). The reversal, then, is more than a contemporary temperance or slum narrative but it constructs the Potts as third world citizens rather than as British expatriates. As a result, the family acquires various features of the non-Western Other. As a sign of this, they are repeatedly described as unwashed and wearing dirty clothes (see, e.g., *AB* 37, 46), a trope that also links them with Otherness and diminishes their status, as does Ruby's uninhibited sexuality leading to pregnancy and abortion. Further, the village inhabitants find the Potts repulsive, even frightening:

> A man, one of the *estrangeiros*, came towards her [Teresa], ducking to clear the orange trees. The black and tan dog was with him. Would everyone in London be so tall? The man wore a filthy vest and he had not shaved. Teresa stepped back to let him pass and for a moment was covered in confusion. (*AB* 137)

My reading emphasizing the Potts' role as the Other is supported by the portrayal of their contribution to the village *festa* – or what "in England [...] would be called a car-boot sale" (*AB* 45). The episode shows how people, both local and foreigners, try to sell "their junk," "useless possessions" including "wooden bowls, lidless teapots, broken furniture, mysterious plastic objects of indeterminate use" (*AB* 45), all signs of poverty and the Potts' entry into the fringes of modernity. The Potts' contribution to the sales is described as follows: "Chrissie sat on the open boot of the Renault 4. On a blanket at her feet she had arranged a few pans with broken handles and some rusting agricultural equipment" (*AB* 46–47); on another occasion she sells peg dolls for two Euros (*AB* 197). This Othering is taken further in Chrissie Potts's words where she sees herself in a different light, understanding now that her own position amidst the Portuguese has been transformed into that of an Other:

> I was thinking about when you see the Asian kids translate for their mums. The mums wear saris or baggy coloured pyjamas or some times a big black bag that covers everything except their eyes, so you don't really expect them to understand anything much. I was thinking I'm like that now. *I'm the bloody foreigner.* (*AB* 204; emphasis added)

In the end the Potts family, however, integrates into the local community and reconstructs itself: China finds work with a local builder and Chrissie works with the poor, conducting "voluntary work fit for a nun" (*AB* 271). Their accommodation may be a sign of the fulfilment of homing desire, a form of reconstructing home by accepting its transformed character in the space of the Other.

In contrast to the Potts, the exiled writer Stanton occupies a different position. On one level he represents a satirical version of the modernist myth of an exiled writer who, when cut off from his own culture, is allegedly able to provide in-depth reflections in his great masterpieces. In addition to, or instead of, trying to write his novel about the Romantic poet William Blake, Stanton spends considerable time in drinking and has affairs with both Chrissie and Ruby Potts – a potentially nationed choice for desire. It is also clear that, rather than offering an enlightened perspective based on critical reflection on the intercultural space of Mamarrossa, Stanton's limited cultural crossings do not enrich his literary imagination. Unlike the Potts family, Stanton contemplates leaving as seen in his thoughts in the final chapter:

> Stanton went out and gazed at the North Star, which appeared unaccountably bright. He cupped the back of his head and

> thought it was time. He wanted to go somewhere cold and preferably Teutonic where writers met in cafés with notebooks and grievances and discourse flowed on the meaning of life and of death. He rather fancied a road trip. He hoped to make it as far as Prague. (*AB* 297)

What the passage reveals is that Stanton's exile in Portugal is a romanticized fantasy to be replaced with a similar one, a fabricated dream of Prague as the site of budding writers. Paradoxically, like Marco Afonso whom he despises, Stanton remains unable to contribute to any community, be they artistic or local, and thus occupies a similar nomadic position with no commitment. While crossing borders and acting amidst foreign cultures, these transcultural experiences generate little change in Stanton. In opting for Prague, Stanton reveals a traditional modernist idea privileging the metropolis as a site of creation. Unlike Mamorrosa, the metropolis offers an imagined community of authors and literary discourse; in such a paradigm, as the cultural critic Caren Kaplan has shown, the European peripheries are void, unable to generate creation and can never be

> sites of modernist cultural production themselves: that is, they provide the raw materials to be synthesized in the generative locations of the modern, Western metropolis or they offer opportunities for spatial exploration on the part of metropolitans in search of metaphysical displacement.[29]

In other words, by remaining a believer in modernist myths of creation and its division into the binary model of centre and periphery, Stanton is unable to attain a transcultural identity or what the postcolonial theorist Homi K. Bhabha refers to as the Third Space.[30] Unlike the non-cosmopolitan travellers and migrants from the periphery whose identities are revealed to be translocal, this representative of the centre clings onto his preconceived values and "Teutonic" (*AB* 297) community. In contrast to Stanton's inability to learn from his cultural borderline crossings, translocal or transcultural identity, while not guaranteeing happiness or providing relief from the pressures of globalization, is at least a shared identity helping people to cope with globalization through community.

Conclusion: A Translocal Narrative

This article has argued that the representation of migration in *Alentejo Blue* shows that a place defined as periphery is embedded in the wider world. The global is present in this village in both the networks of its traditional inhabitants and the various European migrants visiting and staying there. In doing so the novel not only exemplifies the significance of contemporary cosmopolitanism as a principle structuring everyday cultural contacts practically everywhere in the world but continues Ali's explorations of the role of the transnational in the contemporary world. Referring to *Brick Lane*, Pirjo Ahokas has argued that its characters perform transnational identities and thus "challenge the initial binary of 'home' and 'abroad' and prove conducive to the emergence of postmodern female subjectivities characterized by fluidity, multiplicity and heterogeneity."[31] Similarly, the fluidity and multiplicity of the identities and narratives of the inhabitants of Mamarrosa shows how the binaries of "home" and "abroad," and, more specifically, "centre" and "periphery," are problematized and transformed in contemporary Europe characterized by migration and stay abroad. Rather than a failure, or a novel with a limited local focus, *Alentejo Blue* can be described as a translocal narrative as it expands the meaning of the local through the various transnational networks in which its inhabitants participate. At the same time it emphasizes the role of the community and its importance for one's identity.

Notes

1. See Jopi Nyman, *Home, Identity, and Mobility in Contemporary Diasporic Fiction* (Amsterdam: Rodopi, 2009).
2. Monica Ali, *Alentejo Blue* (London: Doubleday, 2006). References to the novel will be given parenthetically, preceded by *AB*.
3. See Suman Gupta, *Literature and Globalization* (Cambridge: Polity, 2009), 10–11.
4. Anthony Giddens, *The Consequences of Modernity* (Cambridge: Polity, 1990), 64.
5. Saskia Sassen, *A Sociology of Globalization* (New York: W.W. Norton, 2007), 5.
6. Sassen, 6.

7. Sassen, 4.
8. See Ulrich Beck, *The Cosmopolitan Vision*, trans. Ciaran Cronin (Cambridge: Polity, 2006).
9. Mike Featherstone, *Undoing Culture: Globalization, Postmodernism and Identity* (London: Sage, 1995), 117.
10. James Clifford, *Routes: Travel and Translation in the Late Twentieth Century* (London: Harvard UP, 1997), 7.
11. Clifford, 7.
12. As one reviewer puts it: "Having loved *Brick Lane* I was very eager to read this but it was a huge disappointment – so much so that I don't normally write reviews for Amazon but I am compelled to say 'save your money!'" Corrinne Milsom-Mann, "Go and read something less boring instead," review of *Alentejo Blue*, by Monica Ali, Amazon.co.uk (16 October 2006), available at: <http://www.amazon.co.uk/gp/cdp/member-reviews/A3R8MQS43S2RHZ> (visited 2 January 2010).
13. Natasha Walter, "Continental Drift," review of *Alentejo Blue* by Monica Ali, *The Guardian*, online ed. (20 May 2006), available at: <http://www.guardian.co.uk/books/2006/may/20/featuresreviews.guardianreview14> (visited 2 January 2010).
14. Natasha Walter, online.
15. See amazon.co.uk: <http://www.amazon.co.uk/Alentejo-Blue-Monica-Ali/dp/0385604866> (visited 29 January 2008).
16. Sissy Helff, "Shifting Perspectives: The Transcultural Novel," in *Transcultural English Studies: Theories, Fictions, Realities*, ed. Frank Schulze-Engler and Sissy Helff (Amsterdam: Rodopi, 2009), 83.
17. Helff, 83.
18. Arjun Appadurai, *Modernity at Large: Cultural Dimensions of Globalization* (Minneapolis: U of Minnesota P, 1996), 33.
19. Appadurai, 33.
20. Helff, 83.
21. Bruce Robbins, "Upward Mobility in the Postcolonial Era: Kincaid, Mukherjee, and the Cosmopolitan Au Pair," *Modernism/Modernity* 1.2 (1994): 137.
22. Robbins, 145.
23. Robbins, 143.
24. Anthony D'Andrea, "Deciphering the Space and Scale of Global Nomadism: Subjectivity and Counterculture in a Global Age," in

Deciphering the Global: Its Scales, Spaces and Subjects, ed. Saskia Sassen (London: Routledge, 2007), 149.

25. Beck, 9.
26. Beck, 103.
27. Beck, 103–105.
28. Beck, 104.
29. Caren Kaplan, *Questions of Travel: Postmodern Discourses of Displacement* (Durham: Duke UP, 1996), 32.
30. Homi K. Bhabha, *The Location of Culture* (London: Routledge, 1994), 36.
31. Pirjo Ahokas, "Constructing a Transnational, Postmodern Female Identity in Bharati Mukherjee's *Desirable Daughters* and Monica Ali's *Brick Lane*," in *Transcultural Localisms: Responding to Ethnicity in a Globalized World*, ed. Yiorgos Kalogeras, Eleftheria Arapoglou and Linda Manney (Heidelberg: Winter, 2006), 165.

Works Cited

Ahokas, Pirjo. "Constructing a Transnational, Postmodern Female Identity in Bharati Mukherjee's *Desirable Daughters* and Monica Ali's *Brick Lane*." In *Transcultural Localisms: Responding to Ethnicity in a Globalized World*. Ed. Yiorgos Kalogeras, Eleftheria Arapoglou and Linda Manney. Heidelberg: Winter, 2006. 165–181.

Ali, Monica. *Alentejo Blue*. London: Doubleday, 2006.

Amazon.co.uk. "Alentejo-Blue-Monica-Ali." Available at: <http://www.amazon.co.uk/Alentejo-Blue-Monica-Ali/dp/0385604866>. (Visited 2 January 2010.)

Appadurai, Arjun. *Modernity at Large: Cultural Dimensions of Globalization*. Minneapolis: U of Minnesota P, 1996.

Beck, Ulrich. *The Cosmopolitan Vision*. Trans. Ciaran Cronin. Cambridge: Polity, 2006. [Orig. *Der kosmopolitische Blick, oder: Krieg ist Frieden*, 2004.]

Bhabha, Homi K. *The Location of Culture*. London: Routledge, 1994.

Clifford, James. *Routes: Travel and Translation in the Late Twentieth Century*. London: Harvard UP, 1997.

D'Andrea, Anthony. "Deciphering the Space and Scale of Global Nomadism: Subjectivity and Counterculture in a Global Age." In *Deciphering the Global: Its Scales, Spaces and Subjects*. Ed. Saskia Sassen. London: Routledge, 2007. 139–153.

Featherstone, Mike. *Undoing Culture: Globalization, Postmodernism and Identity*. London: Sage, 1995.

Giddens, Anthony. *The Consequences of Modernity*. Cambridge: Polity, 1990.

Gupta, Suman. *Literature and Globalization*. Cambridge: Polity, 2009.

Helff, Sissy. "Shifting Perspectives: The Transcultural Novel." In *Transcultural English Studies: Theories, Fictions, Realities*. Ed. Frank Schulze-Engler and Sissy Helff. Amsterdam: Rodopi, 2009. 75–89.

Kaplan, Caren. *Questions of Travel: Postmodern Discourses of Displacement*. Durham: Duke UP, 1996.

Milsom-Mann, Corrinne. "Go and read something less boring instead." Review of *Alentejo Blue*, by Monica Ali. Amazon.co.uk (16 October 2006). Available at: <http://www.amazon.co.uk/gp/cdp/member-reviews/A3R8MQS43S2RHZ>. (Visited 2 January 2010.)

Nyman, Jopi. *Home, Identity, and Mobility in Contemporary Diasporic Fiction*. Amsterdam: Rodopi, 2009.

Robbins, Bruce. "Upward Mobility in the Postcolonial Era: Kincaid, Mukherjee, and the Cosmopolitan Au Pair." *Modernism/Modernity* 1.2 (1994): 133–151.

Sassen, Saskia. *A Sociology of Globalization*. New York: W.W. Norton, 2007.

Walter, Natasha. "Continental Drift." Review of *Alentejo Blue* by Monica Ali. *The Guardian*, online ed. (20 May 2006). Available at: <http://www.guardian.co.uk/books/2006/may/20/featuresreviews.guardianreview14>. (Visited 2 January 2010.)

10

Teaching a Transcultural/ Transgeneric 'Classic'

Hanif Kureishi's *My Beautiful Laundrette*

LAURENZ VOLKMANN

Generic Hybridity: Film Script/Play Text

Working on the film script of *My Beautiful Laundrette*[1] in 1985, Hanif Kureishi received a phone call from Howard Davies, then a director with the Royal Shakespeare Company. He was asked to write an adaptation of Bertolt Brecht's *Mother Courage* for RSC actors. What followed, as Kureishi explains in the introduction to his film script, was a simultaneous tackling of two projects – a stage drama on the one hand, a film on the other. In the case of *My Beautiful Laundrette*, this added even more qualities of the stage play to a script written by one of Britain's then most promising young playwrights. In his words, Kureishi started rewriting

> each scene of the film like a little scene for a play, with the action written like stage directions and with lots of dialogue. Then I'd cut most of the dialogue and add more stage directions, often set in cars, or with people running about, to keep the thing moving, since films require [...] action.[2]

In two significant respects, *My Beautiful Laundrette* marks an important watershed in Kureishi's professional career. For one, its success both with the critics and the public encouraged him to branch out by exploring different non-theatrical media, thus establishing himself as one of Great Britain's leading authors in a variety of media, ranging from screenplays to novels, short stories and essays. Since his success with *My Beautiful Laundrette* (1985) and the ensuing novel *The Buddha of Suburbia* (1990), Kureishi has continued writing and staging plays. However, though he must be considered one of Britain's outstanding artists, he is rarely perceived to be one of its more celebrated playwrights.

My Beautiful Laundrette can be singled out as a prominent *exemplum* of recent cultural trends towards generic hybridity. In the case of Kureishi, this transgression of boundaries and the process of "cross-fertilization" can be noted in the cinematic, visual quality of his narration in novels and short stories. Conversely, his plays have also been seen as highly influenced by techniques of film narrative, as the biographer Kenneth C. Kaleta points out: "Kureishi envisions not for the proscenium arch, but rather through the hand-held camera."[3] As Kureishi himself observes, his transformation from budding playwright to much-fêted author of film scripts was strongly influenced by populist and commercial necessities; in this his change is symptomatic of how the new medium film inevitably supersedes the cultural dominance of the old medium, the theatre.

> I wrote plays in the sixties and seventies, when I was growing up, the theatre was the hot thing in England. We didn't really have a cinema. Coppola and Woody Allen were in the States in the seventies, you know, but we didn't have any cinema in our country, really. It was the emergence of the cinematic stage. The alternative theater was great; it was really cooking, and it was about music and sex and class. There were plenty of theaters all over London. And you got to meet actresses. But the work didn't really suit me. I don't like writing plays. [...] [W]e need a cinema that is both critical and intelligent, sensuous and celebratory, reflecting the diversity and contradictions of our lives. It could exist; it is waiting to happen, except for the fools standing in its way.[4]

In spite of its generic definition and qualities as a film, *My Beautiful Laundrette* cannot deny its strong affinity to drama. Like many independent films or "artistic" films made for TV, it shares with stage productions its limited setting and *dramatis personae.*

Similarly, the film features a more stagnant, immobile and detached camera perspective, which focuses mainly on *mise en scène*. It is dialogue-centred, which constitutes a main element of the film's artistic impact.[5] Like many under-funded stage productions, it relies less on cinema gadgetry and to greater extent on good narration, impressive acting and theatrical devices as for example those of the Brechtian "V-effect," the alienation device of foregrounding the very act of acting and presenting a show – the film thus engages in a kind of "unadorned, low-budget naturalism."[6]

In this sense, reading the script and watching the DVD can provide lessons in cross-generic influences and how dramatic devices can be transplanted to film. Though *My Beautiful Laundrette* may be analysed as an important contribution to low-budget film making in Great Britain and the fertile influence of the theatre community on film making, more salient points of discussion and/or teaching are to be found in its historical importance as a work of art. Its enduring reputation and prestige rest with the fact that it can be perceived as one of the first and finest artistic productions of a promising young artist from a "visible" minority group in Great Britain which reached the mainstream audience and brought hitherto excluded or marginalized topics and social groups to public attention. This was achieved not with a strident agitprop production but rather through an unlikely *Romeo and Juliet* – love story across the demarcation lines of race, class and gender. Neither did it cause major irritations although its content could be viewed as potentially risqué or provocative.

Against this background, my article focuses on how to teach *My Beautiful Laundrette* in a non-native speaker setting with the specific aim of fostering students' intercultural competence. I will briefly trace Kureishi's career before and after he wrote *My Beautiful Laundrette*, assess the artist's prevailing importance in British cultural production, and outline some of his major themes and topics. Following that, the context to the film's production will be delineated, followed by a brief plot summary with a focus on character constellations. One of Kureishi's major narrative strategies – that of subverting his audience's expectations – will be explored, supported by a close reading of one of the film's key scenes. As to teaching aspects, the structure presented here – an approach by focusing on the author, background of film (history, production, and so on), plot, constellation of characters, prominent themes – could also be reflected in teaching situations. Additionally, in the final section, I will provide some practical suggestions for employing various methods of developing students' interest and for approaching the text and the film in both cognitive and affective manners.

Kureishi's Biography and Major Themes

Hanif Kureishi's father Rafiushan came from a wealthy Madras family, whose members moved mostly to Pakistan after the Partition of India in 1947. Rafiushan Kureishi migrated to England first to study law, then to settle for a job at the High Commission of Pakistan. After the marriage to Kureishi's English mother Audrey, the couple settled in Bromley, Kent, where Hanif Kureishi was born in 1954. Raised in a suburban milieu, of both English and Indian origin, Kureishi was educated at local schools (among them Bromley Technical High School), and, after a short stint at King's College, London, he became a professional theatre man and playwright in the late 1970s. His early productions include his first play *Soaking the Heat,* performed at the Royal Court Theatre Upstairs in London in 1976. *The Mother Country* (1980) won the Thames TV Playwright Award, followed in 1981 by two plays about immigrants in London, namely *Outskirts* and *Borderline.* For the latter plays Kureishi received further awards, among them the 1981 Critics Circle Theatre Award for Most Promising Playwright of the Year, and in 1982 he became Writer in Residence at the Royal Court Theatre.

It was with the screenplay for *My Beautiful Laundrette,* written in 1985, that Kureishi, whose career was launched by the theatre, became greatly successful and gained a larger, world-wide audience, as will be detailed below. Ensuing film projects such as *Sammy and Rosie Get Laid* (1987) or *London Kills Me* (1991), both dealing with the topics of dislocation and racial tensions in London, proved less successful with critics and theatregoers. It was the publication of his first novel *The Buddha of Suburbia* (1990) that once more boosted Kureishi's critical and popular acclaim. He had created a "classic" postmodern tale of growing up, with the protagonist

Karim, closely resembling the author, struggling to gain a more complete, cosmopolitan and, eventually, meaningful life. In a tale set against the background of the 1970s pop culture in London, the protagonist moves from the stifling suburbs the vibrant art scene of London, exploring various aspects of his "hybrid" identity such as mixed ethnic background, bi-sexuality and inner tensions between commercial and artistic, hedonistic and spiritual inclinations. The book won the Whitbread First Novel Award and was produced by the BBC as a four-part-television series in 1993. Kureishi's next novel *The Black Album*, dealing with repercussions of the *fatwa* against Salman Rushdie as they impinge on the relationship of a young man of Pakistani origin and his white lover, proved less successful. It was seen by many as an uneven composition, caught between a treatise against Muslim fundamentalism and a sentimental love story across the barriers of race, class and education.[7] In general, Kureishi's recent works have received less critical acclaim. His collections of short stories such as *Love in a Blue Time* (1997), *Midnight All Day* (1999) and the novella *Intimacy* (1998) – which was produced in 2001 as a film directed by Patrice Chéreau – created some controversy due to their sexual explicitness and navel-gazing exploration of personal issues allegedly related to Kureishi's divorce. Described as "male confessionals," Kureishi's recent narratives have met with less approval by his readers, who find themselves antagonized by "politically incorrect" ways of exploring masculinity and male sexuality. Those attracted to his multi-cultural milieus, characters and topics have also been disappointed with the author's increasingly pronounced eschewing of the issue of ethnicity, instead deliberately opting for what has been dubbed a "post-ethnic" attitude towards identity formation in urban and increasingly globalized environments. Kureishi continues to write plays such as *Sleep with Me*, produced in 1999 at the Royal National Theatre and *When the Night Begins* (2004), produced at the Hampstead Theatre in the same year.

While recent publications like the story of adolescent initiation *Gabriel's Gift* (2001) and *My Ear at His Heart* (2004), a book recounting the author's relationship with his father, appear to reconfirm the critical assessment of Kureishi's current artistic stagnation ("Peter Pan's midlife crisis" is the title of one of the more recent articles on the Internet),[8] Kureishi's reputation rests with his early key literary texts, the screenplay *My Beautiful Laundrette* and the novel *The Buddha of Suburbia*. Their reception in Great Britain and abroad has increasingly established them as set texts in classes dealing with contemporary Britain as a multi-cultural society – both for their artistic merits as works of fiction and their qualities of capturing a multifaceted image of the country, particularly its capital London. In EFL teaching contexts, Kureishi's texts have been promoted as "authentic" literary evidence of the growing importance of multiculturalism and have often been appreciated as an "authentic insider's voice" from an ethnic minority group. However, this is not just a problem of wrong literary "labelling". It must also be considered as a rather lopsided if not outright incorrect categorization of the author, his texts and his intended message. Kureishi is bi-cultural with respect to his family background; and he has frequently stressed that he considers himself more a Londoner than being affiliated with any ethnic or national entity, as is substantiated by texts refraining from exclusively examining the lives of members of ethnic minority groups. Rather, it is the complex process of searching for a more fluid, less fixed identity within the co-ordinates of gender and race that Kureishi probes in his cross-cultural fictions. What emerges – similar to Salman Rushdie's concept of hybridity – is an endorsement of notions of hybridity, predicated on plurality rather than singularity or exclusiveness. Theoretically, Kureishi has expounded these ideas of postmodern mutability and fluidity of the self in his persuasive essay "The Rainbow Sign." This essay was first published along with *My Beautiful Laundrette* and explores the ambivalences of identity as defined by colour, culture, immigration, and exile. This is summed up cogently in the following assessment by Merle Tönnies and Claus-Ulrich Viol:

> All of Kureishi's texts express a high degree of skepticism of any kind of homogeneous, closed and immutable society, be it of ethnic, religious or social nature, and advocate open and dynamic relationships which accept heterogeneity.[9]

Notwithstanding Kureishi's persuasive plea for multicultural values and a mobile, fissile and plural individual, the author's prominent role in contributing to a new Asian (that is, Indian and Pakistani) identity in Great Britain should not be underestimated.

Kureishi is one of the most outstanding and widely-read writers born in Britain of "postcolonial origin". However, his reputation among British Asians has remained ambivalent.[10] What has led to both angry rejections and critical appraisals is Kureishi's disavowal of the "politics of representation." Contrary to positions which claim that an author of an ethnic minority or any marginalized group should represent its members only in a positive light to redress the balance of clichéd images in the dominant culture, Kureishi has insisted that he will not play the role of an ambassador representing his minority, preferring to depict the grimmer realities of racism, class division and tensions within minority groups. Nor does he refrain from portraying Asians with mixed, sometimes less benign character traits. This artistic freedom has been met with passionate rejections both by some Pakistani organizations and Asian critics. Their anger is echoed by traditional conservative Britons, who argue along traditionalist lines. According to white British conservatives, Kureishi has painted a grotesquely ugly image of Britain as a cesspool of vice, decay, racism, xenophobia and homophobia – in short, of a nation in decline, morally hollowed out.

For traditional Asians, Kureishi's picture of Asians in Britain portrays them solely as drug dealers, sodomites and callous landlords, as for example in *My Beautiful Laundrette.*[11] In an article with the telling title "Dirty Linen" an enraged Mahmood Jamal decries Kureishi's script as "an example of what Asian filmmakers should try to avoid: the caricature and the reinforcing of stereotypes of their own people for a few cheap laughs."[12] In the words of the critic, the film "expresses all the prejudices that this society has felt about Asians and Jews – that they are money-grabbing, scheming, sex-crazed people. It's not surprising therefore, that it was popular with European audiences."[13]

In general, there is a generational divide to be perceived in Asian reactions to Kureishi as an artist and to his works. With the author's gradual receding from contentious racial issues in his current circling around private and non-ethnic subject matters, he has become less of a polarizing artist. Those who have embraced him as an ethnic author confess a certain degree of disappointment; while others are beginning to appreciate Kureishi's achievements as "the literary godfather to a generation of British Asians", as articles on the Internet phrase it. One paean reads as follows:

> Kureishi himself is a father figure to a whole generation of Asian artists who were inspired by the fearlessness of his writing. A young Meera Syal, author of *Anita and Me*, starred in *My Beautiful Laundrette*. Ayub Khan-Din, author of the play and hit film *East Is East*, was one of the joint leads in *Sammy and Rosie Get Laid*. The band *Cornershop*, whose "Brimful of Asha" is one of the best records ever to top the pop charts, included a song called "Hanif Kureishi Scene" on the B-side of their first single. [...] Gurinder Chadha, director of *Bend It Like Beckham*, says: "When I saw My Beautiful Laundrette I was, like, 'Wow!' Hanif took Asians into another space. He was bringing us up to speed. I remember thinking that we'll never go back to having arranged-marriage stories on the screen."[14]

It is against this background that *My Beautiful Laundrette* must be gauged and discussed. It stands out as an early popular product by an author of an ethnic minority group which elicited both rave reviews and allegations of pandering to white prejudices. Moreover, it has over the last decades become a cornerstone of the history of British Asian artists contributing to today's image of Britain.

The Film: Production Background and Plot Outline

It was in the medium of film that Hanif Kureishi successfully endeavoured to reach a mass audience with an alternative, counter-cultural production. *My Beautiful Laundrette* paradoxically profited from an interest in Indian culture as expressed in a spate of films about the British Raj during the Thatcher era. To Kureishi, "lavish films in exotic settings" such as David Lean's *A Passage to India* (1984, based on the novel by E.M. Forster) or the *Jewel in the Crown* (1983) seemed to exude conservative ideologies. Their partly affirmative recreations of England's imperial past seemed to evoke "an image of Englishness that encapsulated the identity of its élite, ruling class."[15] Against such genteel and embellishing portrayals of Indian-British relations Kureishi intended to pit, as he proclaimed, an image of "the England I know, I mean England is horrible and full of drugs."[16] Originally, Kureishi intended the film to start with the arrival of an immigrant family to England and depict their progress to the present – presenting a semi-documentary family saga of sorts. The result is less epic. The film was shot in six weeks in 1985, produced on a low budget of 600,000 pounds. Commissioned for and funded by the "alternative" Channel 4, a TV channel created in 1982 with the explicit aim of catering to *avant-garde* and minority tastes, it was first *played* at the Edinburgh Film Festival in the autumn of 1985, opened at the London Film Festival on 15 November and was subsequently released at London cinemas. It soon reached a wider public, harvesting awards such as an Oscar nomination for Best Screenplay. Not only did it mark a successful co-operation between Kureishi and director Stephen Frears, which was continued with *Sammy and Rosie Get Laid.* It also helped to boost Daniel Day Lewis's career to stardom and bolstered claims for a renaissance of British cinema. Other innovative and socially critical films produced with financial assistance by Channel 4 include, for instance, *The Draughtman's Contract* (1983), *Dance with a Stranger* (1985), *Letter to Brezhnev* (1985) and *Mona Lisa* (1986).

As briefly outlined above, the audiences' responses to the film may be indicative of the mid-1980s cultural context, the Thatcher era. While the film was fêted for bringing gay and ethnic minority issues to the attention of a mainstream audience by avoiding the dour didactics of issue based cinema and handling potentially contentious topics such as homosexuality and interracial relationships in an off-handed, matter-of-fact manner, conservative Asians took offence and objected to the lack of positive portrayals of Pakistani immigrants in England. There were picket lines around theatres in New York City, exhibiting banners which called the film "the product of a vile and perverted mind".

What these enraged critics also objected to was the darkly funny comedy showing overtly ambitious middle-class Pakistani characters having affairs with white middle-class women or indulging in a homosexual relationship with a white ex-National Front hoodlum. On top of this sexually deviant behaviour, Asian characters successfully emulate the conservative Prime Minister Margaret Thatcher's ideal of entrepreneurial initiative and risk-taking by succeeding in the rough world of enterprise where only money counts and success is defined by wealth and status symbols, regardless of the often amoral means of achieving it. After all, Asians in this film benefit from the free market system in fields as diverse as drug dealing and laundering the dirty clothes of white

Britons – or rather, having the laundromat operated by white subalterns while cashing in on the surplus. The tensions of the Thatcher years – a revival of xenophobia and national pride on the one hand, an individualistic competitive business culture on the other – form the socio-cultural matrix of the plot and prefigure the basic constellation of characters in *My Beautiful Laundrette.* The film's real hero is Omar (played by Gordon Warnecke), a young, restless and ambitious Pakistani Briton, burdened with the obligation to look after his bedridden, self-pitying and alcoholic father, who wants his son to get education, the traditional path for immigrants to climb the social ladder in Great Britain. Omar's mother has recently committed suicide by leaping before a train. Omar gets an eagerly awaited chance for showing his business potential when his Uncle Nasser (Saeed Jeffrey) offers him work, first washing cars, then – as a promotion – to manage one of his dilapidated laundrettes. Nasser, a true wheeler-dealer, has his fingers in many obscure businesses, shows little qualms about evicting penniless tenants from his apartments, acts as a true patriarch in front of his wife and children and enjoys entertaining English friends. He also has a white British mistress, Rachel, whom he keeps in a separate compartment of his life. Their relationship – heterosexual, sensuous and illicit – offers a sub-plot and thus a foil to the main plot of the film, which is Omar's relationship with his street-wise, charming but ex-National Front white friend Johnny (Daniel Day Lewis). Instead of pursuing a relationship with his uncle Nasser's attractive daughter, Omar is increasingly drawn towards his employee Johnny. Theirs is a complex relationship, with Omar employing his former friend as a worker for refurbishing and revamping the laundrette into a dazzling emporium. This is achieved by dubious means, partly by conning Omar's drug dealing uncle Salim, partly (as it is only hinted at) by stealing and peddling consumer items. While the laundrette, as witnessed during the opening ceremony as the film's climax, is turned into a profitable business, Omar and Johnny – whose homosexual and erotic aspects are depicted in a playful and sensitive manner – simultaneously manage to ward off attacks by Johnny's former gang of neo-fascist Paki-bashers and gradually develop a physical relationship, which remains unknown to Omar's Pakistani relatives. Their relationship finds its symbolic fulfilment in the last scene of the film. In it, the two men are splashing around in the washroom of the laundrette, "reminiscent of a ritual ablution: the blood of racist violence is washed off, bodies are purified, bad feelings are purged from souls."[17]

Interpretative Approaches to the Text

There is a wide range of secondary literature available on *My Beautiful Laundrette*. Indebted to cutting-edge critical approaches in various fields of race, class, and gender studies, recent monographs such as the studies by Bart Moore-Gilbert (2001), Ruvani Ranasinha (2002) and Susie Thomas (2005), offer complex discussions of Kureishi's complete *oeuvre*, including succinct analyses of both the script and the play.[18] Additionally, the first book-length study by Kenneth C. Kaleta (1998) offers less theory-oriented but committed interpretations of Kureishi's work plus many passages from interviews with the artist.[19] All books include up-to-date and extensive bibliographies for further, more detailed research. German publishers, for instance, have acknowledged the text's teaching potential in the form of two annotated and commented editions; both are excellent texts for non-native speakers. Indeed, Tönnies and Viol in their afterword offer a lucid interpretation which may well be considered to be the standard introduction to both the script and the film.[20] Apart from the doctoral thesis by Ines Karin Böhner (1996), which offers plentiful additional information on the play and has unfortunately been little noted, there are a number of classroom-oriented interpretations, markedly by Rainer Schüren (1994, 1998).[21] Focusing on the film version of *My Beautiful Laundrette*, Schüren suggests a broad spectrum of innovative approaches and provides some very useful additional texts on ethnic minority groups, racism, multicultural concepts and reviews. Anyone interested in an intertextual approach to the film is well advised to consult and use the material provided in Schüren's articles. Of course, of the interpretations and background information provided in articles and books on *The Buddha of Suburbia*, many can be put to effective use also in connection with teaching or interpreting *My Beautiful Laundrette*.

Considering approaches to interpreting or teaching the text, the overall discursive strategy of *My Beautiful Laundrette* could serve as a guideline. This strategy can be described as a constant play with the reader's (or viewer's) expectations, his or her prejudices, stereotypes and clichés. The text continually and quite deliberately toys with its readers' or audience's notions of race, class and gender. Thus an interpretation can make the reader or viewer aware of how his or her cultural concepts of these categories are based on conventions, traditions and how, in turn, theses categories are culturally "constructed." The text achieves this unsettling effect by "subverting the predictable." Thus, on the one hand, it exposes how its characters are embedded in a conventional social matrix. It reveals the conventional matrix of racial relations and notions of ethnic identity, a class-conscious, hierarchical society and fixed gender roles and expectations.[22] It works with partly overt, partly covert hierarchical juxtapositions of British and Asian communities, white employer and black employee, gay and straight concepts of sexuality. Yet, on the other hand, it subverts these concepts by endorsing different, "alternative" concepts of relations and identities. The text succeeds in establishing these counter-concepts by having them evolve in a rather matter-of-fact manner, without strident political exclamations. On the contrary, the fact that traditional concepts of race relations, class and gender roles are turned upside down is sneakily expanded until the recipients register this reversal as something quite "natural."

Of course, the main reversal of traditional cultural concepts is symbolized in the relationship between Omar and Johnny. Here, the rather infamous and apodictic imperialist motto by Rudyard Kipling that "East is East, and West is West, and never the twain shall meet" is utterly deconstructed by proving the opposite, though in the "inverted" form of the two protagonists' amorous relationship. Symbolically, they stand as representatives of their respective culture, though traditional notions of hierarchy are reversed: Thus, a sophisticated, well-groomed and smartly attired Pakistani entrepreneur employs a rather inarticulate white labourer, sloppily dressed and with dyed hair to do the manual and dirty work for him. A love affair which connects two members from opposite ethnic and social groups ensues; in this case this is not a heterosexual couple but a happy homosexual relationship. In its symbolic function with respect to race, class and gender, their bonding is an ironic comment on the fading of Britain's former colonial glory as it was once perpetrated by male sahibs, with the Asian Omar now exhibiting all the stiff-upper-lip qualities it takes to run an (economic) empire. It is also a utopian fantasy in which all ethnic and sexual barriers to individual fulfilment have been overcome and social inequalities transcended or dissolved.

The importance of this discursive strategy of inversion can be asserted by focusing on a series of aspects of the text. It may be suggested that the following points be foregrounded: the symbolism of the title, different facets of sexual identity, identity formation along the lines of white *vs.* black and English *vs.* Asian as represented by the range of characters in the film, the culture of enterprise as propagated by Prime Minister Thatcher and how this shapes the text's characters. Finally, specific questions such as the semiotics and narrative techniques employed in the film can be discussed. This can be done, for example, by a close reading of a selected scene such as the Opening of the Laundrette Scene, which in essence presents many aspects of the film's visual and narrative techniques as well as its major themes.

As a useful point of departure and a first step towards a closer analysis, one can first turn to the laundrette's naming and its obvious symbolic implications. It is rather evident that the change of name from "Churchills" to "Powders" is indicative of a historical change which has various connotations. The directions in the film script leave no doubt as to the import of both the laundrette's name and its deplorable state: "*It's called 'Churchills'. It's broad and spacious and in a bad condition. It's situated in an area of run-down second-hand shops, betting shops, grocers with their windows boarded-up, etc.*" (*MBL* 49) Obviously, the laundrette here stands for the decay of Britain – the name of the former Prime Minister Winston Churchill being associated with the erstwhile pinnacle of the nation's pride and glory. What is left is a desolate conglomeration of disparate and out-of-order remnants of former industry and greatness. Another comment in the script enforces this view, hinting also at a lack of spiritual or moral direction in an ironic remark: "*Some of the benches in the laundrette are church pews*" (*MBL* 49).

Of course, it is only due to the unrelenting energy and entrepreneurial skills of an Asian that this dilapidated place can be brought to life and glory again. The whole refurbishing process is similarly symbolic, which becomes clear in comments on Johnny's work in the laundrette, where he "demolishes existing structures" (*MBL* 64) – here various figurative meanings are hinted at. (Of course, the ambivalence of the laundrette's new name also alludes to the fact that it was financed mostly by illegal drug dealings.) In Schüren's view, the refurbished laundrette under the ownership of Asians can also be seen as representative of a new, better Britain: "The gloriously refurbished laundrette becomes an ironic microcosm of Thatcher's England, with large sections of the population milling about in it."[23]

Turning from ethnic to gender matters, *My Beautiful Laundrette* can also be read against the background of the spread of the AIDS-epidemic, which began to be noticed as a threat to the whole population in the early 1980s. The early 1980s are also noticeably the era in which gay and lesbian sub-cultures began to become more visible, causing strong backlash effects among conservative circles. These culminated in the demand of a moral regeneration in Britain, a return to "Victorian values" – all of which form the topical background to the film. What distinguishes *My Beautiful Laundrette* from other products of the so-called New Gay Cinema of that era (whose most prominent proponent was Derek Jarman, who produced sexually provocative films such as *The Last of England* [1987] or *Edward II* [1991] and aggressively promoted gay agendas) is that Kureishi does not employ the direct idiom of sexual identity politics. On the contrary, the homosexual relationship between Omar and Johnny appears as something quite "natural," and the "consummation" is only implied in scenes of kissing and tender cuddling. Mostly, their affair remains "closeted"; yet the clandestine nature of it creates comic scenes, using the theatrical device of dramatic irony. While the audience already know about Omar's sexual preferences, his Asian relatives find his homophilia difficult or impossible to grasp. It is indicated that Omar's father has sneaking suspicions when he approaches Nasser with the following utterance: "Try and fix him with a nice girl. I'm not sure if his penis is in full working order" (*MBL* 23). This remark seems to reverberate through the text. Occasionally, sexual irritations create slapstick humour, as is the case when Nasser accidentally hits upon the two gay lovers getting dressed after love making in a hurry before the opening of the laundrette. Here Nasser's remark can be interpreted as naive, blinkered or unwilling to face the obvious: "What the hell are you doing? Sunbathing?" (*MBL* 84).

In a similar vein, Kureishi's portrayal of immigrants playfully questions accepted stereotypes by experimenting with strategies of inversion and hyperbole. While the issues of race and ethnicity – and with it questions of racism, xenophobia and discrimination – retain their status as socio-cultural parameters of the text, its prevailing and contradictory theme is that of money and material success as a gigantic levelling-out machinery. As a cultural conflict this is represented in the two brothers, Nasser and Papa. A fervent socialist, Papa embodies the traditional hope of first-generation immigrants, believing in furthering his son's advancement through education. This credo – "For us education is power" (*MBL* 35) – is later reconfirmed in the following words: "I want my son out of this underpants cleaning condition. I want him reading in college" (*MBL* 99). On the other hand, Uncle Nasser has wholeheartedly embraced the free-market spirit of Thatcherism. A flamboyant and charismatic character, he is not without contradictions in his effort to adapt to materialistic Britain. His ostentatious ravelling in the trappings of monetary gains – a luxurious country house, an expensive automobile and, arguably as his ultimate status symbol, a British mistress – may make him prone to charges of having "sold out" to the British. Yet, notwithstanding Nasser's distinct entrepreneurial skills, which include seemingly heartless evictions of tenants unable to pay the rent, his irreverent and highly ironic attitude towards Britain and the work ethic propagated by the Thatcher government make him an endearing character. As Salim at one point remarks to Nasser: "You're too busy keeping this damn country in the black. Someone's got to do it" (*MBL* 27). In addition, Nasser's exchanges provide the best lines of the script, as when he quips: "In this damn country which we hate and love, you can get anything you want. It's all spread out and available. That's why I believe in England. You just have to know how to squeeze the tits of the system" (*MBL* 32). A similar sense of humour is exhibited in the following exchange, which takes place after Nasser has learnt about Omar employing a white person, Johnny:

Nasser: He's hired someone else to do the work.

Zaki: Typically English, if I can say that. (*MBL* 67)

Indeed, viewing or reading *My Beautiful Laundrette* equals a revisiting of the Thatcher years. And a critical assessment of the text's unwitting or witting participation in the Thatcher spirit of free enterprise is partly dependent on its interpreter's attitude towards the revival of nationalism in the era, social disintegration and belief in the self-regulatory and wealth-creating powers of deregulation and private initiative. If the text and characters like Nasser or Omar seem to embody the spirit of Thatcherism, they certainly do so with a great deal of self-deprecating humour and cynical flippancy. This becomes clear in such remarks as the one by Salim on having his nephew Omar employed: "Mrs Thatcher will be pleased with me" (*MBL* 28). The above-mentioned facet of colour-blindness of money is expressed in Nasser's observation that "we're professional businessmen. Not professional Pakistanis. There's no race question in the new enterprise culture" (*MBL* 78). A darker sub-text is hinted at in Salim's view: "But we're nothing in England without money" (*MBL* 90). Certainly, the seemingly facetious stance towards Britain's new enterprise culture is not without its grotesque, darker dimension. These are, however, according to the generic conventions of this comedy, only alluded to in scenes displaying how the most lucrative business opportunities are in illegal markets, in stealing, drug running and, most rewardingly, laundering dirty money: After all, the dynamic duo's success is based not only on conning drug dealers but also, as a brief scene reveals, on stealing "televisions, stereos, videos, etc. [which are] stacked up in the back room" (*MBL* 104) of the laundrette to be used for retaining "start-up capital." In these scenes, *My Beautiful Laundrette* links itself with the tradition of great comedies of the commercial world like Ben Jonson's *The Alchemist* (1610) or John Gay's *The Beggar's Opera* (1728). It shares with them a critical exposure of the all-pervasive forces of the market that level out legal and illegal ways of gaining wealth. Here, the pernicious commercial spirit of the age seems to pervert all existing values and norms. However, one would surely read the text against the grain and possibly misinterpret it if one were to describe this comedy as a trenchant critique of capitalist practices. Rather, the text retains its open, ambivalent structure, which can best be demonstrated by a closer glance at the most presentable character of the film. As a three-dimensional figure, both a self-indulgent hedonist and a shrewd, occasionally ruthless businessman, Nasser demonstrates all the traits of a trickster. Partly absorbing British values, partly adhering to eastern traditions, especially in his family, Nasser oscillates like the quintessential postmodern chameleon not only between cultures but also between identities. The critical opinion voiced by Kaleta that Nasser "achieved riches despite the price paid in terms of loss of integrity and denial of his heritage"[24] seems to be undercut by the message sent out by the text. Rather, he is a predecessor of Karim's father Haroon, in *The Buddha of Suburbia*, who successfully exemplifies postmodern identity *bricolage by selling himself as an Indian life-style guru to his Western audience.*

It is through the character of Nasser, therefore, that Kureishi most convincingly probes the multifarious complexities of the Asian experience in Britain – without succumbing to demands for a politically correct portrayal of Asian characters. As stated above, Kureishi favours concepts of fluid hybridity and constant refashioning and adaptation processes of the self. This ideal of hybridity is also reflected in the text's and film's hybrid nature. Elements of the theatre of the epic and independent, low-budget and documentary-style films mingle with an ironic narrative mode, which the author describes as "the modern mode, a way of commenting on bleakness and cruelty without falling into dourness and didacticism" (*MBL* 9). So far, most reviewers and critics have only made passing remarks on the ironic and satiric mode of *My Beautiful Laundrette*.[25]

However, one would have to go beyond analysing humour and satire in the text. To take this one step further, any critical reading of both the script and the play would have to elaborate on its techniques of non-realism. These could be discerned, first of all, by asking questions about the basic logic of the plot of the film. Thus the non-realist plot line of the film and its suspension of disbelief could come to the fore. How, for instance, would it be possible that a street smart character like Salim is duped by entrepreneurial amateurs like Omar and Johnny? How could a love relationship between a white ex-fascist and a young immigrant Asian develop – unless one takes into consideration the fact that they are the best-looking characters in the film? Why would the savvy Nasser fork out any money on a dilapidated laundrette? And, finally, are we really to believe that the glitzy, revamped emporium can stay in business in a run-down area of London for any period of time? Such questions reveal, of course, the break with mainstream modes of narrating which aim at creating an aura of verisimilitude. Just as the story constantly recycles accepted notions of sexuality, gender, class, race and ethnicity, it also serves as an integrating force in terms of combining a broad palette of genres, both from film and fiction.

Apart from being a story about a gay growing up and "coming out", the text integrates an ethnic success story: "Emigrating from Pakistan to London with his brother, Uncle Nasser of *My Beautiful Laundrette's* is superficially an assimilated personification of the classic rags-to-riches story."[26] Of course, the same would apply to Omar and his Thatcherite success story. Additionally, the story involves elements of the "buddies narrative", the thriller, and, most notably, a *Romeo-and-Juliet*-type plot line with a spin. It is this incorporating of numerous previously existing story lines, characters, situations and *genres* which contribute to the quality of the film as a cult movie. Following Umberto Eco, viewers would thus detect in the film an abundance of "intertextual frames", that is, "stereotyped situations derived from preceding textual traditions and recorded by our encyclopedia."[27] In other words, it is exactly the many stereotypes and clichés which the film playfully integrates and constantly subverts which help towards producing a (post) modern "classic". For Eco surmises: "Two clichés make us laugh but a hundred clichés move us because we sense dimly that the clichés are talking among themselves, celebrating a reunion."[28]

Key Scene: The Opening of the Laundrette

The crucial and climactic scene of the film takes place when the newly refurbished laundrette is ceremoniously opened. The following excerpt artfully intertwines two strands of the plot. Nasser arrives with his mistress Rachel, whom he intended to keep secret from his daughter Tania. The first meeting between the two results not only in a clash between daughter and mistress, but between cultures and generations. Simultaneously, Nasser, who seems unwilling to grasp the evident, that is the growing love affair between Johnny and Omar, starts a renewed effort at an "arranged" marriage between Tania and Johnny:

> *The laundrette is open now. The ladies and other locals are doing their washing. The machines are whirring, sheets are being folded, magazines read, music played, video games played, etc.*
>
> *Salim arrives with Zaki. They talk as they come in.*
>
> ZAKI. Laundrettes are impossible. I've got two laundrettes and two ulcers.
>
> Plus … piles!
>
> (Genghis, Moose and the rest of the Gang arrive. Moose goes into the laundrette, followed by Genghis. Genghis turns and forbids the rest of the Gang from entering. They wait restlessly outside. Johnny is talking to Rachel.)
>
> RACHEL. What is your surname?
>
> JOHNNY. Burfoot.
>
> RACHEL. That's it. I know your mother.
>
> *(The Telephone Character is on the phone, talking eagerly to his Angela. Through the window, Omar, who is talking to Nasser, sees Tania. She is crossing the road and carrying a bouquet of flowers.)*
>
> OMAR. I thought Papa just might make it today, Uncle.
>
> NASSER. He said he never visits laundrettes.
>
> *(Tania comes in through the door.)*
>
> JOHNNY *(to Rachel)*. Oh good, it's Tania.
>
> RACHEL. I've never met her. But she has a beautiful face.
>
> *(Johnny leaves Rachel and goes to Tania, kissing her. He takes the flowers delightedly. Nasser is disturbed by the sudden unexpected appearance of his daughter, since he is with his mistress, Rachel.)*
>
> NASSER *(to Omar)*. Who invited Tania, dammit?
>
> *(Genghis and Moose shout out as they play the video game.)*
>
> OMAR. I did, Uncle.

(They watch as Tania goes to Rachel with Johnny. Johnny has no choice but to introduce Tania and Rachel.)

TANIA. *(smiles at Rachel).* At last. After so many years in my family's life.

RACHEL. Tania, I do feel I know you.

TANIA. But you don't.

NASSER *(watching this).* Bring Tania over here.

TANIA *(to Rachel).* I don't mind my father having a mistress.

RACHEL. Good. I am so grateful.

NASSER *(to Omar).* Then marry her. *(Omar looks at him.)* What's wrong with her? If I say marry her then you damn well do it!

TANIA *(to Rachel).* I don't mind my father spending our money on you.

RACHEL. Why don't you mind?

NASSER *(to Omar).* Start being nice to Tania. Take the pressure off my fucking head.

TANIA *(to Rachel).* Or my father being with you instead of with our mother.

NASSER *(to Omar).* Your penis works, doesn't it?

TANIA *(to Rachel).* But I don't like women who live off men.

NASSER *(shoving Omar forward).* Get going then!

TANIA *(to Rachel).* That's a pretty disgusting parasitical thing, isn't it?

OMAR *(to Tania).* Tania, come and look at the spin-driers. They are rather interesting.

RACHEL. But tell me, who do you live off? And you must understand, we are of different generations, and different classes. Everything is waiting for you. The only thing that has ever waited for me is your father.

(Then, with great dignity, Nasser goes to Rachel.)

NASSER. We'd better get going. See you boys.

(He shakes hands warmly with Omar and Johnny. And goes out with Rachel, ignoring Tania. [...]*)* (*MBL* 85–87)

The scene clearly serves to characterize Nasser's traditional attitude towards family values, arranged marriages and heterosexuality. The device of dramatic irony is very convincingly employed here, since the gay couple have just had their first intimate exchanges on screen and were almost "caught" by Nasser. So, while there is a conflict between Nasser's outlook and his trying to save an awkward situation – Tania meeting Rachel – by means of verbal aggression towards Omar, the truly moving encounter takes place between two minor characters, two outsiders. Accidentally being in the same room at the same time, they meet as representatives of two separate worlds. Rachel defends her position as Nasser's mistress with pride and dignity, appealing to the feelings of sympathy of the audience for someone who has been marginalized throughout her life and, understandably enough, tries to eke out her moments of private happiness. It is in this scene that different lifestyles and ways of searching for individual happiness are presented in a truly dialogical way. Neither voice gets the exquisite right to present the sole solution, and seemingly "amoral" or "politically incorrect" ways of seeking some measure of happiness are given equal weight without favouring just one option. Identity, happiness, fulfilment – all these human needs are in a flux and need to be constantly re-negotiated with a tolerant attitude towards different models of living, as indicated here.

Further Teaching Suggestions

As has been pointed out, *My Beautiful Laundrette* is a highly didactic film in that it openly privileges concepts of ethnic, sexual and cultural pluralism. It clearly favours open concepts of both the individual and his or her society. In this, it aims at fostering the acclaimed goals of intercultural learning,[29] that is empathy, tolerance and particularly an understanding of marginalized and oppressed groups in the target culture, without painting a completely bleak – and thus in the context of intercultural learning counterproductive – picture of it. It is a hilarious, optimistic and buoyant film, full of positive messages. Yet it has enough depth and serious undertones to save it from accusations of being merely shallow entertainment. Apart from these pedagogic, ethical goals, what are other teaching/learning objectives teachers should aim at when putting the script and the film on the classroom agenda? And what are additional, more practical teaching goals?

The first reason lies in the fact that *My Beautiful Laundrette* has stood the test of time to have achieved the status of a "classic" of British cinema, in the rubrics of gay cinema, ethnic cinema and the section of "how independent movies have gone mainstream." In these fields, it can be credited as being a pioneering achievement which should be viewed by all those interested in popular British culture, multicultural Britain and British sub-cultures. In addition, it opens a window on one of the most controversial yet also pivotal periods in post-war Britain, the Thatcher years – and all the above-mentioned topics connected with those years can be discussed in this context. For students today, these years are historically beyond their grasp and need to be "revived" in the classroom. In this context, to use the film as a gateway to the Thatcher era which would, in turn, add important contours to many facets of contemporary Britain, would mean including other "texts" of the area: rock and punk rock songs, pictures, architecture, historical speeches, documentaries, and so on. Parallel and in addition to this focus on the Thatcher years, a closer look at Britain's history in the context of colonialism, imperialism and postcolonialism including multiculturalism would be necessary. Instead of providing students with lists of historical facts and figures, it would be advisable to encourage them to do individual or group research *via* the Internet on the mentalities that are connected with colonial and postcolonial encounters. It would seem beneficial, in this context, to read some of the key texts of Imperialism and racism, such as a selection of Kipling's verses or short stories, and, for instance, Enoch Powell's infamous "Rivers of Blood" speech. Also known as the Birmingham Speech on 20 April 1968, this notorious speech has often been read as inciting racial hatred by warning against continued immigration to Great Britain.[30] It could well be counterbalanced by some more recent texts by Black British artists, for example by dub poets or musicians.

It is only by means of this historicizing and intertextual approach that students will be able to come to a deeper understanding of the cultural subtext of Kureishi's text and appreciate how, notwithstanding its topicality, it can still carry important messages decades after it was written. However, like any great piece of art, *My Beautiful Laundrette* may be appreciated both for its topical, in this case also ethnic and its universal, timeless appeal. Rainer Schüren attributes the film's enduring success in the EFL classroom exactly to this quality: It is successful

> [...] although it is rooted in two cultures, the English and that of the Indian sub-continent, which raises very complex problems of understanding. But perhaps it is exactly this experienced rootedness of the human condition in the depths of a foreign culture (and history) which accounts for the fascinating aura of such art.[31]

Notes

1. Hanif Kureishi, *Hanif Kureishi: My Beautiful Laundrette: A Screenplay*, "Fremdsprachentexte", ed. Merle Tönnies and Claus-Ulrich Viol (Stuttgart: Philipp Reclam jun., 1999); further references are to this edition, and are given parenthetically in the text, preceded by *MBL*.
2. Merle Tönnies and Claus-Ulrich Viol. "Introduction," in Kureishi, *My Beautiful Laundrette: A Screenplay*. ("Fremdsprachentexte"), ed. Merle Tönnies and Claus-Ulrich Viol (Stuttgart: Philipp Reclam jun., 1999), 4.
3. Kenneth C. Kaleta, *Hanif Kureishi: Postcolonial Storyteller* (Austin: U Texas P, 1998.), 10.
4. Quoted in Kaleta, 38f.
5. Cf. Tönnies and Viol, "Nachwort," 164; Eva Rueschmann, "Film Notes: My Beautiful Laundrette," 2000, available at: <http://helios.hampshire.edu/~erHA/hacu234/laundrette.html> (visited 4 March, 2010).
6. Quoted in Tönnies and Viol, "Nachwort," 164
7. Cf. Ruvani Ranashinha, *Hanif Kureishi*, "Writers and Their Work" (Tavistock: Northcote House, 2002).
8. Jessica Mann, "Peter Pan's Midlife Crisis," *The Sunday Telegraph* (20 October, 2002), available at: <www.telegraph.co.uk/culture/4729043/Peter-Pans-midlife-crisis.html> (visited 7 January, 2010).
9. Tönnies and Viol, "Nachwort," 138 (translation LV).
10. Cf. Bart Moore-Gilbert, *Hanif Kureishi*, "Contemporary World Writers" (Manchester and New York: Manchester UP, 2001).

11. See Tönnies and Viol, "Nachwort," 138.
12. Mahmood Jamal, "Dirty Linen," *Black Film, British Cinema*, ICA Documents (London: British Film Institute, 1988), 21–22; reprinted in Rainer Schüren, "'My Beautiful Laundrette': Multikulturelle Aspekte der Filmarbeit im Englischunterricht der Oberstufe," *Der fremdsprachliche Unterricht–Englisch* 28/14 (1994): 53.
13. Jamal, 53.
14. Sukhdev Sandhu, "Life Lines," *The Telegraph* (28 Aug., 2005), available at: <www.telegraph.co.uk/arts/main.jhtml?xml=/arts/2004/08/28/bokur28.xml> (visited 5 January 2010).
15. Ranasinha 39.
16. Quoted in Ranasinha 39.
17. Rainer Schüren, "Teaching Different Cultures through Film. *Educating Rita* and *My Beautiful Laundrette*," *Journal for the Study of British Cultures* 5.2 (1998): 210.
18. See Moore-Gilbert, Ranasinha, and Susie Thomas, *Hanif Kureishi*, "Readers' Guide to Essential Criticism" (New York: Palgrave Macmillan, 2005). See also Laurenz Volkmann, "Teaching Hanif Kureishi," in *Transcultural English Studies: Theories, Fictions, Realities*, ed. Frank Schulze-Engler and Sissy Helff (Amsterdam: Rodopi, 2009), 393–408.
19. See Kaleta.
20. Tönnies and Viol, "Nachwort," see also Doris Teske, [chapter on Kureishi], *Cultural Studies: GB. Anglistik–Amerikanistik* (Berlin: Cornelsen, 2002), 176–186.
21. Ines Karin Böhner, *'My Beautiful Laundrette' und 'Sammy and Rosie Get Laid': Filmische Reflexionen von Lernprozessen* (Frankfurt am Main: Lang, 1996); see also Schüren, "'My Beautiful Laundrette'" and Schüren, "Teaching."
22. Cf. David Mason, *Race and Ethnicity in Modern Britain*, 2nd ed. (Oxford: Oxford UP, 2000).
23. Schüren, "'My Beautiful Laundrette'," 46.
24. Kaleta, 196.
25. See, e.g., Moore-Gilbert and Ranasinha.
26. Kaleta, 195.
27. Umberto Eco, "*Casablanca:* Cult Movies and Intertextual Collage," in *Modern Criticism and Theory: A Reader*, ed. David Lodge (with Nigel Wood), 2nd ed. (London: Longman, 2000), 396.
28. Eco 401.

29. As discussed by Klaus Stierstorfer, "Literatur und interkulturelle Kompetenz," in *Interkulturelle Kompetenz: Theorie und Praxis des fremdsprachlichen Unterrichts*, ed. Laurenz Volkmann, Klaus Stierstorfer and Wolfgang Gehring (Tübingen: Gunter Narr, 2002), 119–141.
30. Reprinted partly in *Minorities in Britain: Never at Ease?* "Viewfinder", ed. Michael Mitchell (München: Langenscheidt-Longman, 1997), 3.
31. Schüren, "'My Beautiful Laundrette'," 44 (translation LV).

Works Cited

Böhner, Ines Karin. *'My Beautiful Laundrette' und 'Sammy and Rosie Get Laid': Filmische Reflexionen von Lernprozessen.* Frankfurt am Main: Lang, 1996.

Eco, Umberto. "*Casablanca:* Cult Movies and Intertextual Collage." In *Modern Criticism and Theory: A Reader*. Ed. David Lodge (with Nigel Wood). 2nd Edition. London: Longman, 2000. 394–402.

Jamal, Mahmood. "Dirty Linen." *Black Film, British Cinema.* ICA Documents. London: British Film Institute, 1988. 21–22.

Kaleta, Kenneth C. *Hanif Kureishi: Postcolonial Storyteller.* Austin: U of Texas P, 1998.

Kureishi, Hanif. "My Beautiful Laundrette." In Kureishi, *My Beautiful Laundrette and The Rainbow Sign.* London: Faber & Faber, 1986.

Kureishi, Hanif. *Hanif Kureishi: My Beautiful Laundrette: A Screenplay.* "Fremdsprachentexte" Ed. Merle Tönnies and Claus-Ulrich Viol. Stuttgart: Philipp Reclam jun., 1999.

Kureishi, Hanif. *My Beautiful Laundrette. A Screenplay.* ("Viewfinder") Ed. Michael Mitchell. München: Langenscheidt, 1999.

Kureishi, Hanif. "My Son the Fanatic." In *Many Voices–Many Cultures. Multicultural British Short Stories.* "Fremdsprachentexte". Ed. Barbara Korte and Claudia Sternberg. Stuttgart: Philipp Reclam jun., 1997 [1994]. 147–165.

Mann, Jessica. "Peter Pan's Midlife Crisis." *The Sunday Telegraph* (20 October, 2002). Available at: <www.telegraph.co.uk/culture/4729043/Peter-Pans-midlife-crisis.html>. (Visited 7 January, 2010).

Mason, David. *Race and Ethnicity in Modern Britain.* 2nd ed. Oxford: Oxford UP, 2000.

Mitchell, Michael (ed.). *Minorities in Britain: Never at Ease?* "Viewfinder". München: Langenscheidt-Longman, 1997.

Moore-Gilbert, Bart. *Hanif Kureishi.* "Contemporary World Writers". Manchester and New York: Manchester UP, 2001.

Ranasinha, Ruvani. *Hanif Kureishi.* "Writers and Their Work". Tavistock: Northcote House, 2002.

Rueschmann, Eva. "Film Notes: My Beautiful Laundrette." 2000. Available at: <http://helios.hampshire.edu/~erHA/hacu234/laundrette.html>. (Visited 4 March, 2010).

Sandhu, Sukhdev. "Life Lines." *The Telegraph* (28 August, 2005). Available at <www.telegraph.co.uk/arts/main.jhtml?xml=/arts/2004/08/28/bokur28.xml>. (Visited 5 January 2010).

Schüren, Rainer. "'My Beautiful Laundrette': Multikulturelle Aspekte der Filmarbeit im Englischunterricht der Oberstufe." *Der fremdsprachliche Unterricht–Englisch* 28/14 (1994): 44–54.

Schüren, Rainer. "Teaching Different Cultures through Film. *Educating Rita* and *My Beautiful Laundrette.*" *Journal for the Study of British Cultures* 5.2 (1998): 195–214.

Stierstorfer, Klaus. "Literatur und interkulturelle Kompetenz." In *Interkulturelle Kompetenz: Theorie und Praxis des fremdsprachlichen Unterrichts.* Eds. Laurenz Volkmann, Klaus Stierstorfer and Wolfgang Gehring. Tübingen: Gunter Narr, 2002. 119–141.

Teske, Doris. [Chapter on Kureishi]. *Cultural Studies: GB. Anglistik–Amerikanistik*, Berlin: Cornelsen, 2002. 176–186.

Thomas, Susie. *Hanif Kureishi.* "Readers' Guide to Essential Criticism". New York: Palgrave Macmillan, 2005.

Tönnies, Merle and Claus-Ulrich Viol. "Introduction." In Kureishi, *My Beautiful Laundrette: A Screenplay.* ("Fremdsprachentexte"). Eds. Merle Tönnies and Claus-Ulrich Viol. Stuttgart: Philipp Reclam jun., 1999. 3–14.

Tönnies, Merle and Claus-Ulrich Viol. "Nachwort." In Kureishi, *My Beautiful Laundrette: A Screenplay.* ("Fremdsprachentexte"). Eds. Merle Tönnies and Claus-Ulrich Viol. Stuttgart: Philipp Reclam jun., 1999. 133–165.

Tönnies, Merle and Claus-Ulrich Viol (eds.). *Hanif Kureishi: My Beautiful Laundrette: A Screenplay.* ("Fremdsprachentexte"). Stuttgart: Philipp Reclam jun., 1999.

Volkmann, Laurenz. "Teaching Hanif Kureishi." In *Transcultural English Studies: Theories, Fictions, Realities.* Ed. Frank Schulze-Engler and Sissy Helff. Amsterdam: Rodopi, 2009. 393–408.

11

Nations of the Soul and Women's Poetic Activism

LAKSMISREE BANERJEE

The Emergence of Poetic Texts of Women

In the aftermath of the Imperial Era, with the birth of independent postcolonial societies, poetic writings by women have assumed a new literary significance of a novel brand of nationhood, liberalization and democratization. These poetic compositions, cutting across barriers and wide extensions of time and space, manifest a positive, aggressive identity, which may well be defined as a socio-psychological, ethnic, culturally specific and literary configuration or space designated here as "Nations of the Soul." The poetic texts by women across the Commonwealth and Euro-American world evince a certain innovative way of defining the meanings of nation, nationhood and the narrativization of the intersecting points of gender, identity and race. Hence, it is a fruitful, critical exercise to interpret and analyse the singular coalescence of vision, perspectives and creative delineations of this new, emerging theory of "Nation" in the context of evolving feminist and postfeminist historiography. Within the ambit of articles on imaginary homelands and of feminist interpretations of "subaltern" texts in postcolonial discourse, this differentiated category of a women-specific nationhood, unifying varied segments of aesthetic sisterhood across the globe, becomes a significant area of study. This interesting sub-*genre* situates as well as problematizes these "Nations of the Soul" as an extended metaphor and conceptualized space of women's experiences, issues, struggles, perceptions, projections of truths and the creative expressions of suppressed feminist histories and trajectories.

This literary perspective also reflects upon the quintessential questions of homogeneity *versus* heterogeneity, spirit *versus* body, nature *versus* culture, multiculturalism *versus* isolationism, centre *versus* periphery and so on. Though reactionary and resistant to a certain extent, in the prioritization of the female consciousness, these nations of the soul defy temporal and territorial borderlines in their formidable integrations of poetic artistry. Further, they display a certain wholeness of vision etched out of the depths of female creativity and identifiable in the harmonious resonance of women's poetic voices and activism sustaining their State of Universal Sisterhood.

In the course of this article, many paradoxical positions are arrived at, while the epistemological status of this dialectic naturally reinforces the problematic determination that all female creativity and narrativity is monolithic. These debatable viewpoints could well be investigated through the critical framework of such postcolonial critique as that of R. Radhakrishnan's "Nationalism, Gender and the Narrative of Identity," Aijaz Ahmad's reinterpretations in "Jameson's Rhetoric of Otherness and the National Allegory," Rajeswari Sunder Rajan's "Representing Sati: Continuities and Discontinuities" and such other critical focus on the de-colonizing of the mind along with the positivist complicity with "subaltern" insurgency and "feminist" radicalism. The compositions of such varied internationally known women poets as Toru Dutt, Sarojini Naidu, Kamala Das, Emily Dickinson, Christina Rossetti, Elizabeth Barret Browning, Imtiaz Dharker, Tara Patel, Eunice De Souza, Meena Alexander, Rukmini Bhaya Nair, Margaret Atwood, Sujata Bhatt, Sylvia Plath, Gillian Clarke, Elizabeth Bartlett, Adrienne Rich, Stevie Smith, Elaine Feinstein, Edith Sitwell and so on, from diverse temporal and spatial vantage-points, could well be examined and re-evaluated as composite creations of a resurgent poetic activism lending credence and permanent validity to their "Nations of the Soul."

A Newly Enhanced Fabric of Unity

In the postulation of this new idea of a Nation of Womanhood, one notices a definite centralization of women's emancipatory struggles and issues, which run parallel to and often in conflict with the earlier nationalist movements, which gave birth to postcolonial independent states. While recognizing the fluidity of divergent cultural and poetic constructions, one must also keep in mind the absolute definitions used in the framing of any specific *genre* or canon. Says Aijaz Ahmad in his essay on the representation of women in a postmodern situation: "The axiomatic fact about any canon formation, even when it takes shape as a counter-canon, is that when the desired literary typology is constructed, the canonizing agency selects certain kinds of authors, texts and styles, privileging them over others."[1] In this connection, one would have to accentuate and focus upon only those poetic texts which project the selfhood and identity of women as explicit and unambiguous statements of their "Nations of the Soul," born out of the palimpsestic, hitherto suppressed histories of women. While reading these symptomatic women's poetic compositions, one would definitely arrive at an ideological location of a representative universalism and a central poetic alliance despite cultural and historical differences. The earlier fragmentations, alienations, identity crises and divisive forces of victimization, easily dissolve into a newly enhanced fabric of unity and a resonant harmony. One may, in this context, re-examine Muriel Rukeyser's lines:

> When I wrote of the women in their dances and wildness, it was a mask/... when I wrote of the god,/fragmented ... in exile from myself/... There is no mountain, there is no god ... /No more masks!/Now, for the first time, ... /the fragments join in me with their own music.[2]

Maitrayee Chaudhuri's socio-scientific etching of a liberal state based on the role of women as agents, recipients and equal participators in the formation of a nation as well as her perspective on women as the emblems of a specific, differentiated but equalized culture and ethos, completes only half the picture.[3] The other half could well be garnered through the psychoanalytic properties and symbolical elements that Julia Kristeva attributes to poetic language.[4] Our starting point could be obtained from affecting a balance of these two perspectives of a socio-culturally liberated state and the use of a revolutionary, inborn poetic language for re-defining the limitless limits of this new category. The earlier imbalances of gender, race and class being washed off, we derive new tools of creative vision, symbolism and expression in the strong and powerful "We" of Sylvia Plath's "Mushrooms":

> Overnight, very/Whitely, discreetly ... Our toes, our noses/Take hold on the loam,/Acquire the air ... So many of us! So many of us! ... Nudgers and shovers/Inspite of ourselves,/Our kind multiplies;/We shall by morning/Inherit the earth,/Our foot's in the door.[5]

Beyond the political and socio-scientific gamut of definitions and beyond the fallacy of the existence of a theoretical, determinate and unitary locale for a so-called "Nation," we have an entire corpus of such metaphorical and symbolical poetic language and reconstructions of woman-power, laden with the signification for asserting the truth of these conceptualized "Nations of the Soul" as aesthetic embodiments and representations of an entire female community of poets and artists across the globe. The Indian poet Rajlukshmee Debee Bhattacharya, though in a totally different category of identity and ethnicity from Sylvia Plath and worlds apart in both temporal and spatial terms, creates effusively a similar allegory of woman power through her poem "Punarnava," the ever renewing "velvet-green medicinal creeper" climbing up the "lichened wall ... sprouting leaves,/growing in greenness/eternal companion on the rooftop."[6]

In cutting across political, cultural, geographic and time-bound barriers, these internationally known women poets, could now be assessed and acknowledged as a major aesthetic group impacting global transformations through their poetic activism and ratification of the truth, the beauty and the intensity of the woman's world as an integral part of the larger realms of human affairs. In this sense, these "Nations of the Soul" carved out from the depths of authentic poems written by women, are formidable zones of progressive human thinking and democratization born out of mighty pens, which have dissolved and dissipated the agonies of marginalization and brutalization of the Fanonian "Wretched of the Earth".[7] R. Radhakrishnan, in extending the line and scope of Partha Chatterjee's adverse critique of "Indian nationalism" as a problem of male and feudal conservatism, advocates an innovative and radical feminist historiography:

> Feminist historiography is representational in the sense that it speaks for those questions and concerns that stem from women's issues initially, but in doing so, it understands (and expands) 'gender' as a category that is much more comprehensive in its scope and goes beyond its initial commitment to merely one specific constituency.[8]

This propagation of a non-totalizing and non-teleological feminist historiography holds true in the perception of these "Nations of the Soul" as relevant indices for understanding female-specific issues as larger issues of the human world around. In this holistic framework, dealing with the representational questions and concerns of women, the politicization of "gender" does not hold any water. The well-defined, articulated and designated space of women's poetry, taking its birth and growth from the feminine spiritual-artistic consciousness and socio-psychological experiences, transcends regional and local categories to be blended smoothly in a homogenous poetic space. When Emily Dickinson speaks of the supremacy of the domain of her soul in her Poem No. 303: "The Soul selects her own Society … /Then shuts the Door … /Then closes the Valves of her attention" or about the sanctity of her individual Nation of the human spirit in her Poem No. 214: "I taste a liquor never brewed–/From Tankards scooped in Pearl/Not all the Vats upon the Rhine/Yield such an Alcohol!/Inebriate of Air am I/And Debauchee of Dew/Reeling through endless summer days/From Inns of Molten Blue,"[9] one can almost hear Sarojini Naidu's ode to her "Invincible flowering soul" in its myriad colours "reblossoming like a grove" though strengthened "in the flame of sorrow".[10] Naidu's "Indian Dancers" – "now silent, now singing and swaying and swinging … /Now wantonly winding, they flash"[11] – are as strong, as stable and as vibrant as Christina Rossetti's "Earth" written in another frame of time and space: "Earth grown old, yet still so green,/Deep beneath her crust of cold/Nurses fire unfelt, unseen."[12]

Womanhood and Nationhood

A common alliance of poetic souls among women writers of the world becomes an undeniable catalyst in impacting the progression of contemporary society towards more balanced, modernized and democratic goals. The defiance of patriarchy in an identifiably purified and exclusive space, often strikes through undertones rather than overtones, transcreating and merging subtly with the connotations and composites of womanhood and nationhood. Though one might argue that Rossetti, Dickinson and Naidu write in the conventional idiom, diction and metaphor of a bygone age, when female poetry was seeped in traditional romanticism, more in complicity with than interrogating patriarchy, the synergies, synonymities and parallels are often deeply submerged. One may easily connect Naidu's Indian Gypsy "tameless with the bold falcon's agile grace and the lithe tiger's sinuous majesty" with Elizabeth Bartlett's "cataclysmic love" leading into "landscapes and inscapes too, sometimes tracts of unknown counties, most often the one great hill" in a single spanning thought. The all-encompassing, self-assured and belligerent stance of Kamala Das asserting, "It is I who laugh, it is I who make love/ … I am sinner, I am saint. I am the beloved and the/Betrayed. I have no joys which are not yours, no/Aches which are not yours. I too call myself I",[13] finally connects the woman with the world. It is more than evident here, that feministic poetic compositions have traversed through great transformative distances to achieve a total integration with humanistic themes. However, the predominance of the female artistic premise continues to invigorate and illuminate the wider zones of human thought and activity. Consider lines from Gillian Clarke's "Red Poppy": "So she walks out of the rectangles/Of hard, crowded America/And floods the skies … /You can put out the sun with poppy,/ … paints out language, land, sky,/So we can only look and drown in deeps/Of poppy under a thundering sun."[14] The unmistakable nuances, subtext and meta-text of Feminine Nationhood resonates with almost similar lines in Laksmisree Banerjee's "Sky": "When the storm broke in,/she looked through/at the outside jettying in … /No walls, only a heap/of dry, incinerated hopes/ … She started building/once more/This time, not a home but a sky."[15] Hence, "Nation" is no longer a traumatized space for segregation of the oppressed victim but a proclaimed arena of feminine fortitude and spiritual beauty, as wide as the sky, as deep as the ocean and as diversely ornate and multi-hued as a garden.

In investigating the varied linguistic, mythic, historical, cultural and symbolic dimensions and precincts of these "Nations of the Soul," one discovers a happy interlink between every temporal and spatial category of poets who are women from grandmothers, through mothers to daughters. One notices a sharp movement from the earlier traumatized cries, through later war cries to a final emancipatory enlargement of vision and space with a tranquil, imaginative dissolution of earlier imbalances. As Adrienne Rich expostulates in "Frame": "Her body is different now,/It is holding together with more than a hint of fury/and more than a hint of fear."[16] The commonwealth and fellowship of poet-sisters has finally arrived at a point of meaningful convergence. Feminism, with its backlash and a new era of post-feminist humanism, refocuses and redefines imaginative, conceptual and cultural parametres for the understanding of these "Nations of the Soul" in a broader, deeper and more holistic sense. These are no longer ghettoized, gendered spaces but significant spheres of human affairs and experiences grounded in a globalized reality of worlds within and beyond worlds. Though, today's "Draupadi" is "Once more/stripped to the raw nerves and/bared in books and case studies" feeling the weight of "an anachronistic civilization", she is now an epitome and a spokesperson of the entire human race with "the global features on her face" and "her heart arrested at a still point in history."[17] The earlier strife, ordeals, subversions, desperate battle-lines and oppressive silences have given way to a new, radical tranquillity, the formidable depth and stillness of an unconquerable nationhood of women poets.

Notes

1. Aijaz Ahmad, "Salman Rushdie's *Shame*: Postmodern Migrancy and the Representation of Women," in Ahmad, *In Theory: Classes, Nations, Literatures* (Oxford: Oxford UP, 1992), 123.
2. Muriel Rukeyser, "The Poem as Mask," in *No More Masks*, ed. Florence Howe (New York: Harper Perennial, 1973), xxvii.
3. Maitrayee Chaudhuri, "Gender in the Making of the Indian Nation-State," in *Nation and National Identity in South Asia*, ed. S.L. Sharma and T.K. Oommen (Hyderabad: Orient Longman, 2000), 113–114.

4. John Lechte, "Introduction," in *Julia Kristeva* (Routledge, 1990), 5–6.
5. Sylvia Plath, "Mushrooms," in *The Faber Book of 20th Century Women's Poetry*, ed. Fleur Adcock (London: Faber & Faber, 1987), 233.
6. Rajlukshmee Debee Bhattacharya, "Punarnava," in *Poetry India: Emerging Voices*, ed. H.K. Kaul (Delhi: Hind Pocket Books, 1992), 21–22.
7. Frantz Fanon, "The Wretched of the Earth," in *Postcolonial Discourses*, ed. Gregory Castle (Oxford: Blackwell Publishers, 2001), 4–5.
8. R. Radhakrishnan, "Nationalism, Gender and the Narrative of Identity," in *Postcolonial Discourses*, ed. Gregory Castle (Oxford: Blackwell, 2001), 193.
9. Emily Dickinson, Poem Nos. 214 and 303, in *Emily Dickinson: Selected Poems*, ed. Helen McNeil (London: Phoenix Poetry, 2003), 5 and 17.
10. Sarojini Naidu, "Invincible," in Naidu, *The Broken Wing: Songs of Love, Death and Destiny, 1915–1916* (London: William Heinemann, 1917), 40–48.
11. Sarojini Naidu, "Indian Dancers" and "Indian Gypsy," in *Indo-English Poetry in Bengal*, ed. K.C. Lahiri (Calcutta: Writers Workshop, 1974), 130–135.
12. Christina Rossetti, "Advent," in *Christina Rossetti: Selected Poems*, ed. Jan Marsh (London: Phoenix Poetry, 1996), 3.
13. Kamala Das, "Introduction," in *In Their Own Voice*, ed. Arlene Zide (Delhi: Penguin, 1993), 46.
14. Gillian Clarke, "Red Poppy," in *Sixty Women Poets*, ed. Linda France (Newcastleupon Tyne: Bloodaxe Books, 1993), 85.
15. Laksmisree Banerjee, "Sky," in *I am the Woman: I am the World* (Delhi: UBSPD, 2004), 118–119.
16. Adrienne Rich, "Frame," in *No More Masks*, ed. Florence Howe (New York: Harper Perennial, 1973), 204.
17. Lakshmi Kannan, "Draupadi," in *In Their Own Voice*, ed. Arlene Zide (Delhi: Penguin 1993), 97.

Works Cited

Ahmad, Aijaz. "Jameson's Rhetoric of Otherness and the 'National Allegory'." *In Social Text* 17 (1987): 3–25.

Ahmad, Aijaz. "Salman Rushdie's *Shame*: Postmodern Migrancy and the Representation of Women." In *In Theory: Classes, Nations, Literatures.* Oxford: Oxford UP, 1992. 123–124.

Banerjee, Laksmisree. "Sky." In *I am the Woman: I am the World.* Delhi: UBSPD, 2004. 118–119

Clarke, Gillian. "Red Poppy." In *Sixty Women Poets.* Ed. Linda France. Newcastleupon Tyne: Bloodaxe Books, 1993. 85–86.

Bhattacharya, Rajlukshmee Debee. "Punarnava." In *Poetry India: Emerging Voices.* Ed. H.K. Kaul. Delhi: Hind Pocket Books, 1992. 21–22.

Chaudhuri, Maitrayee. "Gender in the Making of the Indian Nation-State." In *Nation and National Identity in South Asia.* Ed. S.L. Sharma and T.K. Oommen. Hyderabad: Orient Longman, 2000. 113–114.

Das, Kamala. "Introduction." In *In Their Own Voice.* Ed. Arlene Zide. Delhi: Penguin, 1993. 46.

Dickinson, Emily. Poem No. 214. In *Emily Dickinson: Selected Poems.* Ed. Helen McNeil. London: Phoenix Poetry, 2003. 5.

Dickinson, Emily. Poem No. 303. In *Emily Dickinson: Selected Poems.* Ed. Helen McNeil.London: Phoenix Poetry, 2003. 17.

Fanon, Frantz. "The Wretched of the Earth." In *Postcolonial Discourses.* Ed. Gregory Castle. Oxford: Blackwell, 2001. 4–5.

Kannan, Lakshmi. "Draupadi." In *In Their Own Voice.* Ed. Arlene Zide. Delhi: Penguin India, 1993. 97.

Lechte, John. "Introduction." In *Julia Kristeva.* Ed. Christopher Norris. London and New York: Routledge, 1990. 5–6.

Naidu, Sarojini. "Indian Dancers." In *Indo-English Poetry in Bengal.* Ed. K.C. Lahiri. Calcutta: Writers Workshop, 1974. 130–131.

Naidu, Sarojini. "Indian Gypsy." In *Indo-English Poetry in Bengal.* Ed. K.C. Lahiri. Calcutta: Writers Workshop, 1974. 133–134.

Plath, Sylvia. "Mushrooms." In *The Faber Book of 20th Century Women's Poetry.* Ed. Fleur Adcock. London: Faber & Faber, 1987. 233.

Radhakrishnan, R. "Nationalism, Gender and the Narrative of Identity." In *Postcolonial Discourses.* Ed. Gregory Castle. Oxford: Blackwell, 2001.193. [Orig. 1992.]

Rich, Adrienne. "Frame." In *No More Masks.* Ed. Florence Howe. New York: Harper Perennial, 1973. 204.

Rossetti, Christina. "Advent." In *Christina Rossetti: Selected Poems.* Ed. Jan Marsh. London: Phoenix Poetry, 1996. 3.

Rukeyser, Muriel. "The Poem as Mask." In *No More Masks.* Ed. Florence Howe. New York: Harper Perennial, 1973. xxvii.

Sunder Rajan, Rajeswari "Representing Sati: Continuities and Discontinuities." In *Real and Imagined Women: Gender, Culture, and Postcolonialism.* London and New York: Routledge, 1993. 40–63.

12

Changing Worlds / Changing Words

The Language of Experiment in Salman Rushdie's *Midnight's Children*[1]

OM PRAKASH DWIVEDI

> One has to convey in a language that is not one's own the spirit that is one's own. One has to convey the various shades and omissions of a certain thought movement that looks maltreated in an alien language.
>
> – Raja Rao[2]

Transnational English Usage

The use of the English language by postcolonial authors has become a matter of great debate in the presentday world. Globalization has clearly transformed the role and use of English throughout the world, especially in the erstwhile colonized countries, where it has now become the language of trade and commerce and where it is successfully playing a vital role in development and integration. In this context, one can easily observe that the English language has played the role of an aggressive political agent or activist in transforming postcolonial nations. English, then, has become a powerful tool, an effective "weapon" which can be, and *is*, used for many purposes – social, political, national and international.

British colonialism paved the way for the spread of the English language throughout the world. But ironically, English had emerged in England as a result of the Anglo-Saxon invasion (after the Romans had left). Undoubtedly, English came to be spoken and written in the colonized countries and has become a powerful tool of expression today. Subsequently, it was put to a fantastic creative application by talented writers of those countries. This fact can be corroborated by Rushdie's famous statement: "Those people who were once colonized by the language are now rapidly remaking it, domesticating it, becoming more and more relaxed about the way they use it."[3] This burgeoning use of English has ostensibly internationalized its role and position in the prevailing transnational era.

English in the Indian Context

In India, English was introduced in educational institutions in 1835 by Lord Macaulay, who in his famous *Minute* advocated the English education for Indians. His explicit purpose was to produce a class of *babus* who could operate as interpreters between the ruling Whites and the colonized Indians. Now, after 175 years of that *Minute*, the English language and literature has attained a prestigious place in the literary world in India. In truth, India "is now one of the world's largest markets for the production and dissemination of English language books, and boosts of several very famous novelists in the language."[4] G.V. Desani, Raja Rao, Salman Rushdie, Anita Desai, Amitav Ghosh, Arundhati Roy and Kiran Desai have been highly instrumental in popularizing the glory of the English language throughout India, thus making an "alien" tongue a "primary instrument of national expression."

In the recent past, the question occupying the centre of postcolonial Indian English literature is: "how far can an Indian English author succeed in evoking a sense of nationalism among the indigenous readers?" V.A. Shahane answers this flummoxing question thus:

> English in India must become sufficiently Indian in order to be an adequate instrument of national consciousness and expression. It may deviate, in the process, from the established norms of Kings'

> English but these deviations should be welcomed by all because they will bestow on Indian English the vitality, vigor, and directness which are the admirable qualities of a living language.[5]

Ostensibly, to speak or to write in a language that is not one's own is a demanding challenge in this era of transnationalism. It requires flexibility and the willingness to accept the cultural and political values of that country, while keeping one's own cultural and political values intact. Placed in such a demanding situation, one cannot but choose a middle path, and in case of the postcolonial Indian authors, they do it by innovating the English language itself or by decolonizing it in a significant manner. This innovation of the language brings to these Indian authors a separate identity, an independent recognition and they explore their own culture by employing the language of their past colonizers, thus appealing to the indigenous readers by inseminating the spirit of nationalism into their minds and hearts. Mark what Pritish Nandy says about the Indianizing nature of English, that it is "a language of our own, yes, an Indian language, in which we could feel deeply, create and convey experiences and responses typically."[6]

And yet, there exists a conflicting relationship between the English language and many Indian English writers. On the one hand, we have writers such as Raja Rao, R.K. Narayan and Kamala Das who are willing to adopt this language and convey their emotions and thoughts in it. In his Foreword to *Kanthapura*, Raja Rao writes about the use of English that "It is the language of our intellectual make-up like Sanskrit or Persian was before."[7] R.K. Narayan, on his part, contends that the use of English in India is "a legitimate development and needs no apology."[8] On the other hand, we have many writers, who are against this proliferation of the English language. B. Rajan states that English is "a language imposed upon India rather than nourished by its soil."[9] Evidently, it highlights the paradoxical attitude of Indian English writers towards English, though some of them have used it rather well in their creative works.

Despite the prevailing contradiction in the application of English, it continues to occupy an important position among the English-speaking intelligentsia in India. Literature written in English has come to assume national importance in India, whereas other literatures – Marathi, Gujarati, Bengali, Tamil, Telugu and so on – continue to retain a regional flavour and colour. English has successfully overtaken almost all the regional languages in India in points of popularity, recognition and national integration. Generally, it is considered as a colonizing tool, but in due course of time, it came to be used a lot, especially in schools, colleges, universities and offices as a powerful means of communication and expression. But, of course, the poor and the illiterate have nothing to do with this language, as it is largely confined to the elitist class in India for discussing matters of national importance, such as political and economic policies and the ways of their implementation. English is the only language in India that bonds all the Indians together, irrespective of their caste, creed and community.

English à la Rushdie

Right from the very beginning of one's life, language plays an increasingly vital role in establishing one's identity. The medium of communication between a parent and a child becomes a tool for siphoning language into the mind of a child, and it is with this particular language that he identifies himself. He starts learning and speaking that language in due course of time. He then goes on to construct a sense of "I/we" and "us". Since English is a colonial language, the question then arises: what identity can a colonial language give to the colonized or their descendants? The answer to this perplexing postcolonial question can be found in the following lines of Kamala Das in her poem "An Introduction":

> I am an Indian very brown, born in
> Malabar, I speak three languages, write in
> Two, dream in one. Don't write in English they said
> English is not your mother tongue
> … … …
> The language I speak
> Becomes mine, its distortions, its queerness
> All mine, mine alone.[10]

Seen from this angle, one can clearly say that language is an integral part of human communication. Language, then, cannot only be learnt but also be creatively used, as Das does in her writings. In the postcolonial context, language is inevitably linked with power. It becomes a site of contestation within which new identities are constructed.

Salman Rushdie created a furore with the publication of his novel, *Midnight's Children* (1981).[11] Its popularity rests on two things: the innovative use of English as a language, and the fantastic representation of history. While Rushdie resorts to the use of *magic realism* to oppose the Eurocentrism of master discourses, the innovativeness of Rushdie's English is prompted by a desire to capture the spirit of Indian culture with all its multiplicity and diversity. As a linguistic experimentalist, Rushdie attempts to destroy "the natural rhythms of the English language" and to dislocate "the English and let other things into it."[12] Rushdie's *Midnight's Children* best illustrates his strategy of "Indianising, revitalising and decolonising the English language."[13] Here in this article, I shall try to highlight the linguistic innovations in Salman Rushdie's *Midnight's Children*.

At first glance, the most inviting feature of Salman Rushdie's language is the bounteous sprinkling of Hindi and Urdu words throughout *Midnight's Children*, and this colourful sprinkling provides a certain amount of oriental flavour to the novel. This is probably done for two specific reasons: firstly, to situate the novel in its geographical location in various cities of India, Pakistan and Bangladesh; and secondly, to subvert a language associated with colonial powers. Evidently, the English of *Midnight's Children* is not the Queen's English (or Standard English); it is the English best suited to express the sensibility of South Asian readers, even if they are living abroad. But though the novel abounds in Hindi and Urdu words, Rushdie has added no notes or glossary to explain them to Western readers, as Raja Rao has done at the end of his monumental novel, *Kanthapura* (1938). Like Vikram Seth in *A Suitable Boy* (1993), Rushdie does not think it necessary to provide explanations. In an interview with T. Vijay Kumar, Rushdie remarks that "to do footnotes or to do notes at the end was a kind of defeat. The story has to tell itself, it must not rely on explanations. If it needs footnotes, it's a failure."[14]

Rather, Rushdie thinks that the text of the novel should be self-explanatory and absorbing in itself. In truth, Raja Rao's English remains Sanskritized, whereas Rushdie's English is an example of the hybrid discourses of a cosmopolitan writer. According to

Tabish Khair, Rushdie is "mostly trying to appropriate a kind of Indian English that his characters are supposed to speak while Rao is *mostly* translating the vernacular spoken by his characters."[15] This fact accounts for a lot of difference between the attitudes of these two writers towards English.

True to his grain, Rushdie makes use of a number of Hindi, Urdu and Hindustani words, phrases and expressions in *Midnight's Children*. Such words, phrases and expressions form a long list, including *ekdum* (at once), *angrez* (Englishman), *phut-aphut* (in no time), *nasbandi* (sterilization), *dhoban* (washerwoman), *feringee* (the same as "angrez"), *baba* (grandfather), *garam masala* (hot spices), *rakshasas* (demons), *fauz* (army), *badmaas* (badmen), *jailkhana* (prison), *baap-re-baap* (o, my father), *hai hai* (exclamatory expression), *sab kuch* (all things), *bas* (enough is enough), *chi-chi* (an expression of contempt), *yaar* (friend), *gora* (white-skinned one), *pyar kiya to darna kya* (why to fear in love), *goondas* (musclemen), *hubshee* (negro), *ooper nichey* (up and down), *sarpanch* (head of a village), *kahin* (said), *bhai-bhai* (brother-brother), *it* (end), *zenana* (harem), *crorepatis* (a man of crores, a multi-millionaire), *ayah* (nurse), *nimbu-pani* (lemon-juice), *paan* (betel), *khichri* (mixed food), *gur* (molasses), *rasgullas* (a kind of sweet), *gulabjamuns* (another variety of sweet), *jalebis* (a variety of sweet), *barfi* (a sweet), *bhel-puri* (a sort of tasty snack) [16], and many others. The use of such words and expressions provides an amount of authenticity and credibility to the novel. It also enhances the quantum of reality that is so much needed in a historical novel like *Midnight's Children*.

In her Introduction to *Rushdie's Midnight's Children: A Book of Critical Readings* (2003), Meenakshi Mukherjee mentions "linguistic risks" that Rushdie took with utter abandon, defining them as "getting away with the use of the mongrel street language of cities, daring to translate idioms and puns mediated by no apology, no footnote, no glossary."[17] Though Mukherjee's contention that Rushdie "get[s] away with the use of the mongrel street language of cities" is difficult to accept, as Rushdie occasionally resorts to film-songs and film-language in this novel, her observation that he is "daring to translate idioms and puns mediated by no apology, no footnote, no glossary" is definitely sustainable. She commends *Midnight's Children* as "a theoretical discourse about nation, history and their narrativity," as "the paradigmatic postcolonial text subverting the notions of received historiography and indigenising both the language and the narrative mode of the colonising culture," and as "the quintessential fictional embodiment of the postmodern celebration of de-centring and hybridity."[18] Rushdie's English is decidedly postcolonial and postmodern. It gives us glimpses into his conscious craftsmanship, which aims at decentring and hybridity. And his skill at "decentring" and "hybridity" is best seen when he, at the lexical level, employs some Latin and Arabic words. Some of the outstanding examples of this are: "*mucuna pruritis*," "*feronia elephanticus*," "*sunt lacrimae rerum*" (all Latin), "*kan ma kan, fi qadim azzaman*," "*tilk al-gharaniq al-'ula wa inna shafa'ata-hunna la-turtaja*" (all Arabic).

Sometimes Rushdie combines words and phrases to make compounds, a style later appropriated by Arundhati Roy in her novel *The God of Small Things* (1997). Such compounds are galore in *Midnight's Children*, such as "overandover," "updownup," "downdowndown," "suchandsuch," "noseholes," "birthanddeath," "whatdoyoumeanhowcanyousaythat," "blackasnight," "nearlynine," "nearlynineyearold," "almostseven," and "godknowswhat."[19] These compounds display the extent of Rushdie's inventiveness and show his mastery of the English language. He employs it as he wishes to suit his purpose. But the danger of deviations from the traditional English, especially in matters of grammar and syntax, lies in creating unwanted difficulties for readers. Also, the novelist who is out to demonstrate his sharp perception of the language in order to dazzle his readers might be branded as modist or a faddist. Rushdie may be a trendsetter of "mongrel English," but his writing smacks of a touch of artificiality and appropriation. Hence, Tabish Khair rightly points out:

> The only Englishes which could be dubbed 'not artificial' and 'unproblematically Indian' would probably be the types used by Narayan or by Ghosh in *The Calcutta Chromosome*, who more or less write their minimally stylized version of the English grapholect.[20]

In a way, Khair suggests here that Rushdie uses a highly "stylized version of the English grapholect." And as Ben Jonson said of Shakespeare, Rushdie is "not a safe model" for the future writers of English because of his "chutnification" of the language. Rushdie uses slang mostly Indian – very often in the text of *Midnight's Children*; for example, "funtoosh," "goo," "gora," "zenana," "hubsee," and so on. Occasionally, Rushdie resorts to deliberate misspellings of words, as for example in "unquestionabel," "straaange," "existance," and "ees." He also uses some incorrect words, from the grammatical viewpoint, such as "mens," "lifeliness," and "informations." All these deliberate misspellings point to the use of English by Indians in their daily lives. Such lapses are, probably, deliberate in order to flout the traditionally accepted norms of grammar. The use of "once upon a time" in the passage quoted above seems to be redundant, though it serves to create the impression of a fairytale. This kind of expression tends to create magic realism in the novel, for *Midnight's Children* is both history and fantasy at the same time.

In *Midnight's Children*, Rushdie tries to destroy "the notion of the purity or centrality of English" by inventing new forms of existing English words or by effecting "creative hybridization." Though one can find a number of examples of this in the text of the novel: "dislikeable," "doctori," "unbeautiful," "sonship," "memoryless," "historyless," "dupatta-less," or "chutnification," to mention only a few. A remarkable feature of Rushdie's linguistic experiment is the repetition of words, phrases, even descriptions of events. In fact, a fine example of the repetition of words, phrases and even descriptions of events can be witnessed at the very beginning of the novel, where Rushdie writes about Saleem's birth in a grandiloquent manner:

> I was born in the city of Bombay ... once upon a time. No, that won't do, there's no getting away from the date; I was born in Doctor Narlikar's Nursing Home on August 15th, 1947. And the time? The time matters, too. Well then: at night. ... On the stroke of the midnight, as a matter of fact. Clock-hands joined palms in respectful greeting as I came. Oh, spell it out, spell it out: at the precise instant of India's arrival at independence, I tumbled forth into the world. There were gasps. And, outside the window, fireworks and crowds. (*MC* 3)

A parallel description of the birth of Saleem Sinai's son is found towards the close of the novel:

> He was born in Old Delhi ... once upon a time. No, that won't do, there's no getting away from the date: Aadam Sinai arrived at a night-shadowed slum on June 25th, 1975. And the time? The

> time matters, too. As I said: at night. No, it's important to be more ... On the stroke of midnight, as a matter of fact. Clockhands joined palms. Oh, spell it out, spell it out: at the instant of India's arrival at Emergency, he emerged. There were gasps; and, across the country, silences and fears. And owing to the occult tyrannies of that benighted hour, he was mysteriously handcuffed to history, his destiny indissolubly chained to those of his country. (*MC* 419)

By using such repetitions, Rushdie successfully associates the history of the individual to the history of the nation, and thus Saleem is "handcuffed to history" (*MC* 1) right from his birth.

An important matter to be discussed is Rushdie's narrative style. He makes use of the first-person narration in *Midnight's Children*. Right from the beginning to the end of the novel, one can easily mark the unfolding of the story in the first person; for instance, "I was born in the city of Bombay" (*MC* 3), "I permit myself to insert a Bombaytalkie style close-up" (*MC* 414). The use of the personal pronoun "I" renders the narration authentic and trustworthy. It is through the eyes and the language of the narrator Saleem Sinai that various events, turns in history and characters are seen. Rushdie uses a childlike idiosyncrasy to create the character of Saleem. The language which he uses for this purpose is what Tabish Khair calls "a stylized staged-cum-spoken-English." There is a dramatic element in Rushdie's prose style, and it contains the flavour of speech. Rushdie uses the ironic pidgin English as spoken in certain middle class urban circles in and outside India. At times he translates literally from Indian languages. He also makes use of incorrect English (as pointed out in the preceding paragraph) as spoken by semi-literate Indians. The first person narration displays the involvement of the narrator in the happenings around (and this is diametrically opposed to the sense of detachment usually found in the third-person narration).

Indian and English

In her well-known critique of Indian English fiction, *The Twice Born Fiction* (1974), Meenakshi Mukherjee comments that "the most significant challenge is the task of using the English language in a way that will be distinctively Indian and still remain English."[21] Rushdie has faced this challenge squarely and churned out an

Indian English that is a peculiar mixture. This could be possible for him because of his tendency for amalgamation or, in Rushdie's own words, 'chutnification' of various narrational registers. At times Rushdie makes use of the language of films, as in the following:

> I permit myself to insert a Bombay-talkie-style close-up – a calendar ruffled by a breeze, its pages flying off in rapid succession to denote the passing of the years; I superimpose turbulent long-shots of street riots, medium slots of burning buses. (*MC* 414)

The expression "zooming out into long shot. … Merrily it rolls along, rolls along, rolls along. … (Fade out)" (*MC* 283) also has a ring of the filmy language about it. The use of such language clearly shows Rushdie's postmodern interest in mass culture. Occasionally, Rushdie indulges in verbal fantasy (and 'fantasy' is an integral part of his structural strategy along with 'reality').

Rushdie frequently uses lengthy and complex sentences in *Midnight's Children.* One may mark the following extract in this connection:

> O, spell it out, spell it out; the operation whose ostensible purpose was the draining of my inflamed sinews and the once-and-for-all clearing of my nasal passages had the effect of breaking whatever connection had been made in a washing chest; of depriving me of nose-given telepathy; of banishing me from the possibility of midnight's children. (*MC* 304)

Clearly, Rushdie has become wordy and rhetorical here, and his description of the operation on Saleem's nasal passage tends to be lengthy, witty, humorous, and complex.

To conclude, Rushdie's numerous experiments with the English language have made *Midnight's Children* a highly challenging and complex work of fiction. Along with the content and its marvellous treatment, these linguistic experiments have enabled Rushdie to capture the topmost position among the winners of the Booker Prize over the past twenty-five years. His linguistic experiments in *Midnight's Children*, strange and startling at times as they are, have attracted readers and reviewers the world over, and have placed Indian English fiction on a sound footing in the presentday highly competitive literary scene.

Notes

1. An earlier version published as "Linguistic Experiments in Rushdie's *Midnight's Children*," in *Transnational Literature* 1:1 (2008). Available at: <http://dspace.flinders.edu.au/dspace/bitstream/2328/3244/1/Dwivedi.pdf>. (Visited 3 May, 2010.)
2. Raja Rao, "Author's Foreword," in Rao, *Kanthapura* (New York: New Directions, 1963), vii.
3. Jahan Ramazani, *The Hybrid Muse: Postcolonial Poetry in English* (Chicago: U Chicago P, 2001), 14.
4. Aijaz Ahmad, *In Theory: Classes, Nations, Literatures* (New Delhi: Oxford UP, 1994), 73.
5. V.A. Sahane, *Points of View* XV:1 (2008), 52.
6. Pritish Nandy, *Indian Poetry in English Today* (New Delhi: Sterling, 1973), 8.
7. Rao vii.
8. R.K. Narayan, *A Writer's Nightmare* (Harmondsworth: Penguin, 1988), 197.
9. B. Rajan, "India," in *Literatures of the World in English*, ed. Bruce King (London: Routledge & Kegan Paul, 1974), 179.
10. Kamala Das, "An Introduction," in *Kamala Das: A Selection with Essays on Her Work*, ed. Syd C. Harrex and Vincent O'Sullivan (Adelaide: CRNLE, 1986), 7.
11. Salman Rushdie, *Midnight's Children* (New York: Avon, 1982); references are to this edition, and they are given parenthetically, preceded by *MC*.
12. Sisir Kumar Chatterjee, '"Chutnification": The Dynamics of Language in *Midnight's Children*', *Salman Rushdie's 'Midnight's Children': A Reader's Companion* (New Delhi: Asia Book Club, 2004), 253.
13. Chatterjee 253.
14. Salman Rushdie, "An Interview with Salman Rushdie," with T. Vijay Kumar, in *Rushdie's* Midnight's Children*: A Book of Readings*, ed. Meenakshi Mukherjee (New Delhi: Pencraft International, 2003), 217.
15. Tabish Khair, "Language Problems of Dialogue and Mapping," in *Babu Fictions: Alienation in Contemporary Indian English Novels* (New Delhi: Oxford UP, 2005), 110.
16. Chatterjee 253–254.
17. Meenakshi Mukherjee, "Introduction," in *Rushdie's Midnight's Children: A Book of Readings*, ed. Meenakshi Mukherjee (New Delhi: Pencraft International, 2003), 10.
18. Mukherjee 9.

19. Chatterjee 254.
20. Khair 109–110.
21. Meenakshi Mukherjee, *The Twice Born Fiction* (New Delhi: Arnold-Heinemann, 1974), 165.

Works Cited

Ahmad, Aijaz. *In Theory: Classes, Nations, Literatures.* New Delhi: Oxford UP, 1994.

Chatterjee, Sisir Kumar. "'Chutnification': The Dynamics of Language in *Midnight's Children.*" In *Salman Rushdie's Midnight's Children: A Reader's Companion.* New Delhi: Asia Book Club, 2004. 253.

Das, Kamala. "An Introduction." In *Kamala Das: A Selection with Essays on Her Work.* Ed. Syd C. Harrex and Vincent O'Sullivan. Adelaide: CRNLE, 1986. 7.

Mukherjee, Meenakshi. "Introduction." In *Rushdie's Midnight's Children: A Book of Readings.* Ed. Meenakshi Mukherjee. New Delhi: Pencraft International, 2003.

Mukherjee, Meenakshi. *The Twice Born Fiction.* New Delhi: Arnold-Heinemann, 1974.

Nandy, Pritish. *Indian Poetry in English Today.* New Delhi: Sterling, 1973.

Narayan, R.K. *A Writer's Nightmare.* Harmondsworth: Penguin, 1988.

Rajan, B. "India." In *Literatures of the World in English.* Ed. Bruce King. London: Routledge and Kegan Paul, 1974. 178–195.

Ramazani, Jahan. *The Hybrid Muse: Postcolonial Poetry in English.* Chicago: U Chicago P, 2001.

Rao, Raja. "Author's Foreword." In *Kanthapura.* New York: New Directions, 1963. vii–viii. (Orig. 1938.)

Rushdie, Salman. "An Interview with Salman Rushdie." With T. Vijay Kumar. In *Rushdie's Midnight's Children: A Book of Readings.* Ed. Meenakshi Mukherjee. New Delhi: Pencraft International, 2003. 217.

Rushdie, Salman. *Midnight's Children.* New York: Avon, 1982. (Orig. 1981.)

Sahane, V.A. *Points of View* XV:1 (2008), 52.

13

Salman Rushdie's Transnational Layers

JOEL KUORTTI

"I'll Show Them All": Salman Rushdie and the Secret of the Fish Bones

The Indian-born Salman Rushdie is one of the most disputed figures of contemporary British literature, literature that he entered as a kind of heir to the British Empire – although he is also labelled an Indian, or a Pakistani writer. In his books, Rushdie often deals with England, English, and Englishness. How do they appear in his writing? What kind of British literary landscapes emerges from his writings? What kind of a "British" writer does Rushdie see himself, or is perceived? It is, thus, interesting to probe the ways in which transnational markers of language and literature are there in his writings – how Rushdie has been conquering England, a conquest that has been a conquest of the English language.

One of Rushdie's formative experiences of England was a kipper served for breakfast. He did not know how to eat it. This autobiographical anecdote is also in Rushdie's novel *The Satanic Verses* (1988),[1] in which one of the two main protagonists,

Salahuddin Chamchawala – Saladin Chamcha for short – experiences a similar challenge at his first English breakfast:

> He sat there staring at it, not knowing where to begin. Then he cut into it, and got a mouthful of tiny bones. And after extracting them all, another mouthful, more bones. His fellow-pupils watched him suffer in silence; not one of them said, here, let me show you, you eat it in this way. It took him ninety minutes to eat the fish and he was not permitted to rise from the table until it was done. By that time he was shaking, and if he had been able to cry he would have done so. Then the thought occurred to him that he had been taught an important lesson: "England was a peculiar-tasting smoked fish full of spikes and bones, and nobody would ever tell him how to eat it." (*SV* 44)

Further, he discovered that he was a bloody-minded person: "I'll show them all," he swore and continued: "You see if I don't." The eaten kipper was his first victory, the first step in his conquest of England.

For Rushdie, that was his last kipper breakfast but in his literary endeavours he has continued his conquest of the "peculiar-tasting smoked fish."[2] Rushdie has handled the British society and its history in many ways in his works. His point of view has always been critical, whether he is writing about the effects of colonialism, or immigration policies. Rushdie has succeeded in "showing them all" that Saladin in the previous quotation wanted to and has found himself a place in British literature. He has not contented himself by adapting to and imitating the colonial power and its language but has reformed them for his own purposes. It has been especially important for Rushdie to enrich the English language with Indian English – specifically in his first books – and he has not only familiarized himself with English but has tried, and succeeded in, changing it.

Grand Narratives, Small Stories

Today, Rushdie is an established writer living in the United States, but earlier he was somewhat an oddity in the British literary circles. He worked with the fringe theatre and advertising, and dreamt of a career as a writer. In 1975 he published his first novel *Grimus*, which he had written particularly for a science fiction writing competition organized by the publishing company Victor Gollancz. The novel was withdrawn from the contest because the publisher did not want Rushdie to be labelled as a Sci-Fi writer. The judges of the competition – the eminent writers Brian Aldiss, Kingsley Amis and Arthur C. Clarke – would have given the prize to Rushdie, and Aldiss admits that this would have meant that Rushdie would be marginalized as a writer catering to a small circle of readers.[3] *Grimus* pleased neither the readers nor Rushdie, although its wider themes are familiar to readers of his later works: questions of identity, emphasis on multiplicity and the interplay of different cultural, mythological and literary materials. The book is also funny, even though its satire is juvenile as compared to that in the later books. As an example one could give the description of the title of a pompous book by one Professor Ignatius Quasimodo Gribb, *The All-Purpose Quotable Philosophy*, in which we can find statements like "The sands of time are steeped in new Beginnings."[4] According to Gribb, individual statements gain new meanings and new depth when they are presented in new contexts. Even though the idea of ambiguity is here proposed tongue-in-cheek, it is nevertheless a major theme present in some form or the other in all of Rushdie's books. It is also one of the most interesting elements in his books. The texts are full of intertextual references to world literature, comics, music and cinema, as well as to historical characters and events. These references intensify a given narrative and they offer new experiences of discovery for the reader: they are a cornucopia that continues to produce new and enchanting interpretations and connections.

For Rushdie, the grand narratives of history – be they political, religious, or ideological – do not constitute a meaningful reference. They derive their meaning from the lives of the people, intertwined through countless small stories, continuously changing into something else. This aspect is especially clear in *Haroun and the Sea of Stories* (1990), most of all because it does not aspire to be a Great Novel but rather a fantastic tale. In the book, there is the "Ocean of the Streams of Story," which held all the stories of the world "in fluid form, [so that] they retained the ability to change, to become new versions of themselves, to join up with other stories and so become yet other stories."[5] Rushdie wrote this popular and slender book while he was hiding from the threats on his life due to the controversy caused by the publication of his novel *The Satanic Verses*. Although *Haroun* is often relegated as a "youth novel," it nevertheless deals with the issues of freedom of speech and the meanings of story telling, which are central themes in his *oeuvre*. Then again, many readers do find it the most pleasing of his books for its brevity and fairy-tale-like atmosphere.

In 1981, Rushdie was awarded the prestigious Booker prize for his novel *Midnight's Children* (1981).[6] With that book, he opened up a new way to define British literature that was to be written by numerous postcolonial writers all over the former Empire, the present Commonwealth. While Rushdie had remarkable precursors – such as the Booker Prize winners V.S. Naipaul from Trinidad (for *In a Free State* in 1971), Nadine Gordimer from South Africa (for *The Conservationist*, 1974) and the multinational but largely recognized as an Indian writer, Ruth Prawer Jhabvala (for *Heat and Dust*, 1975) – it was *Midnight's Children* that became the key work to transform the literary field.

Since Rushdie, postcolonial literatures have had a remarkable position in the UK. This is confirmed for example if one looks at the list of subsequent Booker Prize winners: the South African J.M. Coetzee (*The Life and Times of Michael K*, 1983 and *Disgrace*, 1999), the New Zealander of Maori descent Keri Hulme (*Bone People*, 1985), the Nigerian Ben Okri (*The Famished Road*, 1991), the Canadian Sri Lankan Michael Ondaatje (*The English Patient*, 1992), the Indian Arundhati Roy (*The God of Small Things*, 1997), the Indo-American Kiran Desai (*The Inheritance of Loss*, 2006), and most recently the Indian Aravind Adiga (*The White Tiger*, 2008). Furthermore, in 1993, *Midnight's Children* was nominated as the Booker of Bookers, as the best awarded book in the 25-year-history of the prize. By redefining British literature, Rushdie and other writers have opened up such doors for the readers that did not even exist before. Literature defined in strictly national terms has got on its side a whole new field of new transnational, multicultural, or global literary tradition emerging from a hybrid combination of nationalities, ethnicities, and histories.

Rushdie's main works so far are *Midnight's Children* and *The Satanic Verses*. *Midnight's Children* is the story of Saleem Sinai, born in the midnight hour on 15 August, 1947, at the moment when the British leave India and let the Indians rule their own country. The story is not a romanticized story of postcolonial bliss but a multi-layered and even tragic look at the history of India during its first two decades of independence. *Midnight's Children* represents magical realism in which the realistic and historical narrative framework incorporates incidents that are magical and illogical, but which are however treated as natural. In the book, during the first hour of independent India, 1,001 children are born and who by that reason alone have naturally magical abilities (*MC* 195). Saleem, one of the two children born exactly in the midnight hour, describes this situation as follows:

> So among the midnight children were infants with powers of transmutation, flight, prophecy and wizardry ... but two of us were born on the stroke of midnight. Saleem and Shiva, [...] to Shiva, the hour had given the gifts of war [...] and to me, the greatest talent of all – the ability to look into the hearts and minds of men. (*MC* 229)

With his telepathic abilities, Saleem narrates his own story, which is simultaneously the story of India for, after all, he had been "mysteriously handcuffed to history" (*MC* 3). The novel is often seen as a national allegory, an allegory of the birth of a nation, for Saleem, together with his opposite Shiva, stands for the classical Indian mythological opposition between Brahma and Shiva. For Saleem, however, the direction of history is from the national to the private: Indian history takes place because of and through him and his family. Thus for example "the hidden purpose of the Indo-Pakistani war of 1965 was nothing more nor less than the elimination of my benighted family from the face of the earth" (*MC* 338).

In *The Satanic Verses*, too, the real and the magical come together. The book begins with terrorists blowing up an aeroplane over the English Channel, resulting in the fall of the two main protagonists Saladin Chamcha and Gibreel Farishta into the sea unharmed. Saladin's "conquest of England" is ironically compared to that of William the Conqueror in 1066, and subsequently he is beaten up by the police and immigration officers. For the reader, the story sets up – among other things – the fight between good and evil, in which Saladin's counterpart is Gibreel. In this fight, the traditional roles have been shifted so that good is represented by the "devilish" Saladin and evil by the "angelic" Gibreel. While

Gibreel's motto is one truth and the unity of identity, Saladin vouches for the multiplicity of identity and truth. All this leads to a fight of spirits all over London and Britain, and, through Gibreel's dreams, also an interpretation of the early history of Islam in Arabia. The book ends with a "final combat" in which Saladin remains alive with his lover. Among such grand narratives in Rushdie's books, we find also love, although he often takes an ironic view of love as well as eroticism.[7]

Of all Rushdie's books, *The Satanic Verses* is the most multidimensional, varying and rewarding. As its history shows, it is also the most daring in its discussion of Islam and the Prophet Mohammed in a way that has not been acceptable to many Muslims. It is exactly the juxtaposing of different worlds and stories that gives the book its special, enchanting flavour.

In his books, Rushdie approaches the grand themes through individual stories and destinies. If in *Midnight's Children* the fates of Saleem and India coincide, in *Shame* (1982)[8] the lives of Omar Khayyam Shakil and Sufiya Zenobia are linked to the political realities of Pakistan in the 1970s and 1980s – to President Zulfikar Ali Bhutto and General Zia Ul-Haq. When Saladin Chamcha and Gibreel Farishta are locked in their mutual fight in *The Satanic Verses*, it also suggests a critique of British Thatcherite immigration policy – and through its dream sequences, also looks at Islamic history. In *Shalimar the Clown* (2005) the Kashmiri terrorist Shalimar's revenge attack fuses the private with the public political history in the debated border area of Kashmir between India and Pakistan.[9] In Rushdie's latest novel *The Enchantress of Florence* (2008), the life of the Mughal Emperor Akbar is mingled surprisingly with the Florentine Niccolò Machiavelli's life.[10] These are the kinds of connections that are born in the Ocean of the Streams of Story, bringing out the multilayered nature of reality as well as the human capabilities either for good or bad.

The Secret Lives of Sir Salman

Rushdie's literary output has been rich and successful, yet he is best known worldwide for issues other than his books. Most of all, this is due to the "death sentence", or *fatwa* that was issued on him in 1989 for the publication of *The Satanic Verses*. Ironically enough (intentionally or unintentionally), the *fatwa* was issued on the Valentine's Day, February 14 1989, by the late Iranian religious leader Ayatollah Ruhollah Khomeini. He issued an Islamic religious ruling, sentencing Rushdie to be killed for blasphemy and disgracing Islam and especially the Prophet. Having studied Islamic history at Cambridge, Rushdie does discuss this religious topic critically and satirically, in the tradition of Western postmodern literary style, but also in the tradition of historical demythologization within Biblical studies. Especially the section of the so-called "satanic verses," which challenges the divine revelatory nature of *The Qur'an*, caused serious conflicts. Literary excuses were not taken favourably by the defenders of the Islamic faith, ensuing in a long and destructive dispute.

The book had already faced problems earlier when it was banned in India in October 1988 and in South Africa in November 1988. In January 1989, there was a book burning organized in the British Muslim centre of Bradford in protest against it. "The *Satanic Verses* Affair" escalated into an international diplomatic crisis, and turned into a clash between Islam and the West – triggering a Clash of Civilizations.[11] The crisis continued more or less unabated for about ten years until in 1998 Iran announced publicly that it does no more support murder attempts on Rushdie. Since then Rushdie has been able to move about more, although not completely, freely.

During the time of his hiding, Rushdie was at first covered daily in the media. Later this became less persistent but nevertheless his person became public property. During the years of hiding, Rushdie met heads of state and other dignitaries in order to gather support for himself in particular and for the freedom of speech in general. Displays of support led also to violence: Rushdie's Japanese translator Hitoshi Igarashi was stabbed to death in 1991. The same year the Italian translator Ettore Capriolo survived an attempted stabbing, and in 1993 there was an assassination attempt on Rushdie's Norwegian publisher William Nygaard who was seriously injured. Rushdie himself has escaped physical violence but has faced mental suffering and character assassination.

The public figure of Rushdie is coloured not only by the *fatwa* but also by his unashamed ambition and alleged arrogance. He has not lain low but has remained constantly in the limelight. He has been awarded numerous prizes in a dozen or so countries and he has featured both in cinema (Sharon Maguire' *Bridget Jones's Diary*, 2001 and Helen Hunt's *Then She Found Me*, 2007) and music videos ("The Ground Beneath Her Feet" by U2, 2000 and "Falling Down" by Scarlett Johansson, 2008). These have obviously been inspiring opportunities for Rushdie who is a movie enthusiast; and he did once contemplate on making a movie with the singer Bono from U2.

Rushdie moved from London to New York in September 2000. The departure from England was turbulent for Rushdie felt that he was accused of having caused himself his problems and the accrued costs of millions of pounds spent over the years for security and over 30 safe houses used to hide him. Furthermore, he also felt being unfairly accused for the dozens of deaths in the numerous demonstrations against him.[12] One year later, he already regarded New York as his own as he wrote about the terrorist attacks of 9/11 that the terrorists "broke *our city*. I'm among the newest of New Yorkers, but even people who have never set foot in Manhattan have felt its wounds."[13]

Furthermore, Rushdie's fame has been underlined by his numerous literary and political disputes as well as his personal relationships and multiple marriages and divorces. Open political disagreement with both Indira Gandhi and Margaret Thatcher marked him out as a member of the critical leftist literati, and *Midnight's Children* faced a court order for libelling the Gandhis and was censored. Rushdie has also quarrelled with V.S. Naipaul; when Naipaul received his Nobel Prize for Literature in 2001, Rushdie accused him of fraternizing with the Hindu fundamentalists and bringing shame to the Nobel Prize. For its part, the Nobel Prize committee had refused to give support to Rushdie and in consequence three of its members – Kerstin Ekman, Lars Gyllensten and Werner Aspenström – declined to work within the committee. Rushdie himself has been seen as a probable candidate for the prize – and he is always ever so disappointed for not being an awardee.

In summer 2007, another furore was created over the decision by Queen Elizabeth II to grant Rushdie the title of Knight Bachelor for his services to literature. In the Islamic world, giving the title to

Sir Salman was an open support for Rushdie against Islam. In the West, there was confusion about the eagerness of Rushdie – known for his republican and leftist inclinations – to accept the honour. All in all, Rushdie's global reputation is based not only on his literary merits but on other concerns as well. However, Rushdie is most of all a novelist and it is specifically his novels that have brought him fame as a writer.

Images of Rushdie

If one were to decide on a single feature connecting Rushdie's novels, it would most likely be their multilayeredness. There are many other features striving for that position but especially the intertwining stories, multicultural elements, intertextual references and allusions, as well as contextually varying interpretations are common to all the novels. It is also these aspects that the readers have found to be most enthralling, captivating and appealing. In his books, Rushdie combines story-telling traditions of many cultures, times and styles in a skilful way. The stories of the *Thousand and One Nights* are mixed with the worlds of science fiction movies, and myths around the world are staged in the streets of modern metropolises. In *Grimus* this multilayeredness is described philosophically as follows:

> There are a million possible Earths with a million possible histories, all of which actually exist simultaneously. In the course of one's daily life, one weaves a course between them, if you like, but that does not destroy the existence of pasts or futures we choose not to enter.[14]

The idea of a layered world is, thus, not seen only as a mere literary device but the source of richness in everyday lives of people. One of the more interesting images used to portray this layered world can be found in the novel *The Moor's Last Sigh* (1995). Already in the cover art we find Dennis Leigh's palimpsest image in which (at least) two pictures lay within each other. In the novel, the protagonist the Moor, or Moraes Zogoiby, comes forward with an idea to his father that his, the Moor's, mother Miranda's image could be recovered underneath the picture painted over it:

> Painted over. *The Artist as Boabdil, the Unlucky (el-Zogoybi), Last Sultan of Granada, Seen Departing from the Alhambra. Or, The Moor's Last Sigh.* That tearful equestrian chocolate-box picture which Mummyji said was worse than even a bazaar painter's scrawl. To remove it would be no loss. And then we would have her back.[15]

This layering over of a reality by other realities – and the thought of the possibility of even their partial retrieval – has fascinated Rushdie and his readers in all of his books. In many places, his books function as *romans de clef* so that the reader can try to recognize the more or (as sometimes is the case) less camouflaged person or incident (or persons/incidents). However, as often it is a question of such a mixture of real and false leads, misrememberings and sheer fiction that it is impossible to trace the "original" picture. This was evidenced also by Rushdie himself when he was tracing, without success, a portrait of his mother in the BBC documentary film "The Lost Portrait" (1995):[16] the lost past cannot be recovered by other means than imagining. The painting is not found but instead the famous Indian painter Bhupen Khakhar is seen painting Rushdie's own portrait that ends up in the National Portrait Gallery in London.

Even though movies have been a central and significant influence on Rushdie, his books have not yet been filmed. Their multiplicity and scope is so wide that it has so far proved impossible to make them into films even though some attempts have been made. BBC planned a TV-movie on *Midnight's Children* in 1997 but was not able to complete it;[17] a new attempt is planned under the direction of Deepa Mehta. In the theatres, Rushdie productions have been seen a couple of times. For example in 2003, The Royal Shakespeare Company staged a version of *Midnight's Children* dramatized by Rushdie together with Simon Reade and Tim Supple in London. A dramatized version of *Haroun and the Sea of Stories*, then, had its premiere at the Royal National Theatre already in September 1998.

Rushdie's books are graphic, winding and demanding. Their literary, cultural and cinematic references and allusions alone make them a challenge for the reader who tries to enter their worlds. However, by being challenging they are at the same time rewarding, and feed the imagination with new ideas and connections. Even though Rushdie's *oeuvre* shares certain features, he has not restricted himself to particular themes, times, or places. Whatever this might have meant for his reception, he has reached audiences, and is a widely read author all over the world.

Rushdie's fate has often been linked with that of his characters, and it has been seen as reflected in his books. As an example of such parallelism, in *The Satanic Verses* we encounter a highly realistic description of the "Supreme Being":

> Gibreel's vision of the Supreme Being was not abstract in the least. He saw, sitting on the bed, a man of about the same age as himself, of medium height, fairly heavily built, with salt-and-pepper beard cropped close to the line of the jaw. What struck him most was that the apparition was balding, seemed to suffer from dandruff and wore glasses. (*SV* 318)

It is no coincidence that this description reads like a spitting image of Rushdie himself, for he often plays with the concept of author, and the questions of authorial authority. When in the Islamic section of the novel the Prophet Mahound finally captures his adversary, Salman Farsi, he comments matter-of-factly: "Your blasphemy, Salman, can't be forgiven. Did you think I wouldn't work it out? To set your words against the Words of God" (*SV* 374). Especially in this case, many critics interpreted the reference directly to Rushdie, thus confirming his responsibility – even though the text explicitly plays with the multiplicity of meanings and their susceptibility.

Rushdie's works tell of people and a time connected by a global historical transformation from the colonial times into a transcultural, transnational world. These people are, broadly speaking, "midnight's children" whose "privilege and the curse [is] to be both masters and victims of their times, to forsake privacy and be sucked into the annihilating whirlpool of the multitudes, and to be unable to live or die in peace" (*MC* 463).

As such a midnight's child, Rushdie has both anticipated and produced the future in his works. Their transnational, transcultural multiplicity captivates the reader and introduces both unforeseen sceneries as well as old and familiar places and spaces seen from new perspectives. The books confront complicated topics, globally traumatic issues, and significant ideas while at the same time in their linguistic playfulness they laugh at the face of death, reveal the emperors' new clothes and in their diversity, position humanity and freedom as the highest moral good.

Notes

1. See Salman Rushdie, *The Satanic Verses* (London: Viking Penguin, 1989 [1988]); further references are to this edition and will be given parenthetically in the text, preceded by *SV*.
2. See Gerald Marzorati, "Salman Rushdie: Fiction's Embattled Infidel," *The New York Times Magazine* (29 January,1989), available at: <http://www.nytimes.com/books/99/04/18/specials/rushdie-maginfidel.html> (visited 22 February, 2010).
3. Bryan Appleyard, "Why Don't We Love Science Fiction?" *The Sunday Times* (2 Dec., 2007), available at: <http://entertainment.timesonline.co.uk/tol/arts_and_entertainment/books/article2961480.ece> (visited 22 Feb., 2010).
4. Salman Rushdie, *Grimus* (London: Paladin, 1989 [1975]), 130.
5. Rushdie, *Haroun and the Sea of Stories* (London: Granta Books, 1990), 72.
6. Salman Rushdie, *Midnight's Children* (London: Jonathan Cape, 1982 [1981]; further references are to this edition and will be given parenthetically in the text, preceded by *MC*.
7. Although Rushdie's books are by no means overtly erotic he has also discussed the positive influence of pornography in Islamic countries, see Salman Rushdie, "The East Is Blue," in *XXX: 30 Porn-Star Portraits*, ed. Timothy Greenfield-Sanders (Bulfinch Press, 2004), 98–99.
8. See Salman Rushdie, *Shame* (London: Jonathan Cape, 1983 [1982]).
9. See Salman Rushdie, *Shalimar the Clown* (New York: Random House, 2005).
10. See Salman Rushdie, *The Enchantress of Florence* (London: Jonathan Cape, 2008).
11. Although the media prefer the label "The Rushdie Affair", my preference is "*The Satanic Verses* Affair" as it focuses on the book, not the person; see Joel Kuortti, *Place of the Sacred: The Rhetoric of the* Satanic Verses *Affair* (Frankfurt an Main: Peter Lang, 1997), 15–16.
12. See D.T. Max, "Manhattan Transfer," *The Observer* (24 September, 2000), available at: <http://www.guardian.co.uk/books/2000/sep/24/fiction.salmanrushdie/print> (visited 22 February, 2010); also Salman Rushdie, "Why I Left," *The Guardian* (27 September, 2000).

13. Salman Rushdie, "Let's get back to life," *The Guardian* (6 October, 2001), available at: <http://www.guardian.co.uk/books/2001/oct/06/fiction.afghanistan>; repr. in Salman Rushdie, *Step across This Line: Collected Nonfiction 1992–2002* (New York: Random House, 2002), 336 (emphasis added).
14. Rushdie, *Grimus*, 53.
15. Salman Rushdie, *The Moor's Last Sigh* (Jonathan Cape, 1996 [1995]), 323–324.
16. "Salman Rushdie and the Lost Portrait," directed by Chris Granlund and edited by Michael Poole (1995) (BBC/RM Arts co-production, 1995).
17. A screenplay exists of this project, however, see Salman Rushdie, *The Screenplay of Midnight's Children* (London: Vintage, 1999).

Works Cited

Appleyard, Bryan. "Why Don't We Love Science Fiction?" *The Sunday Times* (2 Dec., 2007). Available at: <http://entertainment.timesonline.co.uk/tol/arts_and_entertainment/books/article2961480.ece>. (Visited 22 Feb., 2010.)

Granlund, Chris (dir.) and Michael Poole (ed.) 1995: "Salman Rushdie and the Lost Portrait." BBC/RM Arts co-production, 1995.

Gurnah, Abdulrazak. Ed. *The Cambridge Companion to Salman Rushdie.* Cambridge: Cambridge UP, 2007.

Kuortti, Joel. *The Salman Rushdie Bibliography: A Bibliography of Salman Rushdie's Work and Rushdie Criticism.* Frankfurt aM etc.: Peter Lang, 1997.

Kuortti, Joel. *Place of the Sacred: The Rhetoric of the* Satanic Verses *Affair.* Frankfurt aM etc.: Peter Lang, 1997.

Kuortti, Joel. *Fictions to Live In: Narration as an Argument for Fiction in Salman Rushdie's Novels.* Frankfurt aM etc.: Peter Lang, 1998.

Marzorati, Gerald. "Salman Rushdie: Fiction's Embattled Infidel." *The New York Times Magazine* (29 January, 1989). Available at: <http://www.nytimes.com/books/99/04/18/specials/rushdie-maginfidel.html>. (Visited 22 February, 2010.)

Max, D.T. "Manhattan Transfer." *The Observer* (24 September, 2000). Available at: <http://www.guardian.co.uk/books/2000/sep/24/fiction.salmanrushdie/print>. (Visited 22 February, 2010.)

Rushdie, Salman. "The East Is Blue." In *XXX: 30 Porn-Star Portraits.* Ed. Timothy Greenfield-Sanders. Boston and New York: Bulfinch Press, 2004. 98–99.

Rushdie, Salman. *Grimus.* London: Paladin, 1989 [1975].

Rushdie, Salman. *The Enchantress of Florence.* London: Jonathan Cape, 2008.

Rushdie, Salman. *The Ground Beneath Her Feet.* London: Jonathan Cape, 1999.

Rushdie, Salman. *Haroun and the Sea of Stories.* London: Granta Books, 1991 [1990].

Rushdie, Salman. *Imaginary Homelands: Essays and Criticism, 1981–1991.* London: Granta Books & Penguin, 1992.

Rushdie, Salman. "Let's get back to life." *The Guardian* (6 October, 2001). Available at: <http://www.guardian.co.uk/books/2001/oct/06/fiction.afghansta>. Repr. in Rushdie, *Step across This Line: Collected Nonfiction 1992–2002.* New York: Random House. 2002.

Rushdie, Salman. *Midnight's Children.* London: Jonathan Cape, 1982 [1981].

Rushdie, Salman. *The Moor's Last Sigh.* London: Jonathan Cape, 1996 [1995].

Rushdie, Salman. *Salman Rushdie's Haroun and the Sea of Stories.* Dramatized by Tim Supple and David Tushingham. London: Faber & Faber, 1998.

Rushdie, Salman. *Salman Rushdie's Midnight's Children.* Dramatized by Salman Rushdie, Simon Reade and Tim Supple. London: Modern Library, 2002.

Rushdie, Salman. *The Satanic Verses.* London: Viking Penguin, 1989 [1988].

Rushdie, Salman. *The Screenplay of Midnight's Children.* London: Vintage, 1999.

Rushdie, Salman. *Shalimar the Clown.* New York: Random House, 2005.

Rushdie, Salman. *Shame.* London: Jonathan Cape, 1983.

Rushdie, Salman. *Step across This Line: Collected Nonfiction 1992–2002.* New York: Random House, 2002.

Rushdie, Salman. "Why I Left." *The Guardian* 27 September, 2000.

Index